AWS Certified Solutions Architect - Associate (SAA-C03) Exam Guide

Aligned with the latest AWS SAA-C03 exam objectives to help you pass the exam on your first attempt

Michelle Chismon

Kate Gawron

AWS Certified Solutions Architect - Associate (SAA-C03) Exam Guide

Copyright © 2024 Packt Publishing

Authors: Michelle Chismon and Kate Gawron

Reviewer: Saibal Ghosh

Publishing Product Manager: Sneha Shinde

Senior Development Editor: Ketan Giri

Development Editor: Kalyani S.

Digital Editor: M Keerthi Nair

Presentation Designer: Salma Patel

Editorial Board: Vijin Boricha, Megan Carlisle, Simon Cox, Saurabh Kadave, Alex Mazonowicz, Gandhali Raut, and Ankita Thakur

First Published: November 2024

Production Reference: 1291124

Published by Packt Publishing Ltd.
Grosvenor House
11 St Paul's Square
Birmingham
B3 1RB
ISBN: 978-1-83763-000-4

www.packtpub.com

Contributors

About the Authors

Michelle Chismon is a Senior Cloud Architect with a diverse background that spans the fields of bioinformatics, consulting, and education. After completing her Ph.D. in genetics and molecular medicine, Michelle transitioned into the world of cloud consulting, where she leveraged her unique background to provide innovative cloud infrastructure solutions for clients in various industries. Michelle's dedication to continuous learning and improvement drove her to master the AWS ecosystem, and she subsequently became an AWS Authorized Instructor, delivering training on behalf of AWS worldwide.

During the 2020 pandemic and lockdown, Michelle trained a successful cohort of students in the AWS re/Start program, giving several people from disadvantaged backgrounds their jumpstart into the tech industry. She now works full-time at AWS working with some of the largest companies globally to solve their cloud infrastructure challenges.

LinkedIn profile: `https://www.linkedin.com/in/beaumontmichelle/`

Kate Gawron is a full-time Senior Cloud Consultant. She has worked with applications and databases for 18 years and AWS for 5 years. She holds four AWS certifications, including the *AWS Certified Solution Architect–Associate* certification, and two Google Cloud certifications. Kate currently works as a senior cloud architect, helping customers to migrate and refactor their applications and databases to work optimally within the AWS cloud. Kate has published a highly regarded exam guide for the *AWS Certified Database – Specialty* with Packt in 2022. She is also a part-time future racing driver. She was a competitor in Formula Woman, and she aspires to become a professional Gran Turismo (GT) racing driver.

LinkedIn profile: `https://www.linkedin.com/in/katehollow`

About the Reviewer

Saibal Ghosh is a seasoned professional with extensive expertise in Databases, Machine Learning, Cloud Security, Docker, Kubernetes, and the AWS Cloud.

He previously specialized as an Oracle DBA but has since expanded his expertise to include a broader range of databases beyond Oracle. His current focus also encompasses Data Engineering and Machine Learning.

As a Senior Technical Account Manager at Amazon Web Services, Saibal leverages his deep knowledge of cloud technologies to simplify AWS Cloud's complexities for customers, empowering them to effectively address their business challenges.

He is also the author of *Docker Demystified* published by BPB Publications, which underscores his ability to convey complex technological concepts clearly. Throughout his career, Saibal has embraced diverse roles, including developer, database administrator focused on performance tuning, trainer, and technical writer. His recent work deals with cloud technology, cloud security, telecommunications, and database management. With over two decades of experience combining technical expertise and business acumen, Saibal excels at delivering solutions that balance technical excellence with organizational goals.

Table of Contents

3

Identity and Access Management   57

4

Compute   71

6

DNS and Load Balancing   119

7

Data and Analytics   137

8

Migrations and Data Transfer   177

9

Serverless and Application Integration   191

10

Security   207

11

Management and Governance   221

12

Design Secure Architectures   243

13

Design Resilient Architectures   253

14

Design High-Performing Architectures   265

15

Design Cost-Optimized Architectures   287

16

Accessing the Online Practice Resources   299

Preface

The *AWS Certified Solutions Architect - Associate (SAA-C03)* exam is a key certification for IT professionals looking to demonstrate their ability to design and deploy scalable, highly available, and secure systems on AWS. This book is crafted to provide essential knowledge, practical exercises, and the insight needed to confidently pass the SAA-C03 exam. Whether you are an experienced professional or new to cloud computing, this guide will help you navigate the complexities of the exam with ease.

Why This Book?

The SAA-C03 exam covers a wide array of topics, from fundamental AWS services to advanced architectural concepts. This book simplifies these topics into digestible sections, providing real-world examples and hands-on labs to ensure that you can not only understand the material but also apply it effectively. By the end of this book, you will be well prepared to take the exam and implement your skills in real-world scenarios.

What This Book Covers

Chapter 1, Understanding Cloud Fundamentals, helps you get a clear understanding of the fundamentals of cloud computing.

Chapter 2, Virtual Private Cloud, teaches you about the intricacies of VPCs, giving you an in-depth understanding of their structure and functionality.

Chapter 3, Identity and Access Management, provides you with a comprehensive understanding of IAM's capabilities and mechanisms.

Chapter 4, Compute, explores the diverse compute options available, ranging from traditional instances to modern container services.

Chapter 5, Storage, delves deeper into the specifics of AWS's storage options, ensuring that you are able to choose the most appropriate solution for your needs.

Chapter 6, DNS and Load Balancing, covers the core concepts of DNS, Route 53, load balancing, and ELB to help you make optimal design decisions when architecting highly available applications on AWS.

Chapter 7, Data and Analytics, explores the various AWS data and analytics services, teaching you how to evaluate the choices available.

Chapter 8, Migrations and Data Transfer, teaches you about the processes and tools for migrating and transferring data to AWS.

Chapter 9, Serverless and Application Integration, delves deep into the core principles and services that underpin the serverless paradigm, focusing on equipping you with the skills required to design and implement efficient, cost-effective, and resilient serverless applications.

Chapter 10, Security, provides an overview of the key AWS security services.

Chapter 11, Management and Governance, explains how to create compliance rules so that you can be alerted when rules are broken, how to auto-remediate broken rules, and how to enforce permissions across an entire cross-region, multi-account platform, among other things.

Chapter 12, Design Secure Architectures, shows you how the services covered in previous chapters fit into the *Design Secure Architectures* exam domain.

Chapter 13, Design Resilient Architectures, covers the two task statements from the *Design Resilient Architectures* exam domain.

Chapter 14, Design High-Performing Architectures, focuses on the *Design High-Performing Architectures* exam domain and explores the key considerations across various components that contribute to building solutions that not only perform well under current loads but are also scalable.

Chapter 15, Design Cost-Optimized Architectures, covers the four task statements from the *Design Cost-Optimized Architectures* exam domain.

How to Get the Most Out of This Book

This book is crafted to equip you with the skills necessary to excel in the SAA-C03 exam through practical explanations of major domain topics. It covers the core domains critical to the expertise that candidates need to pass the exam. For each domain, you will work through content that reflects real-world challenges and also complete hands-on labs for some. At the end of each chapter, you will assess your understanding by taking chapter-specific quizzes. This not only prepares you for the SAA-C03 exam but also allows you to dive deeper into the topics.

Online Practice Resources

With this book, you will unlock unlimited access to our online exam-prep platform (*Figure 0.1*). This is your place to practice everything you learn in the book.

> **How to access the resources**
>
> To learn how to access the online resources, refer to *Chapter 16, Accessing the Online Practice Resources,* at the end of this book.

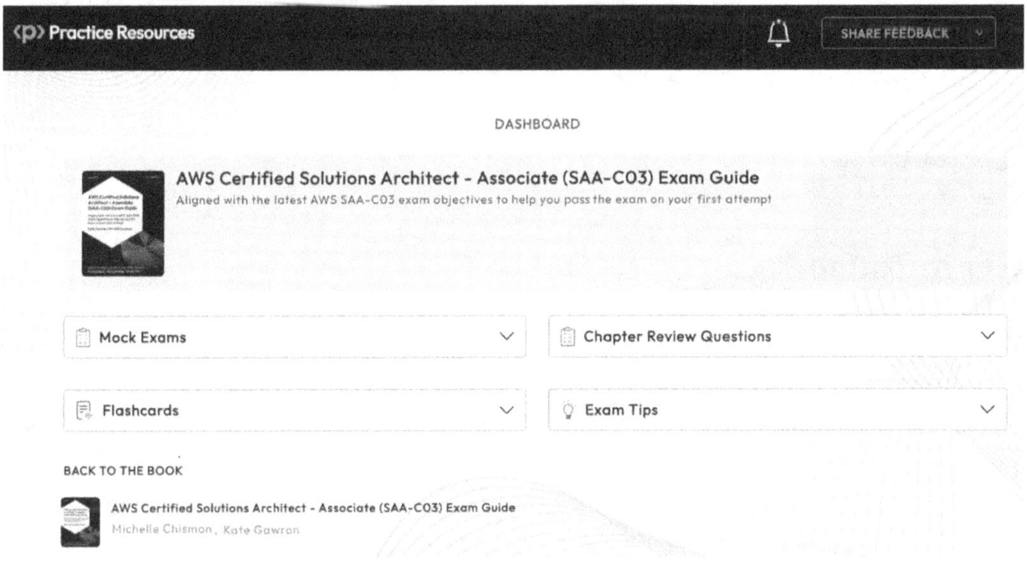

Figure 0.1 – Online exam-prep platform on a desktop device

Sharpen your knowledge of AWS SAA-C03 concepts with multiple sets of mock exams, interactive flashcards, and exam tips accessible from all modern web browsers.

Download the Color Images

We also provide a PDF file that has color images of the screenshots/diagrams used in this book.

You can download it here: https://packt.link/SAAC03graphicbundle

Conventions Used

Code words in the text, database table names, folder names, filenames, file extensions, screen text, pathnames, dummy URLs, user input, and X handles are shown as follows: "Type aws—version in the Terminal."

A block of code is set as follows:

```
aws ec2 create-vpc --cidr-block 10.0.0.0/16
```

New terms and important words are shown like this: "In its early days, it offered **Simple Storage Solution (S3)** for storage and **Elastic Compute Cloud (EC2)** for computing power."

> **Tips or important notes**
> Appear like this.

Get in Touch

Feedback from our readers is always welcome.

General feedback: If you have questions about any aspect of this book, mention the book title in the subject of your message and email us at customercare@packt.com.

Errata: Although we have taken every care to ensure the accuracy of our content, mistakes do happen. If you have found a mistake in this book, we would be grateful if you would report this to us. Please visit www.packtpub.com/support/errata, selecting your book, clicking on the Errata Submission Form link, and entering the details. We ensure that all valid errata are promptly updated in the GitHub repository, with the relevant information available in the Readme.md file. You can access the GitHub repository at https://packt.link/SAAC03github.

Piracy: If you come across any illegal copies of our works in any form on the Internet, we would be grateful if you would provide us with the location address or website name. Please contact us at copyright@packt.com with a link to the material.

If you are interested in becoming an author: If there is a topic that you have expertise in and you are interested in either writing or contributing to a book, please visit authors.packtpub.com.

Technical Requirements

To fully engage with the content and exercises in this book, you will need to meet the following technical requirements:

- AWS account with root access:

  - You will need an AWS account with root access to complete the exercises in this book. Most of the services and examples fall under the AWS Free Tier, allowing you to experiment without incurring costs, provided your account is within the first 12 months of creation.

  - If you do not have an AWS account, you can create one at https://aws.amazon.com/free/.

- **Command-line interface (CLI) access:**

  - The AWS CLI will be used frequently throughout this book for interacting with AWS services from the command line.

  - To set up the AWS CLI, do the following:

    1. **Download the AWS CLI**: Get the latest version from the CLI Install page: https://docs.aws.amazon.com/cli/latest/userguide/install-cliv2.html.

    2. **Create an IAM user**: Follow the steps in the User Creation Guide, https://docs.aws.amazon.com/IAM/latest/UserGuide/id_users_create.html, to create an IAM user with administrative access and generate an access key.

    3. **Configure the AWS CLI**: Use the aws configure command to set up your CLI profile with the necessary credentials. Detailed instructions can be found in the AWS CLI Configuration Guide: https://docs.aws.amazon.com/cli/latest/userguide/cli-configure-quickstart.html.

- **A basic understanding of AWS services**: While this book will teach you everything you need to know for the SAA-C03 exam, having a basic understanding of core AWS services such as EC2, S3, RDS, and IAM will be beneficial.

In addition to these technical requirements, it is important to have hands-on practice. Passing the SAA-C03 exam requires not just theoretical knowledge but also practical experience. Be sure to complete the exercises, experiment with AWS services, and apply your learning to real-world scenarios.

With these technical requirements met, you will be ready to begin your journey toward passing the *AWS Certified Solutions Architect - Associate (SAA-C03)* exam. Let's dive in and unlock your full potential in cloud architecture, starting with an overview of the exam.

AWS Certified Solutions Architect - Associate (SAA-C03) Exam Overview

To assist in your preparations for the exam, it is worth looking at both the format of the exam and the topics that will be covered. This can guide you through your revision by allowing you to focus on the areas you are least confident in.

In this section, you are going to read about the following:

- **Exam format**: What type of questions here are and how long you will have during the exam
- **Exam domains**: The areas you will be tested on during the exam

First, let's look at the exam format so you know what to expect after you have booked the exam.

Exam Format

All AWS exams are taken electronically, either at a test center or remotely via an online proctoring session.

The exam lasts 130 minutes and there will be 65 questions. If English is your second language or you have a disability that may impact your ability to complete the exam in 130 minutes, you can request an additional 30 minutes of exam time.

The pass mark will vary slightly between each exam, but the minimum will always be 720 out of 1,000. This variation is due to the questions being rated with varying difficulty, so they are weighted for fairness. As a rough guide, a pass should be obtained by answering 50 questions correctly.

Each exam has 15 questions that are not scored. These are used to evaluate questions for future versions of the exam. These unscored questions are not identified in the exam, so you should answer every question.

You are not penalized for incorrect answers and therefore you should attempt to answer all questions, even if you do not know the answer.

When you start the exam, you will first need to confirm your details, check that you have the right exam, and then sign a **Non-Disclosure Agreement** (**NDA**) that you will not share the exam questions. Once this is done, you will be given a brief overview of the exam and shown how to navigate through the screens.

The majority of the questions are situational, requiring you to be able to interpret the question to work out the correct answer.

The questions are all multiple choice, with two different styles:

- **Multiple choice**: One correct answer and three incorrect answers.
- **Multiple answer**: Two or more correct answers out of five or more options. The question will state how many answers are expected.

You can mark any questions for review at the end.

At the end of the exam, there is a survey about the exam and your preparation for it. You must complete this before receiving your exam result.

You will not typically receive your pass or fail result immediately, and you will only receive your full results and score once they have been verified. This verification normally takes three working days. Once the verification is complete, you will receive an email to your registered address and you will be able to obtain your full score report, which shows you how well you performed in each domain. This is particularly useful if you do not meet the passing grade as you will be given areas to focus your studies on for the next attempt.

You have learned the exam format and style of the questions. Now, take a look at the topics that will be covered in the exam, which this book will guide you through.

Exam Domains

The AWS Certified Solutions Architect – Associate (SAA-C03) exam covers four high-level topics encompassing a wide range of subjects and AWS services and solutions. These are as follows:

Domain	Percentage
Domain 1: Design Secure Architectures	30%
Domain 2: Design Resilient Architectures	26%
Domain 3: Design High-Performing Architectures	24%
Domain 4: Design Cost-Optimized Architectures	20%
TOTAL	100%

Table 0.1: The four exam domains in the SAA-C03 exam

The percentage refers to the most likely number of questions that will be asked in the exam. You can expect roughly the following number of questions in each domain:

Domain	Questions
Domain 1: Design Secure Architectures	19
Domain 2: Design Resilient Architectures	17
Domain 3: Design High-Performing Architectures	16
Domain 4: Design Cost-Optimized Architectures	13
TOTAL	65

Table 0.2: Rough number of questions from each domain

The AWS Certifications team provides a high-level description of each domain, including the key AWS services and technologies you will need to know to pass the exam. However, this exam expects you to be able to use multiple services to architect solutions based on scenarios, so simply knowing the names of AWS services is unlikely to be enough to earn a pass. In the next section, you are going to learn what each domain really means and the key topics within each. This can be used to help guide you while you study and prepare for the exam. Let's begin with domain 1: *Design Secure Architectures*.

Domain 1: Design Secure Architectures

Building secure AWS architectures is vital for protecting data, applications, and infrastructure from threats. This requires knowledge of AWS services, infrastructure, and security best practices, including access control, identity services, and flexible authorization. In this section, we will cover three key task statements for designing secure systems:

- *Design Secure Access to AWS Resources*
- *Design Secure Workloads and Applications*
- *Determine Appropriate Data Security Controls*

Design Secure Access to AWS Resources

Designing secure access to AWS resources requires understanding access controls, federated identity services, AWS infrastructure, security best practices, and the shared responsibility model. Key skills include applying IAM best practices, creating flexible authorization models, implementing role-based access control, managing security for multiple accounts, using resource policies effectively, and integrating directory services with IAM roles when needed.

You will need to know how to design and appropriately apply the following:

- Adhering to AWS security best practices for IAM users and root users, which includes the use of **multi-factor authentication (MFA)** when appropriate.

- Designing a flexible authorization model. This includes IAM users, groups, roles, and policies.

- Creating a role-based access control strategy that incorporates **AWS Security Token Service (AWS STS)**, role switching, and cross-account access.

- Creating a security strategy for multiple AWS accounts, including AWS Control Tower and **service control policies (SCPs)**.

- Deciding the right use of resource policies for AWS services.

- Deciding when to integrate a directory service with IAM roles.

Design Secure Workloads and Applications

Designing secure workloads and applications requires understanding application security, AWS service endpoints, protocols, network traffic, secure access, and external threats. Key skills include creating secure VPC architectures, planning network segmentation, integrating AWS security services, and securing external connections to and from AWS.

This includes the following topics:

- Creating **virtual private cloud (VPC)** architectures with security components, including security groups, route tables, **network access control lists (NACLs)**, and **network address translation (NAT)** gateways.

- Planning network segmentation strategies, which involves determining how to structure your network using public and private subnets.

- Integrating various AWS services to enhance the security of applications. This includes AWS Shield, **AWS Web Application Firewall (AWS WAF)**, **AWS Single Sign On (AWS SSO)**, and AWS Secrets Manager.

- Securing external network connections to and from the AWS cloud, including VPN and AWS Direct Connect.

Determine Appropriate Data Security Controls

Determining appropriate data security controls requires knowledge of data access, governance, recovery, retention, classification, and encryption with key management. Key skills include meeting compliance requirements with AWS technologies, encrypting data at rest and in transit, managing access policies for encryption keys, implementing backups and data lifecycle policies, rotating encryption keys, and renewing certificates.

The following areas are covered in this section:

- Aligning AWS technologies to meet compliance requirements
- Using AWS **Key Management Service** (**KMS**) to encrypt data stored on AWS
- Encrypting data in transit using **AWS Certificate Manager** (**AWS ACM**) and **Transport Layer Security** (**TLS**)
- Setting up access policies for encryption keys
- Setting up automated backup and data replication strategies
- Implementing policies for data access, lifecycle, and protection
- Regularly rotating encryption keys and renewing certificates to maintain security

In conclusion, domain 1 of the SAA-C03 exam covers the design of secure architectures on AWS. It requires knowledge of various AWS services, security best practices, and the shared responsibility model. It also tests your skills in designing secure access to AWS resources and secure workloads and applications. To succeed in this domain, you will need to have a deep understanding of AWS security, networking, and identity and access management.

Let's now look at the second domain in the exam, *Design Resilient Architectures*.

Domain 2: Design Resilient Architectures

Designing resilient architectures is crucial for organizations utilizing AWS to ensure their systems can withstand failures and maintain high availability. Resilient architectures are designed to be scalable, fault-tolerant, and capable of handling disruption, allowing businesses to deliver reliable services to their users. In this section, you will explore two task statements within the domain of designing resilient architectures:

- *Design Scalable and Loosely Coupled Architectures*
- *Design Highly Available and/or Fault-Tolerant Architectures*

Design Scalable and Loosely Coupled Architectures

Creating scalable and loosely coupled architectures involves designing systems that can handle varying workloads and adapt to changing demands. It entails building components that can scale independently, enabling resource adjustments based on specific requirements. Important considerations in this area include the following:

- Leveraging AWS services such as Auto Scaling to automatically scale resources based on workload fluctuations

- Implementing loosely coupled architectures using services such as AWS Lambda, Amazon **Simple Queue Service (SQS)**, or **Amazon Simple Notification Service (SNS)** to decouple components and enhance flexibility and scalability

- Utilizing services such as **Amazon Elastic Container Service (ECS)** or **Amazon Elastic Kubernetes Service (EKS)** to manage containerized workloads efficiently and facilitate scaling

Design High Availability and/or Fault-Tolerant Architectures

Designing highly available and fault-tolerant architectures ensures system operability even in the face of failure or disruption. It involves implementing redundancy, fault isolation, and automated failover mechanisms. Key considerations in this area include the following:

- Deploying solutions such as **AWS Elastic Load Balancer (ELB)** or Amazon Route 53 to distribute traffic across multiple instances or regions, ensuring continuous availability

- Utilizing AWS services such as Amazon RDS Multi-AZ, which provides automated synchronous replication of databases to ensure data availability during failures

- Incorporating fault isolation principles using concepts such as **Availability Zones (AZs)** or multi-region deployments to mitigate the impact of failures

- Implementing automated failover mechanisms through services such as Amazon Route 53 DNS failover or AWS Elastic Beanstalk rolling deployments

In summary, domain 2 of the SAA-C03 exam focuses on designing resilient architectures on AWS. It requires expertise in designing multi-tier architectures for high availability and fault tolerance, as well as ensuring business continuity through disaster recovery and failover strategies. To succeed in this domain, you will need to have a thorough understanding of AWS services such as EC2, ELB, Route 53, and CloudFormation, as well as experience in designing highly available and fault-tolerant architectures.

Let's now learn what domain 3, *Design High-Performing Architectures*, covers.

Domain 3: Design High-Performing Architectures

Designing high-performance architectures is vital for ensuring the smooth and efficient functioning of workloads on AWS. It involves identifying and selecting the right compute, storage, and networking solutions for your workload. To design high-performance architectures, you need to be familiar with various AWS services and understand their capabilities and limitations.

In this section, you will read about the five task statements related to designing high-performance architectures:

- *Determine High-Performance and/or Scalable Storage Solutions*

- *Design High-Performance and Elastic Compute Solutions*

- *Determine High-Performance Database Solutions*

- *Determine High-Performance and/or Scalable Network Architectures*

- *Determine High-Performance Data Ingestion and Transformation Solutions*

Determine High-Performance and/or Scalable Storage Solutions

Selecting the right storage solutions is essential to achieve high performance and scalability in your architecture, ensuring efficient data storage, retrieval, and durability. When designing high-performance architectures, you need to consider the specific requirements of your workload, including data volume, access patterns, latency needs, and durability expectations.

You will need to understand how to do the following:

- Evaluate AWS storage services such as Amazon S3, Amazon EBS, and Amazon EFS based on the specific performance needs of your workload

- Implement caching mechanisms using services such as Amazon ElastiCache and Amazon CloudFront to enhance storage performance

- Utilize sharding or partitioning techniques to distribute data across multiple storage instances for improved scalability

Design High-Performance and Elastic Compute Solutions

Designing high-performance and elastic compute solutions involves a careful evaluation of various compute resources provided by AWS and optimizing their performance to meet the requirements of your workload. This includes considering factors such as computational power, memory capacity, storage options, and networking capabilities.

You will be tested on your knowledge of the following:

- Choosing AWS compute services such as Amazon EC2, AWS Lambda, and AWS Fargate based on workload characteristics and performance requirements

- Implementing auto-scaling configurations to dynamically adjust compute resources based on workload demands

- Leveraging AWS services such as **Amazon Elastic Container Service** (**ECS**) and Amazon **Elastic Kubernetes Service** (**EKS**) to efficiently manage containerized workloads and enhance performance

Determine High-Performance Database Solutions

Selecting the right database solutions is crucial for achieving high performance and scalability in your architecture, enabling efficient data storage, retrieval, and management. When designing high-performance architectures, it is essential to consider factors such as data volume, throughput requirements, latency sensitivity, and scalability needs.

The exam will feature questions on how to do the following:

- Evaluate AWS database services such as Amazon RDS, Amazon DynamoDB, and Amazon Aurora based on the specific performance and scalability requirements of your workload
- Implement read replicas or sharding techniques to distribute database load and improve performance
- Utilize caching mechanisms using services such as Amazon ElastiCache to reduce database access latency and enhance performance

Determine High-Performance and/or Scalable Network Architectures

Designing high-performance and scalable network architectures is vital for achieving optimal performance across your infrastructure, ensuring reliable and efficient communication between various components of your system. A well-designed network architecture can minimize latency, reduce bottlenecks, and provide high bandwidth to support the demands of your workload.

You will need to learn how to do the following:

- Design your network using Amazon VPC to provide isolated and secure communication between resources
- Implement AWS services such as AWS Direct Connect and AWS Global Accelerator to optimize network connectivity and reduce latency
- Utilize **content delivery networks** (**CDNs**) such as Amazon CloudFront to cache and deliver content closer to end users, improving performance

Determine High-Performance Data Ingestion and Transformation Solutions

Efficiently handling data ingestion and transformation is crucial for high-performance architectures, enabling seamless and timely processing of data to drive actionable insights and meet business requirements. In today's data-driven landscape, organizations need to effectively handle the continuous influx of data from various sources and transform it into valuable information.

You will be tested on how to do the following:

- Evaluate AWS services such as Amazon Kinesis and AWS Data Pipeline for real-time or batch data ingestion
- Utilize services such as AWS Glue or Amazon EMR for data transformation and processing at scale
- Implement parallel processing techniques and distributed computing frameworks to optimize data ingestion and transformation performance

To summarize, domain 3 of the SAA-C03 exam delves into the design of high-performance architectures on AWS. This domain encompasses a broad range of topics, including determining high-performing and scalable storage solutions, designing high-performing and elastic compute solutions, selecting high-performing database solutions, crafting high-performing and scalable network architectures, and determining efficient data ingestion and transformation solutions. To excel in this domain, you need to possess a comprehensive understanding of AWS services such as Amazon S3, Amazon EC2, Amazon RDS, Amazon VPC, and AWS Glue. Additionally, hands-on experience in designing architectures that prioritize performance, scalability, and efficiency will prove invaluable.

We will now look at domain 4, *Design Cost-Optimized Architectures*, the final exam domain.

Domain 4: Design Cost-Optimized Architectures

Designing cost-optimized architectures is an important aspect of cloud computing, as it can help organizations maximize the value of their AWS investments while reducing unnecessary expenses. In order to design cost-effective architectures, you need to be familiar with various AWS services, understand how to balance performance requirements with cost, and have expertise in data lifecycle management. In this section, we will cover four task statements related to designing cost-optimized architectures:

- *Design Cost-Optimized Storage Solutions*
- *Design Cost-Optimized Compute Solutions*
- *Design Cost-Optimized Database Solutions*
- *Design Cost-Optimized Network Architectures*

Design Cost-Optimized Storage Solutions

Designing cost-optimized storage solutions involves a meticulous approach to selecting the most suitable storage services and strategies that not only meet the performance requirements of the workload but also optimize costs. It requires a thorough understanding of the data access patterns, usage frequency, and expected growth of the storage needs. By considering these factors, organizations can make informed decisions to strike the right balance between performance and cost. Key considerations in this area include the following:

- Assessing data access patterns and leveraging appropriate storage classes, such as Amazon S3 Standard, Amazon S3 Glacier, and Amazon EBS, to match the needs of different data types

- Implementing data lifecycle management techniques, such as transitioning infrequently accessed data to lower-cost storage tiers or archiving data for long-term retention

- Utilizing AWS storage services such as Amazon S3 Intelligent-Tiering to automatically optimize costs by moving data between storage tiers based on usage patterns

Design Cost-Optimized Compute Solutions

Designing cost-optimized compute solutions involves a strategic approach to selecting compute resources that align with the performance requirements of the workload while optimizing costs. It entails understanding the specific needs of the application or workload and making informed decisions to maximize efficiency and cost-effectiveness. Consider the following:

- Choosing the appropriate instance types based on workload characteristics, such as CPU, memory, and networking requirements

- Utilizing AWS services such as Amazon EC2 Spot Instances, which offers cost savings by leveraging spare capacity

- Implementing auto-scaling configurations to dynamically adjust compute resources based on demand, avoiding over-provisioning and reducing costs

Design Cost-Optimized Database Solutions

Designing cost-optimized database solutions requires the careful evaluation of database services and configurations to ensure they align with the performance needs of the workload while optimizing costs. It involves considering factors such as data volume, query patterns, and desired response times to make informed decisions that strike the right balance between performance and cost efficiency. Consider the following:

- Choosing the appropriate database service based on workload characteristics, such as Amazon RDS, Amazon DynamoDB, or Amazon Aurora

- Right-sizing database instances to match workload demands and avoid unnecessary costs

- Implementing database caching techniques, such as Amazon ElastiCache, to improve performance and reduce database load

Design Cost-Optimized Network Architectures

Designing cost-optimized network architectures involves a comprehensive approach to optimizing network configurations and services in order to minimize costs while meeting the performance and security requirements of the workload. It requires a deep understanding of the network infrastructure and the specific needs of the applications or services running on it. Consider the following:

- Utilizing AWS networking services, such as Amazon VPC, to design efficient and cost-effective network topologies

- Implementing traffic management strategies, such as CDNs like Amazon CloudFront, to reduce data transfer costs and improve content delivery performance

- Leveraging AWS Direct Connect or VPN connections effectively to optimize network connectivity costs

Domain 4 of the exam covers the design of cost-optimized architectures on AWS. This domain requires you to identify cost-effective compute and database services, use cost-effective storage solutions, and design solutions that can optimize costs for operational efficiency based on business requirements. To succeed in this domain, you will need to have a solid understanding of AWS pricing models, cost optimization strategies, and how to balance cost with performance and other business needs.

Now that you have learned about all the domains of the exam, it's time to dive in and learn all about AWS.

Share Your Thoughts

Once you've read *AWS Certified Solutions Architect - Associate (SAA-C03) Exam Guide*, we'd love to hear your thoughts! Scan the QR code below to go straight to the Amazon review page for this book and share your feedback.

https://packt.link/r/1837630003

Your review is important to us and the tech community and will help us make sure we're delivering excellent quality content.

Download a Free PDF Copy of This Book

Thanks for purchasing this book!

Do you like to read on the go but are unable to carry your print books everywhere?

Is your eBook purchase not compatible with the device of your choice?

Don't worry, now with every Packt book you get a DRM-free PDF version of that book at no cost.

Read anywhere, any place, on any device. Search, copy, and paste code from your favorite technical books directly into your application.

The perks don't stop there, you can get exclusive access to discounts, newsletters, and great free content in your inbox daily.

Follow these simple steps to get the benefits:

1. Scan the QR code or visit the link below:

https://packt.link/free-ebook/9781837630004

2. Submit your proof of purchase.
3. That's it! We'll send your free PDF and other benefits to your email directly.

Understanding Cloud Fundamentals

In this chapter, we will delve into the fundamental concepts of cloud computing. Whether you are new to solutions architecture or have experience with traditional on-premises deployments, this chapter aims to provide you with a solid foundation to understand cloud computing and its key principles. While this chapter is part of an **Amazon Web Services (AWS)** exam guide, it aims to give a general overview of the concepts of cloud computing across all cloud providers, with a specific section on AWS specifics.

To become a successful cloud solutions architect, it is vital that you understand the reasons why cloud computing exists and what challenges it aims to resolve before you start diving into deeper technical implementations. In the exam, there are often questions that require you to understand the main benefits of migrating to the cloud from on-premises. By the end of this chapter, you will be able to confidently answer the exam questions focused on the benefits of cloud computing.

Making the Most of This Book – Your Certification and Beyond

This book and its accompanying online resources are designed to be a complete preparation tool for your **AWS Certified Solutions Architect - Associate (SAA-C03) exam**.

The book is written in a way that means you can apply everything you've learned here even after your certification. The online practice resources that come with this book (*Figure 1.1*) are designed to improve your test-taking skills. They are loaded with timed mock exams, chapter review questions, interactive flashcards, case studies, and exam tips to help you work on your exam readiness from now till your test day.

> **Before You Proceed**
>
> To learn how to access these resources, head over to *Chapter 16, Accessing the Online Practice Resources*, at the end of the book.

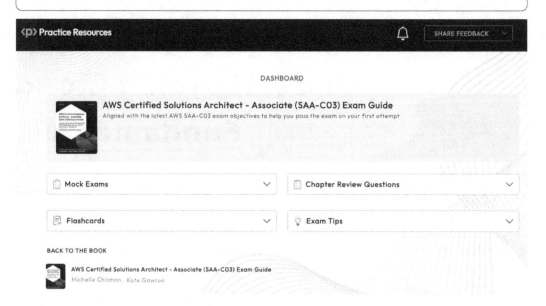

Figure 1.1: Dashboard interface of the online practice resources

Here are some tips on how to make the most of this book so that you can clear your certification and retain your knowledge beyond your exam:

1. Read each section thoroughly.

2. **Make ample notes**: You can use your favorite online note-taking tool or use a physical notebook. The free online resources also give you access to an online version of this book. Click the BACK TO THE BOOK link from the dashboard to access the book in **Packt Reader**. You can highlight specific sections of the book there.

3. **Chapter review questions**: At the end of this chapter, you'll find a link to review questions for this chapter. These are designed to test your knowledge of the chapter. Aim to score at least **75%** before moving on to the next chapter. You'll find detailed instructions on how to make the most of these questions at the end of this chapter in the *Exam Readiness Drill – Chapter Review Questions* section. That way, you're improving your exam-taking skills after each chapter, rather than at the end of the book.

4. **Flashcards**: After you've gone through the book and scored **75%** or more in each of the chapter review questions, start reviewing the online flashcards. They will help you memorize key concepts.

5. **Mock exams**: Revise by solving the mock exams that come with the book till your exam day. If you get some answers wrong, go back to the book and revisit the concepts you're weak in.

6. **Exam tips**: Review these from time to time to improve your exam readiness even further.

In this chapter, we are going to cover the following main topics:

- Cloud computing
- The AWS cloud
- AWS architecture and key infrastructure
- Cloud economics
- Let's get started

Cloud Computing

Cloud computing is particularly important today due to its ability to offer scalability and flexibility, which are essential in our rapidly changing market environments. Organizations can scale their IT resources up or down based on demand, providing a critical competitive advantage in responding swiftly to opportunities or challenges, which, in turn, drives faster innovation. Additionally, cloud computing promotes cost efficiency by allowing businesses to minimize capital expenses. Instead of investing in extensive hardware setups and ongoing maintenance, companies can use cloud services to access advanced computing capabilities, paying only for what they use. This shift not only reduces overhead costs but also enables businesses to allocate resources more strategically to foster innovation and growth.

A possible definition of cloud computing is that it is a framework designed to offer ubiquitous, user-friendly, and instant access to a collectively available and adaptable set of computing resources, encompassing networks, servers, storage, applications, and services. These resources can be swiftly allocated and de-allocated, requiring minimal administrative oversight and interaction with service providers.

Cloud computing represents a significant shift in the way that organizations and individuals utilize computing resources. This means that rather than having to install a suite of software for each computer, users can access their applications and data from any device with an internet connection. This approach to computing offers enhanced flexibility and scalability, making it increasingly popular among businesses and individuals alike.

The evolution of cloud computing marks a significant departure from the traditional IT infrastructure, which was characterized by on-premises hardware and software. In the past, companies needed to invest heavily in physical servers and dedicated IT teams to manage and maintain them. This model was not only costly but also lacked flexibility and scalability. The advent of cloud computing revolutionized this, enabling businesses to access computing resources as a service via the internet. This shift meant that organizations could scale resources up or down based on their needs, without the need for significant upfront investment. The evolution of cloud computing is also marked by advancements in virtualization technology, which allows multiple virtual machines to operate on a single physical server, enhancing the efficiency and cost-effectiveness of computing resources. Take a look at *Figure 1.2*, which shows the basics of cloud computing:

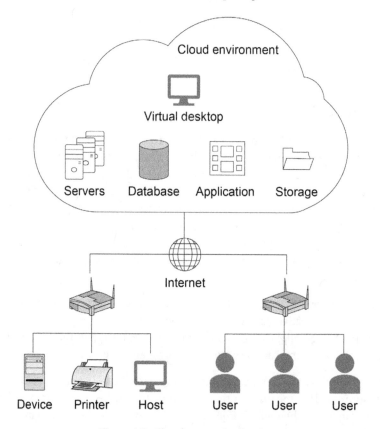

Figure 1.2: Cloud computing basics

Cloud computing is defined by several key characteristics that distinguish it from traditional computing models. These include the following:

- **On-demand self-service**: Users, such as developers, can automatically provision computing resources, such as server time and network storage, as needed, without requiring manual intervention from the service provider. This allows companies to react faster, as they can get the resources they need without lengthy procurement processes.

- **Network access**: Services are accessible over a network and can be utilized through standard protocols (for example, transmission control protocol/internet protocol or application programming interface calls) that support usage across a wide range of different client platforms, whether thin or thick (e.g., mobile phones and laptops).

- **Resource sharing**: The computing resources of the provider are shared across multiple consumers using a multi-tenant model. Different physical and virtual resources are dynamically assigned and reassigned, based on consumer demand. This generally makes cloud computing more cost-effective, as the service providers can offer economies of scale that would be difficult for smaller organizations to match.

- **Elasticity**: Capabilities can be swiftly and elastically provisioned, sometimes automatically, to rapidly scale both outward and inward, in alignment with the fluctuating demand.

- **Service charges**: Cloud systems automatically optimize resource usage through metering, allowing a pay-per-use model and ensuring cost efficiency.

There is a common misbelief that when you discuss cloud computing, you always refer to a cloud service that is managed by someone else. This is not correct. Cloud computing architectures and philosophies can be created and managed within your existing data centers, but this would require a large amount of coding, automation, and expense. In fact, there are four different types of cloud deployment, which you will learn about next.

Cloud Deployment Models

Understanding the various cloud deployment models is crucial for businesses and individuals looking to leverage cloud technology effectively. There are four different types of cloud computing available – private, community, public, and hybrid:

- **Private cloud**: This is designed for exclusive use by a single organization, offering enhanced control and security

- **Community cloud**: This serves a group of organizations with common goals and requirements

- **Public cloud**: This is the most common type, providing services over the internet to the public or large industry groups, often delivering scalability and cost-effectiveness

- **Hybrid cloud**: This blends elements of both the private and public clouds, offering a balanced approach that maximizes both security and flexibility, as shown in *Figure 1.3*:

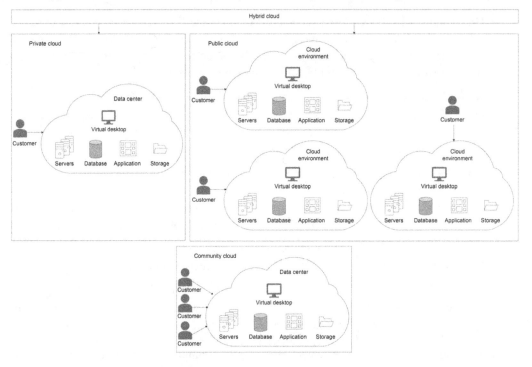

Figure 1.3: Cloud deployment models

Let's take a deeper look at the four cloud deployment models and how they work, starting with the private cloud.

Private

A private cloud is a cloud computing environment dedicated solely to one organization. It offers the following:

- **Exclusivity**: Serves only one organization, providing tailored IT solutions
- **Control and customization**: Gives you full control over the cloud setup, enabling specific customizations for business needs
- **Enhanced security**: Offers higher security levels, beneficial for sensitive data and compliance with regulatory standards

- **Reliable performance**: With dedicated resources, it ensures efficient and stable performance

- **Higher costs**: Typically, it is more expensive than public clouds due to the costs of infrastructure, maintenance, and management

- **Deployment flexibility**: Can be hosted either on-premises or by a third-party provider, but it is used exclusively by one organization

- **Limited scalability**: Offers scalability, although it is not as extensive as public clouds as you are constrained to the servers you own

Private clouds are best suited for organizations needing specific control, high security, and customization in their cloud infrastructure, but they come with higher costs and limited scalability compared to public clouds. Organizations such as banks, government bodies, and the military may consider using a private cloud to meet their security requirements.

Community

A community cloud is a cloud computing model shared by several organizations with common goals or requirements. Its main features include the following:

- **Shared infrastructure**: Designed for a specific community of users with similar needs, allowing cost and resource sharing

- **A collaborative environment**: Facilitates collaboration and data sharing among member organizations, often benefiting from collective expertise

- **Customized security and compliance**: Offers a level of security and compliance tailored to the specific community, often more focused than public clouds but less exclusive than private clouds

- **Cost-effectiveness**: More cost-efficient than private clouds, as expenses are shared among the participating organizations

- **Scalability and flexibility**: Provides scalability and flexibility to accommodate the needs of the community, although it may not match the scale of public clouds

Community clouds are ideal for groups of organizations with shared interests and requirements, offering a balance of security, collaboration, and cost savings.

Public

A public cloud is where services and infrastructure are provided over the internet and shared among multiple users, offering limited customization. Key characteristics include the following:

- **Shared resources**: Operated by third-party providers, it serves multiple clients using the same shared infrastructure; however, there are strict guardrails between customer environments
- **Scalability and flexibility**: Offers high scalability, easily accommodating fluctuating demands
- **Cost-effectiveness**: Typically operates on a pay-as-you-go model, which can be more cost-effective than maintaining private infrastructure
- **Ease of access**: Users can access services and manage their accounts via the internet
- **Minimal maintenance**: Users are not responsible for hardware and software maintenance, as this is managed by the service provider

Public clouds are well-suited for businesses seeking cost-effective, scalable, and easily accessible cloud services without the need for direct management of the infrastructure.

Hybrid

A hybrid cloud combines private and public cloud elements, offering a versatile cloud computing model. Its main features are as follows:

- **The integration of private and public clouds**: Blends the control and security of private clouds with the scalability and cost-efficiency of public clouds
- **Flexibility and scalability**: Allows businesses to keep sensitive data in a private cloud while leveraging the expansive resources of a public cloud for less sensitive operations
- **Cost-effective and efficient**: Provides a balance between cost and performance, allowing organizations to optimize their cloud spending
- **Customizable security and compliance**: Offers tailored security and compliance options, meeting specific organizational needs
- **Complex management**: Management can be more complex due to the integration of different cloud environments

Hybrid clouds are ideal for organizations that need both the security of a private cloud and the scalability and cost benefits of a public cloud.

Once you have chosen which cloud deployment model works best for your organization, you then need to choose the type of service you wish to exploit.

Types of Cloud Services

In addition to choosing which cloud deployment you want to use, you will also need to decide how best to run your services. The three fundamental service models – **Infrastructure as a Service (IaaS)**, **Platform as a Service (PaaS)**, and **Software as a Service (SaaS)** – are offered by most cloud providers and allow users to choose what level of control they need, versus the operational benefits of using a fully managed service. IaaS provides the most basic level of cloud services, offering fundamental computing infrastructure such as servers, storage, and networking resources on demand. PaaS builds upon this by adding a layer of tools and software, allowing developers to create and deploy applications without managing the underlying infrastructure. At the top is SaaS, delivering fully functional software applications over the internet, eliminating the need for users to install or run applications on individual devices. Unlike the cloud deployment model, you can choose a different type of service for each use case that you have, allowing you to customize your service to your specific business needs. *Figure 1.4* shows the three service models:

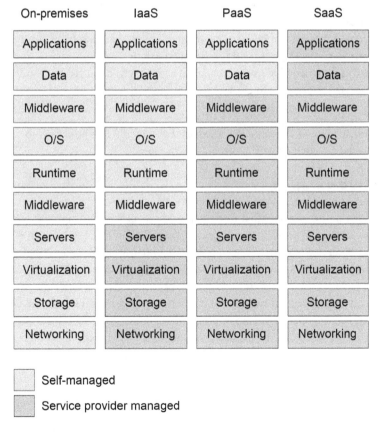

Figure 1.4: IaaS, PaaS, and SaaS

So, now that you can explain the different types of cloud providers and the different types of services available on those clouds, you will learn how AWS handles its own services and offerings.

The AWS Cloud

AWS entered the cloud computing arena in 2006. It was the first public cloud provider. It was initially created to support the growing Amazon.com business, but it was quickly realized that AWS could provide services for other businesses, too. In its early days, it offered **Simple Storage Solution** (**S3**) for storage and **Elastic Compute Cloud** (**EC2**) for computing power. As the years went by, AWS expanded its portfolio to include cutting-edge technologies such as artificial intelligence, machine learning, and the **Internet of Things** (**IoT**). This growth trajectory was not just about diversifying services; it fundamentally reshaped how businesses approach scalability and adaptability, offering unprecedented efficiency and flexibility.

In today's cloud computing landscape, AWS stands as a dominant force, consistently ranking as a top provider globally. Its comprehensive suite of services, known for reliability and scalability, has made it the preferred choice for a diverse spectrum of clients, ranging from emerging start-ups to established enterprises. AWS's impact on the cloud computing sector is significant. It has not only captured a substantial market share but also played a pivotal role in driving cloud adoption across various industries, thus spearheading a wave of digital transformation and fostering a culture of continuous technological innovation.

We will now look at some of the key AWS services that you will need to know for the exam. All of them will be covered in much greater depth in later chapters.

The Core AWS Services

AWS offers a wide range of services that form the backbone of its cloud computing platform, letting businesses choose from multiple robust and versatile tools. At the time of writing, AWS offers over 200 different services. A service may include a combination of hardware, software, storage, and tooling to support a business in its goals. Key services include **Virtual Private Cloud** (**VPC**) for secure and isolated network configuration, EC2 for scalable computing capacity, S3 for reliable data storage solutions, Lambda to run code in response to events without managing servers, and **Relational Database Service** (**RDS**) for the easy setup, operation, and scaling of databases. These services collectively provide a comprehensive, integrated cloud environment that supports a wide range of business applications and workflows, demonstrating AWS's commitment to offering scalable, efficient, and flexible cloud solutions.

VPC

AWS VPC enables you to create a logically isolated area of the AWS cloud where you can deploy your workloads:

- **Custom network configuration**: Set up an IP address range, subnets, and gateways for secure and custom network environments

- **Enhanced security controls**: Control network access to instances and subnets for improved security

- **Seamless AWS integration**: Easily connect with other AWS services, maintaining a secure and efficient cloud ecosystem

EC2

EC2 provides resizable servers or compute in the AWS cloud, allowing you to rapidly deploy and scale your compute needs:

- **Flexible compute options**: A wide range of instance types for different computational needs

- **Scalable resources**: Easily scale capacity up or down as needed

RDS

RDS simplifies the setup, operation, and scaling of relational databases in the cloud:

- **Automated management**: Handles routine database tasks like provisioning, patching, backup, and recovery

- **Multiple database engine support**: Compatible with engines such as MySQL and PostgreSQL

- **Scalability**: Adjust compute and storage resources with minimal downtime

S3

S3 provides scalable object storage, ideal for a wide range of storage applications:

- **High durability and availability**: Ensures data is stored reliably across multiple facilities

- **Simple and scalable**: A user-friendly interface to store and retrieve vast amounts of data

- **Cost-effective**: Store large volumes of data at a low cost, scaling as per requirement

Lambda

AWS Lambda enables you to run code without server management, with billing for the compute time used:

- **Serverless execution**: Automatically manages computing resources
- **Event-driven**: Triggers execution in response to various events
- **Scalable**: Adjusts automatically to handle the workload

Now that you know of some key services that AWS offers, you can start to imagine how you would use them to support the different applications that your organization runs. You should also be able to see that Lambda is a PaaS service, whereas EC2 is an IaaS, as you have more control with EC2 than with Lambda.

AWS Global Infrastructure

AWS has established a vast and robust global infrastructure to support its cloud services, ensuring high availability, low latency, and strong data sovereignty compliance for its users worldwide. This infrastructure is meticulously designed and strategically distributed across various geographical locations. It includes multiple components, such as Regions, **Availability Zones (AZs)**, Edge Locations, and Outposts, each serving a specific purpose to enhance the performance, reliability, and scalability of AWS services. *Figure 1.5* displays the AWS global infrastructure:

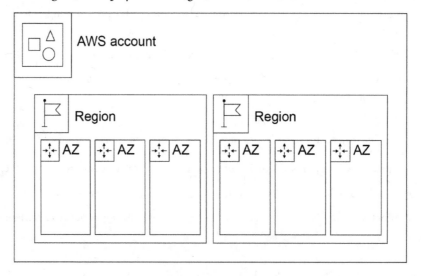

Figure 1.5: AWS global infrastructure

Regions

AWS Regions are geographical areas that host multiple AWS data centers. Each Region is a separate geographic area, isolated and independent from the other Regions to prevent service failures from affecting multiple Regions. This design enhances fault tolerance and stability, ensuring that even if there is a disaster, data integrity and service continuity are maintained. Regions also help you to adhere to data residency requirements, as customers can choose where their data is stored.

Availability Zones

Within each AWS Region, there are AZs. An AZ is a cluster of data centers, each with its own off-grid power, networking capabilities, and connectivity, located in separate buildings that are far enough apart to be protected from a local event (for example, a flood) that could cause an outage. These AZs offer protection against failures of individual servers or entire data centers. By distributing resources across multiple AZs within a Region, AWS provides high availability and fault tolerance to applications and databases.

Edge Locations

Edge Locations are endpoints for AWS that are used to cache content. This aspect of AWS's global infrastructure is primarily used by Amazon CloudFront (AWS's content delivery network) to distribute content to end users with lower latency. These locations are positioned in major cities and highly populated areas around the world, and they bring AWS services closer to the end users, reducing latency and improving the speed of data delivery.

Outposts

AWS Outposts brings multiple AWS services, including its infrastructure, operating methods, and APIs, to your own data center or on-premises facility. It is part of AWS's hybrid cloud solutions, allowing businesses with low latency or high-security requirements to integrate between on-premises data centers and AWS's cloud services. This allows them to run local workloads as if they were on AWS.

We will now take a look at the best practices to deploy and build on AWS. These best practices are known as the Well-Architected Framework.

AWS Architecture

Designing cloud architecture on AWS revolves around a set of fundamental principles aimed at building efficient, resilient, and scalable systems. Key among these is scalability, ensuring that the architecture can handle varying levels of demand without compromising performance or incurring unnecessary costs. AWS provides a range of scalable services, such as Auto Scaling and Elastic Load Balancing, that automatically adjust the computing capacity in response to traffic fluctuations. Fault tolerance is another critical principle, where the architecture is designed to gracefully handle and recover from failures, ensuring continuous operation. This is achieved through redundant and decoupled components, as well as regular backup strategies. High availability is also a priority, focusing on minimizing downtime and maintaining operational performance despite system failures. This is often addressed through the use of multiple AZs to distribute resources and mitigate the impact of outages.

The AWS **Well-Architected Framework (WAF)** plays a crucial role in helping cloud architects design reliable, secure, and efficient systems in the cloud. This framework is built around six pillars:

- Operational excellence
- Security
- Reliability
- Performance efficiency
- Cost optimization
- Sustainability

Each pillar emphasizes aspects such as automating changes, preparing for failure, securing data and applications, optimizing resources, being sustainable, and understanding and controlling costs. The framework encourages architects to think critically about their architectures in the context of these principles, ensuring that their AWS-based systems are scalable, fault-tolerant, and highly available. By adhering to these principles and utilizing the WAF, organizations can build cloud architectures that not only meet their current needs but are also prepared for future challenges and growth. *Figure 1.6* shows the pillars of WAF:

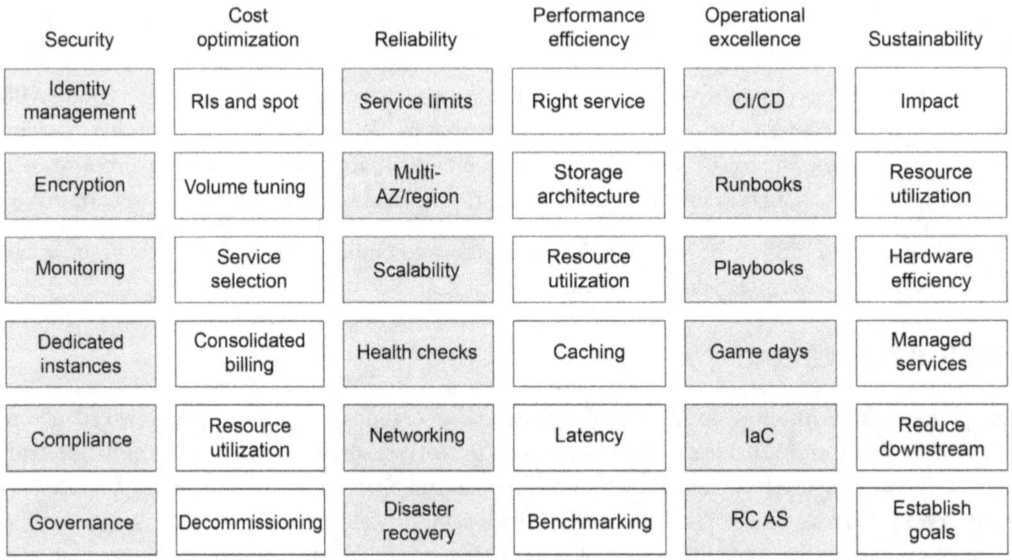

Security	Cost optimization	Reliability	Performance efficiency	Operational excellence	Sustainability
Identity management	RIs and spot	Service limits	Right service	CI/CD	Impact
Encryption	Volume tuning	Multi-AZ/region	Storage architecture	Runbooks	Resource utilization
Monitoring	Service selection	Scalability	Resource utilization	Playbooks	Hardware efficiency
Dedicated instances	Consolidated billing	Health checks	Caching	Game days	Managed services
Compliance	Resource utilization	Networking	Latency	IaC	Reduce downstream
Governance	Decommissioning	Disaster recovery	Benchmarking	RC AS	Establish goals

Figure 1.6: WAF pillars

If you have looked at the *AWS Certified Solutions Architect – Associate (SAA-C03) Certification* exam guide, you may have noticed that many of the domains share names and themes with the WAF. Therefore, having good knowledge of the WAF and its best practices will assist you in the exam.

Let's now look at those exam domains and see how they relate to WAF.

Design Secure Architecture

Creating secure architecture on AWS involves implementing robust security measures to protect data, manage access, and ensure compliance. This domain is critical for building trust and maintaining the integrity of cloud-based systems:

- **Identity and access management (IAM)**: Manage user access and encryption keys to protect data
- **Data protection**: Implement encryption, tokenization, and data masking to secure data
- **Network security**: Utilize firewalls, private networks, and secure access points

This domain aligns with AWS WAF's security pillar and is vital to ensure data integrity and confidentiality, which is covered in the *AWS Certified Solutions Architect – Associate (SAA-C03) Certification* exam.

Designing Resilient Architecture

Resilient architecture is designed to maintain operational capabilities in the face of disruptions, such as system failures or external threats. This aspect is crucial for ensuring continuity and minimizing downtime in cloud environments:

- **High availability**: Use multiple AZs and Auto Scaling for uninterrupted service
- **Backup and disaster recovery**: Implement data backup and disaster recovery strategies that meet your business requirements
- **Decoupling**: Separate components to prevent cascading failures, ensuring one component's failure does not impact others

Integral to the AWS WAF's reliability pillar, this concept is heavily emphasized in the Solutions Architect Associate exam.

Designing High-Performing Architecture

High-performing architecture focuses on optimizing the efficiency and effectiveness of cloud resources. This involves leveraging AWS services to achieve the best performance for applications and workloads.

- **Elasticity and scalability**: Dynamically allocate resources to meet demand without over-provisioning
- **Content distribution**: Use **content delivery networks (CDNs)** to reduce latency
- **Optimized compute and storage**: Select appropriate instance types and storage solutions for the workload requirements

This domain relates to the performance efficiency pillar of the AWS WAF and is a key component of the Solutions Architect Associate exam.

Designing Cost-Optimized Architecture

Cost-optimized architecture aims to reduce costs while maximizing the value delivered. It involves careful planning and management of AWS resources to ensure economic efficiency:

- **Cost-effective resource allocation**: Choose the most cost-effective AWS resources for a task

- **Budgeting and cost monitoring**: Implement tools for monitoring and managing AWS spending

- **Elasticity and scalability**: Use scaling and elasticity to align costs with actual demand

This approach is aligned with the cost optimization pillar of AWS WAF and is an essential aspect of the *AWS Certified Solutions Architect – Associate (SAA-C03) Certification* exam.

All the exam domains will cover the operational excellence and sustainability pillars as well. If you look at the chapter lists in this exam guide, you will see chapters for each exam domain. This is to ensure that you not only have an understanding of the individual services that AWS offers but also know how to integrate and design them across a wider range of services, which will be tested in the exam.

Next, you will learn about cloud economics and why organizations choose to use the cloud, particularly when they are aiming to save costs.

Cloud Economics

Cloud economics fundamentally transform the financial model of IT infrastructure, offering a more flexible and often cost-effective alternative to traditional IT systems. Understanding the nuances of cloud costs is vital for businesses considering implementing cloud solutions or already doing so. It involves understanding the pay-as-you-go pricing model, contrasting it with conventional IT cost structures, and recognizing the efficiency gains that cloud computing can offer.

Understanding Cloud Costs

The economic landscape of cloud computing is shaped by its unique pricing model. Understanding this model is key to unlocking the full potential of cloud cost savings. We will now look at the main cost differentiators between the cloud and an on-premises deployment.

Infrastructure Management

The approach to infrastructure management is a fundamental differentiator between cloud and on-premises solutions, impacting cost and operational efficiency:

- **Cloud**: Offloads infrastructure management to providers, enhancing focus on innovation and core activities
- **On-premises**: Requires direct management of hardware and software, increasing complexity and costs

Capital Expenses

The distinction between operational and capital expenses is a critical financial consideration in the cloud versus on-premises choice:

- **Cloud**: Operates on an **operational expenditure (OpEx)** model, minimizing upfront costs
- **On-premises**: Involves significant **capital expenditure (CapEx)** for hardware and software, impacting initial investment requirements
- *Figure 1.7* lists the difference between CapEx and OpEx:

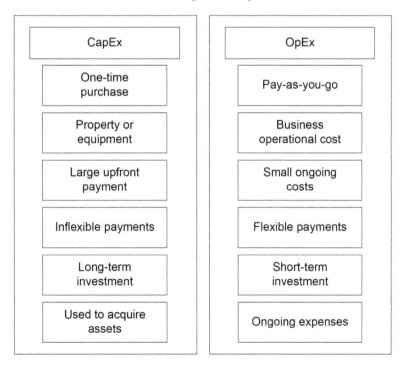

Figure 1.7: CapEx versus OpEx

Scalability

Scalability is a key factor in cost management and resource optimization, differing significantly between cloud and traditional infrastructure:

- **Cloud**: Offers easy and cost-effective scalability, aligning resource use with demand
- **On-premises**: Scaling can be costly and complex, often leading to resource overprovisioning

Flexibility

The level of flexibility in adapting to business needs and technological changes is a crucial aspect of cloud economics:

- **Cloud**: Provides extensive flexibility with a range of services and tools for rapid adaptation
- **On-premises**: May have limited flexibility, hindering swift response to market and technological shifts
- You now have an understanding of cloud economics, and we can now take a look at cost optimization strategies specific to AWS.

Cost Optimization Strategies

- Cost optimization strategies in cloud computing, especially within AWS, focus on utilizing various techniques and tools to effectively manage and minimize expenses. These strategies are crucial for organizations looking to leverage the full potential of cloud computing while maintaining control over their spending. Implementing these cost optimization methods ensures efficient resource utilization, ultimately leading to a more economical and sustainable cloud environment. We will now look at how you can optimize costs within an AWS deployment.

Optimizing Costs in AWS

AWS offers several techniques to help users optimize their spending, ensuring efficient use of resources without compromising on performance and scalability. Some examples of cost optimization are as follows:

- **Reserved instances**: Purchasing reserved instances offers discounts compared to on-demand pricing, suitable for workloads with predictable usage
- **Auto-scaling**: This feature dynamically adjusts resources to maintain performance, reducing costs by ensuring only necessary resources are used
- **Right-sizing resources**: Regularly assessing and adjusting resource allocation can lead to significant savings by ensuring resources are optimally sized for current needs

You can use these techniques to help reduce your costs, but you also need to be able to accurately monitor them. This is where AWS tooling can help.

AWS Cost Management and Optimization Tools

AWS provides a suite of tools designed specifically for cost management and optimization, aiding users in maintaining budget control and financial efficiency:

- **AWS Cost Explorer**: An easy-to-use interface to visualize and understand AWS spending patterns
- **AWS Budgets**: Allows users to set custom budgets and receive alerts when costs or usage exceed predefined thresholds
- **AWS Trusted Advisor**: Offers recommendations for cost reduction, performance improvement, and enhancing security

Total Cost of Ownership (TCO) and Return on Investment (ROI)

When trying to calculate an accurate cost comparison between on-premises and the cloud, it is important to consider all aspects of running the service rather than just the direct costs of the assets. Cost comparisons often miss the extra hidden costs of running on-premises, such as electricity, physical security, and operational staff costs.

TCO and ROI are two crucial financial metrics, each serving different purposes in evaluating and guiding investment decisions.

TCO

TCO refers to the total cost of purchasing, operating, and maintaining a product or system over its entire life cycle. In the context of technology and cloud computing, this includes hardware and software purchasing, operational costs such as management and technical support, communications, end-user expenses, and more indirect costs such as downtime, training, occupied space, and the costs associated with renting a data center or cooling it.

TCO is used to assess the full cost implications of a technology investment. It is particularly useful when comparing different purchasing options – for instance, choosing between different technology solutions or deciding between cloud-based and on-premises infrastructure. TCO provides a comprehensive picture of the cost burdens associated with each option, helping businesses understand the long-term financial impact.

ROI

ROI measures the profitability or efficiency of an investment. It is calculated by dividing the net profit of an investment by its total cost. In technology projects, ROI helps quantify the financial benefits (such as increased revenue, reduced costs, and improved productivity) against the investment made in technology.

ROI is typically used to evaluate the effectiveness of an investment and compare the efficiency of several different investments. In a business setting, ROI can be crucial for justifying technology investments, particularly when the benefits are expected to be substantial relative to the costs. It is a key metric when a company needs to prioritize between different projects or when seeking to demonstrate the financial value of IT investments to stakeholders.

When to Use Which

When the primary concern is understanding the full, long-term cost of a technology solution, choose TCO. It is ideal for budgeting and cost management purposes, especially when comparing the financial implications of different deployment models or technologies.

When the focus is on the profitability and efficiency of an investment, choose ROI. It is suitable for making business cases, justifying expenditure, and in decision-making scenarios where you need to demonstrate the financial gain relative to an investment's cost.

In summary, TCO is about the cost (what you will spend) while ROI is about the benefits (what you will gain). Both metrics are complementary and often used together for a well-rounded financial analysis of technology investments.

Calculating TCO

Calculating TCO involves a systematic approach to quantifying costs and benefits. Let's take a look at a simplified example.

TCO

In this scenario, a company is considering migrating to a cloud-based server from an on-premises server.

Let's identify the costs over five years:

On-premises server:

- Initial cost (e.g., hardware and software licenses): $10,000
- Annual maintenance and support costs: $2,000
- Energy costs per year: $500
- Staff costs (IT management) per year: $3,000
- **Total cost:**
- Initial cost: $10,000
- Recurring costs (maintenance, energy, and staff): ($2,000 + $500 + $3,000) * 5 = $27,500
- TCO for 5 years = $10,000 (initial) + $27,500 (recurring) = **$37,500**

Cloud-based server:

- Monthly subscription fee: $500

- No additional maintenance or energy costs

- **Total cost**:

- Subscription costs: $500 * 12 months * 5 years = $30,000

- TCO for 5 years = **$30,000**

The TCO for the cloud-based server over five years is $30,000, whereas the on-premises server is $37,500.

Now that you have learned how to evaluate and compare costs between on-premises and the cloud, as well as how to cost-optimize your cloud computing services, it is time to get started with AWS. In the next section, you will create an AWS account and set up the AWS CLI. If you already have this configured, you can skip it.

Creating an AWS Account

In later chapters in this book, you will be able to complete hands-on labs using the AWS tools and services. To complete these labs, you will need an AWS account.

Creating and setting up an AWS account, generating access keys, and installing the AWS CLI involves several steps. Here is a detailed guide to walk you through the process:

1. Go to the AWS home page: `https://aws.amazon.com/`.

2. Click on `Create an AWS Account`, as shown in *Figure 1.8*:

Figure 1.8: Creating an AWS account

3. Fill in your email address, password, and account name.

4. Choose `Personal` or `Professional` and provide the necessary contact information.

5. Enter your credit card details. AWS will make a small charge to verify the card, which is later refunded.

6. Confirm your identity via a phone call and by entering the PIN displayed on the screen.

7. Select an appropriate support plan. The basic plan is free.

8. Once the account is created, sign into your new AWS account.

Creating an IAM User and Access Keys

You can follow the given instructions to create an IAM User and Access Keys:

1. In the AWS Management Console, go to `Services` and select `IAM` as shown in *Figure 1.9*:

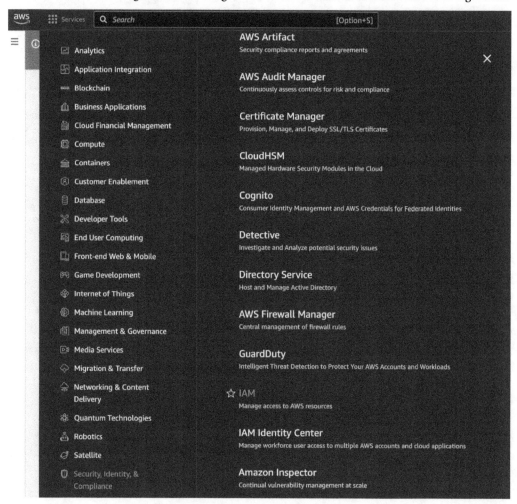

Figure 1.9: Navigate to IAM

2. Click on `Users` and then `Add user`.

3. Enter a username and select `Programmatic access` for the AWS Management Console access type.

4. Attach existing policies directly and select `Administrator Access` for full access. Alternatively, choose specific permissions based on your needs.

5. Review the details and create the user.

6. Once the user is created, download the `.csv` file or store the access key ID and secret access key. This is needed to use the AWS CLI.

Installing the AWS CLI

To install the AWS CLI for Windows, follow these steps:

1. Go to the AWS CLI installation page and download the appropriate version for Windows.

2. Open the downloaded MSI installer and follow the installation prompts.

3. Open the Command Prompt and type `aws—version` to ensure that it's installed.

To install the AWS CLI for macOS/Linux, follow these steps:

1. In your Terminal, use the following command:

```
curl "https://awscli.amazonaws.com/AWSCLIV2.pkg" -o
"AWSCLIV2.pkg"
sudo installer -pkg AWSCLIV2.pkg -target /
```

2. Type `aws—version` in the Terminal.

Configuring the AWS CLI

You can follow the given instructions to configure AWS CLI:

1. On Windows, use Command Prompt or PowerShell. On macOS/Linux, use the Terminal.

2. Type `aws configure` and press `Enter`.

3. Input your access key ID and secret access key.

4. Enter your preferred AWS region (e.g., `us-west-2`).

5. Enter the desired output format (e.g., JSON).

Verify the Configuration

Run a simple AWS CLI command to list all the S3 buckets as a test – `aws s3 ls`.

If configured correctly, this should display a list of S3 buckets (if any exist) or return nothing without errors.

You now have an AWS account set up with an IAM user, and the AWS CLI is installed and configured on your machine, ready for use. Remember to handle your credentials securely and adhere to AWS's best practices for IAM users and permissions.

Summary

In this chapter, you have gained a comprehensive understanding of the fundamentals of cloud computing, including its key characteristics, service models, deployment models, benefits, and cloud economics. This knowledge is crucial because it forms the foundation for your journey into AWS solutions architecture and prepares you for the *AWS Certified Solutions Architect* exam.

You have learned how cloud computing revolutionizes IT infrastructure management, offering scalability, cost-efficiency, flexibility, accessibility, and security. You have explored the significance of cloud service models and deployment models, helping you make informed decisions about resource allocation and architecture choices.

You have now created and configured an AWS account that can be used for the hands-on labs and demos throughout this guide. You will use this account straight away because, in the next chapter, we will dive into the first building block of AWS infrastructure, the VPC. This critical component will enable you to create isolated network environments in the AWS cloud, setting the stage for designing and architecting scalable and resilient cloud solutions.

You will learn about the Virtual Private Cloud in the next chapter.

Exam Readiness Drill – Chapter Review Questions

Apart from mastering key concepts, strong test-taking skills under time pressure are essential for acing your certification exam. That's why developing these abilities early in your learning journey is critical.

Exam readiness drills, using the free online practice resources provided with this book, help you progressively improve your time management and test-taking skills while reinforcing the key concepts you've learned.

HOW TO GET STARTED

- Open the link or scan the QR code at the bottom of this page

- If you have unlocked the practice resources already, log in to your registered account. If you haven't, follow the instructions in *Chapter 16* and come back to this page.

- Once you log in, click the START button to start a quiz

- We recommend attempting a quiz multiple times till you're able to answer most of the questions correctly and well within the time limit.

- You can use the following practice template to help you plan your attempts:

Working On Accuracy		
Attempt	Target	Time Limit
Attempt 1	40% or more	Till the timer runs out
Attempt 2	60% or more	Till the timer runs out
Attempt 3	75% or more	Till the timer runs out
Working On Timing		
Attempt 4	75% or more	1 minute before time limit
Attempt 5	75% or more	2 minutes before time limit
Attempt 6	75% or more	3 minutes before time limit

The above drill is just an example. Design your drills based on your own goals and make the most out of the online quizzes accompanying this book.

First time accessing the online resources? 🔒

You'll need to unlock them through a one-time process. **Head to** *Chapter 16* **for instructions**.

Open Quiz	
https://packt.link/SAAC03Ch01 OR scan this QR code →	

2
Virtual Private Cloud

This chapter delves into the intricacies of AWS **Virtual Private Clouds** (**VPCs**), offering you an in-depth understanding of their structure and functionality. You will gain valuable insights into how VPCs provide a dedicated, isolated section within the AWS cloud, empowering you with full control over your network architecture. From setting up IP address ranges and creating subnets to managing intricate network settings, this chapter is designed to equip you with the knowledge and skills needed to efficiently harness the potential of AWS VPCs in your cloud-based projects.

In this chapter, you will cover the following main topics:

- Introduction to AWS VPCs
- VPC configuration basics
- Security in AWS VPCs
- VPC connectivity

You will start by learning the basics of VPCs and what they are designed to do.

Introduction to AWS VPCs

AWS VPCs represent a foundational infrastructure element, providing you with a dedicated, logically isolated section of the AWS cloud. Within this virtual network, you have full control over the network architecture, enabling you to design, configure, and manage your network resources as per your specific needs.

At its core, an AWS VPC is a virtual network that allows you to define your IP address range, create subnets, and manage network settings. It serves as a private cloud environment where you can launch and operate various AWS resources while maintaining network isolation from other AWS accounts.

An analogy for an AWS VPC is a gated community within a city. In a city, you have various neighborhoods with their own houses and streets, much like the different VPCs within AWS. Each neighborhood (VPC) is self-contained and has its own rules and regulations. The houses (AWS resources) within each neighborhood can communicate with each other freely, but there are gates (security groups and NACLs) controlling who can enter or exit the neighborhood.

Just as you can customize the appearance and layout of your house within a neighborhood, you can configure the IP addressing and network structure within your VPC. Additionally, you can connect multiple neighborhoods (VPC peering) or establish secure tunnels (VPN connections) between your neighborhood and other places, such as your workplace or a friend's house (on-premises networks).

This analogy helps illustrate the idea that a VPC is a controlled and isolated environment within the broader AWS cloud, where you have control over your network while benefiting from the security and services offered by the AWS infrastructure.

Key Components of AWS VPCs

AWS VPCs are made up of several components to allow flexibility, connectivity, and security. You will now look at the most critical components that you will need to know for the exam. You will learn about all of these in more depth later in this chapter:

- **IP addressing**: VPCs enable you to define your IP address range, granting you the flexibility to design your network's IP schema. These are similar to house numbering systems that govern how houses are numbered following a pattern across the entire estate. You cannot have two houses with the same street name and number.

- **Subnets**: Subnets are subdivisions within a VPC, located in specific **Availability Zones** (**AZs**). They play a crucial role in organizing resources and ensuring fault tolerance. To use our house analogy, subnets are like streets in our estate. Each house must have a unique number on the street.

- **Route tables**: Route tables dictate the traffic flow between subnets and control how traffic is routed within the VPC. A route table is like a set of signposts on our estate that helps users find the best path between the houses. It can also point you to the nearest main road to find other estates.

- **Security groups**: Security groups function as virtual firewalls, allowing you to manage inbound and outbound traffic to your EC2 instances and other resources. These could be described as being like an individual homeowner's security system, only allowing pre-authorized visitors.

- **Network Access Control Lists** (**NACLs**): NACLs provide an additional layer of network security by acting as packet filters, governing traffic at the subnet level. NACLs could be compared to a neighborhood watch scheme or a checkpoint at the end of each street.

Stateful Versus Stateless

NACLs and security groups control the flow of packets around your VPC using two different methods, stateful and stateless. Stateful means that the security control remembers which packets and interactions were allowed past in one direction and allows them back through the other way. Imagine you are a customer in a restaurant and the receptionist remembers you and lets you leave and come back at will. Stateless means that the security control has no memory of previous events and therefore a packet that has been let past in one direction will not be let back through unless specifically authorized. In the restaurant example, you would need to show some identification or a receipt to the receptionist each time you wanted to leave or re-enter the restaurant. Security groups are stateful, and therefore you only need to create inbound rules to handle these; outbound rules is automatically authorized with the same criteria. NACLs are stateless and therefore both inbound and outbound rules must be created.

Figure 2.1 is a basic architecture diagram of a simple but commonly used VPC with four subnets, two of which are private (cannot be accessed from the internet) and two of which are public (can be accessed from the internet). You can see how the subnets sit in different **AZs**, ensuring high availability in case of an AZ failure.

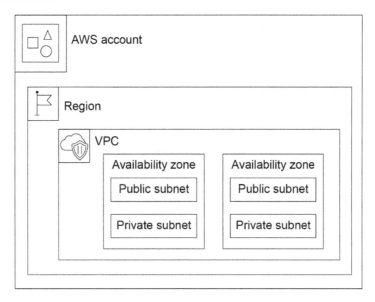

Figure 2.1: AWS VPC architecture

You will also notice that a VPC sits within a region; you cannot create a cross-region VPC. Later in this chapter, you will learn how you can link or connect VPCs together across regions if needed.

VPC Configuration Basics

To effectively use AWS VPCs, you need to understand the available VPC configuration options, which include IP addressing, subnetting, the use of AZs and Regions, and the choice between default and custom VPCs. You will first learn about how IP addresses are assigned and how **Classless Inter-Domain Routing (CIDR)** notation is used to control the available IPs within subnets.

CIDR Notation

CIDR notation is a compact and efficient way to represent IP address ranges and subnet masks in IPv4 addressing. It is widely used for network design, routing, and specifying IP address allocations. CIDR notation is particularly valuable because it allows for flexibility in dividing and allocating IP addresses without relying on traditional class-based addressing (class A, B, and C networks).

In CIDR notation, an IP address range is represented as follows:

`IPAddress/PrefixLength`

- `IPAddress`: This is the base IP address that represents the network or subnet. It identifies the starting point of the range.

- `PrefixLength`: This is the number of bits (from left to right) that represent the network or subnet. It indicates the size of the network or subnet and is often represented as a number following a forward slash (`/`).

Here are a few examples to illustrate CIDR notation:

- **Single IP address** – `192.168.1.5/32`: This represents a single IP address – in this case, `192.168.1.5` – with a prefix length of 32 bits, indicating that it is not part of a subnet (equivalent to a subnet mask of `255.255.255.255`).

- **Small subnet** – `10.0.0.0/24`: This represents a subnet starting at `10.0.0.0` with a subnet mask of `255.255.255.0`. In CIDR notation, the prefix length of 24 bits indicates that the first 24 bits are dedicated to the network portion, allowing for 256 host addresses within the subnet ($2^8 = 256$).

- **Large subnet** – `172.16.0.0/16`: This represents a large subnet starting at `172.16.0.0` with a subnet mask of `255.255.0.0`. In CIDR notation, the prefix length of 16 bits indicates that the first 16 bits are dedicated to the network portion, allowing for a significantly larger address space than the previous example.

CIDR notation is especially useful when designing complex networks, summarizing routes for efficient routing table management, and specifying firewall rules. CIDR is a shorthand method of describing IP ranges, and it is much easier to read than some of the alternatives, such as Classful (which allows fewer options), using a subnet mask (255.0.0.0) to control the allowed ranges, or having to specify an entire network range (192.168.0.0-192.168.255.255). It also allows network administrators and architects to allocate IP address resources more efficiently and precisely by specifying the network size in a flexible and concise format. CIDR notation is used with an AWS VPC to define the IP ranges available for the servers and services to use.

CIDR notation is likely to be featured in the AWS exam as it can often cause architecture problems and confusion. You can now take a look at why understanding subnet masking and CIDR notation is so important.

IP Addressing and Subnetting in VPCs

In AWS VPCs, IP addressing and subnetting form the bedrock of your network architecture and provide the foundational structure for your VPC, allowing you to tailor it precisely to your organization's requirements.

IP address allocations are an important concept in networking, as they help devices communicate over the internet and within local networks. IP addresses act as unique identifiers for devices such as computers, printers, or even your fridge, similar to phone numbers or home addresses. Just like how a postal service uses a street address to deliver mail, IP addresses are used to route data to the right destination. They also play a key role in organizing networks, enhancing security, controlling access, and supporting network growth. Security is enhanced by using IP addresses as you can control where data is sent rather than allowing open access to all devices.

When setting up AWS VPCs, you need to define the IP range and it is difficult to change later. You need to decide on the IP ranges you want and need before you create the VPC to avoid running into problems later. Many AWS customers create a VPC with too small a CIDR and then they run out of IP addresses and cannot scale. However, too large a CIDR range could leave IP addresses unused in one VPC, costing money and making it more difficult to connect to other VPCs as it's likely the IP ranges will overlap.

If you incorrectly define your IP addresses within your subnets, you could end up with an IP address conflict. An IP address conflict occurs when two devices on the same network end up with the same IP address. Because IP addresses are unique identifiers used for routing data, this situation can lead to various issues, such as, primarily, when there is a conflict, it can disrupt communication and cause network problems. This is a particular problem when you need to connect outside of your VPC or connect to on-premises systems.

Here is an example to illustrate what happens in the case of an IP address conflict. Imagine you have two AWS VPCs with an EC2 (server) instance running in each. These instances need to communicate with each other. Both VPCs have been configured with the same CIDR range of 10.0.1.0/28.

Both EC2 instances are assigned the same IP address (10.0.1.5) at the same time. Data sent to 10.0.1.5 might reach either one of the instances, causing inconsistencies and communication errors. It can lead to application failures and confusion in your VPC.

Within your VPC, you have full control over IP address allocation. You can define your IP address range, ensuring that it aligns with your network's specific needs. This level of customization means you can create a network infrastructure that mirrors your on-premises environment or adopt a completely new addressing scheme to suit your cloud architecture. Once you have defined your IP ranges for each subnet, it is difficult and complex to change them, therefore it is critical to define your subnets carefully and with full understanding of your business needs both now and in the future.

Subnet Design Flexibility

Subnetting within a VPC allows you to logically divide your IP address range into smaller, manageable segments. You start by defining the IP range for your entire VPC. Typically, you would allocate a large subnet range, such as 120.0.0.0/16, which would give you 65,536 IP addresses, or 56.24.0.0/24, which would give you 254 IP addresses. After defining the VPC, you would then define the subnets. By doing so, you can organize your resources effectively. For instance, you can create public subnets for resources that require direct internet access and private subnets for those that should remain isolated from the internet. Any subnets open to the internet can be targeted by hackers, so the fewer servers, databases, or applications that can be reached from outside your VPC, the more secure they will be. In general, the typical design is to only put internet-facing applications into a public subnet, and all other servers and databases should be put in private subnets. *Figure 2.2* shows a basic configuration and how the IP addresses for each subnet are controlled by the VPC subnet mask.

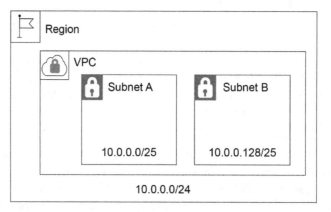

Figure 2.2: VPC and subnet IP ranges

You can have different numbers of IP addresses in each subnet, allowing you to only define precise numbers of IP ranges for each group. This helps prevent the wastage of unused but allocated IPs. Many organizations are currently faced with an issue of IP addresses running out due to business growth, so correctly sizing your subnets will allow you to grow with fewer compromises. Subnets can also be used to isolate certain applications or servers from others, which, when coupled with correctly defined **Security Groups** (**SGs**) and NACLs, improves security and access controls. You will learn about SGs and NACLs later in this chapter.

AZs and Regions

AWS VPCs are designed to be highly available and fault-tolerant, thanks to the concepts of AZs and Regions.

A Region is made up of multiple AZs, and an AZ is made up of multiple data centers that are located close to one another, typically within 100 km.

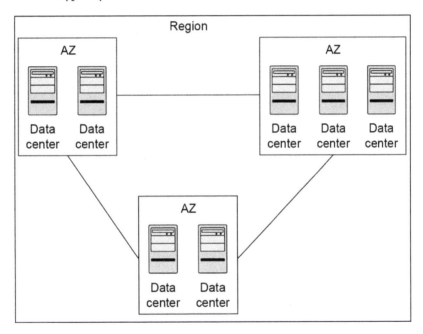

Figure 2.3: Regions and AZs diagram

Now, take a look at a comparison between AZs and Regions in *Table 2.1*:

Feature	Availability Zones (AZs)	Regions
Definition	Distinct, isolated data centers within a region.	Separate geographic areas containing multiple AZs.
Purpose	Provide fault tolerance and redundancy within a region.	Provide geographical distribution and redundancy on a broader scale.
Fault Tolerance	If one AZ has an issue, operations can failover to another AZ in the same region without significant disruption.	If there's a regional outage, operations can switch to another region to maintain continuity.
Latency	Generally lower latency between resources in the same region's AZs due to physical proximity.	Latency varies more significantly due to the greater physical distances between regions.
Use Case	Ideal for applications requiring high availability within the same region.	Suitable for applications needing resilience against regional failures or for serving global audiences with localized infrastructure.
Data Resilience	Data can be replicated across multiple AZs within the same region to prevent data loss from AZ-specific failures.	Data can be replicated across regions to protect against large-scale disasters or regional disruptions.
Scalability	Resources can scale within a region while maintaining close network proximity.	Scalability across regions can manage demand from users distributed around the globe.

Table 2.1: AZs versus Regions

AZs represent distinct, geographically isolated data centers within a Region. Deploying resources across multiple AZs ensures redundancy and fault tolerance. If one AZ experiences an issue, your applications can seamlessly fail over to resources in another AZ, maintaining uninterrupted service availability.

AWS Regions are separate geographic areas containing multiple AZs. By deploying your VPC resources across different Regions, you can achieve regional redundancy. In case of a large-scale disaster or regional outage, your VPC can continue operating from another geographic location, ensuring business continuity.

Default VPC Versus Custom VPC

When you first create an AWS account, AWS automatically sets up a default VPC for your convenience. However, understanding the differences between the default and custom VPC options is crucial for tailoring your network environment to your specific needs. *Table 2.2* shows the main differences between a default and a custom VPC:

Feature	Default VPC	Custom VPC
Subnet Setup	Automatically comes with a subnet in each Availability Zone within the Region	Requires manual setup of subnets, offering flexibility in how you organize and control your network resources
Internet Connectivity	Comes pre-configured with an Internet Gateway (IGW) for immediate internet access	Internet access must be manually set up by attaching an IGW or using other connectivity methods
Security Configuration	Default security settings, which generally allow all outbound traffic and block unsolicited inbound traffic	Custom security settings can be configured, tailoring security groups and NACLs according to specific security needs
Route Tables	Pre-configured with a main route table that includes routes to reach the internet	Custom route tables must be created and configured, allowing precise control over routing between subnets and external connections
IP Addressing	Automatically assign public IP addresses to instances launched in default subnets (can be modified)	Control over public and private IP address assignment based on subnet settings
DHCP Options Set	Uses a default DHCP option set which can be adequate but is not customizable	Allows for the creation of custom DHCP option sets, providing flexibility in domain name, DNS servers, and more
Ease of Use	Ready to use upon AWS account setup; ideal for beginners or quick deployments	Requires more initial setup and understanding of AWS networking, offering more granular control

Table 2.2: Default versus custom VPC

The default VPC is a preconfigured VPC that comes with default settings, including a default IP address range, subnets, route tables, and security groups. While it offers a quick start, it may not align perfectly with your organization's requirements around network design or IP ranges. The default VPC is shared among all AWS accounts in your Region, which might not be ideal for security and isolation.

Custom VPCs are designed for applications and organizations that require more control and flexibility over their network architecture. All production workloads should be placed in a custom VPC to ensure you maintain your security standards and controls and are not restricted by a default VPC. With a custom VPC, you define every aspect of the network, including IP address ranges, subnets, route tables, and security groups. This level of customization allows you to align your VPC precisely with your business needs, security policies, and compliance requirements.

Security in AWS VPCs

Securing your AWS VPC is the most important area of cloud architecture. It is crucial to understand your role within the shared responsibility model, which defines the division of security responsibilities between AWS and customers.

In the realm of AWS VPCs, security is a collaborative effort. AWS shoulders the responsibility for securing the underlying infrastructure, while customers are entrusted with safeguarding their applications and data hosted on AWS resources. This shared responsibility model underscores the need for customers to implement robust security measures to protect their cloud-based assets effectively. In practice, this means that AWS will take responsibility for the security of the cloud, so if someone gained unauthorized access to an AWS-held root or administration account, AWS would be accountable. However, if someone gained unauthorized access to a customer-held root or admin account, the customer would be liable. *Figure 2.4* shows the different areas of responsibility:

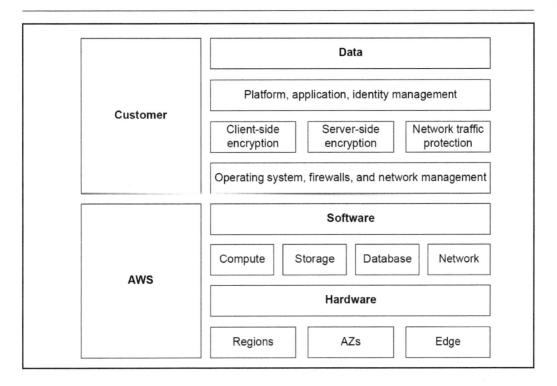

Figure 2.4: AWS shared responsibility model

Security Groups (SGs)

SGs serve as stateful firewalls within AWS VPCs. Stateful means the SG remembers that the traffic was authorized to pass through in one direction and therefore lets the response return the other way. You do not need to specifically define those rules. These virtual barriers exert control over inbound and outbound traffic to and from instances residing within a VPC. SGs act as the first line of defense, allowing customers to meticulously specify which types of traffic are permitted to access their resources.

By defining rules within SGs, customers can enhance the security posture of their VPCs by only allowing necessary and authorized traffic flows. SGs act at the instance level and can be configured to act over more than one subnet at any one time.

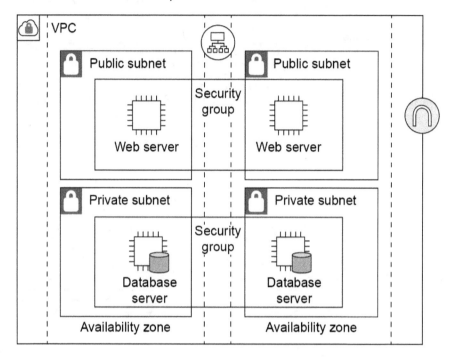

Figure 2.5: SGs across multiple subnets

You will now look at NACLs to see how they differ from SGs.

NACLs

NACLs constitute an additional layer of security operating at the subnet level within an AWS VPC. These NACLs function as stateless packet filters, imparting granular control over the flow of traffic entering and exiting subnets. Stateless means that NACLs do not remember which service sent the inbound request. Therefore, you need to define specific outbound rules, or all outbound traffic is blocked. By crafting specific rules, customers can determine precisely which traffic is allowed and which is denied at the subnet level. NACLs provide an added layer of security defense, increasing the protection of resources within the VPC and helping to enforce network-level security policies effectively. Customers can use NACLs to offer more precise controls and to provide a baseline that cannot be overridden by an SG. This is very useful for customers who have different teams working on VPC configuration, as using NACLs stops anyone from accidentally allowing wide access by misconfiguring an SG.

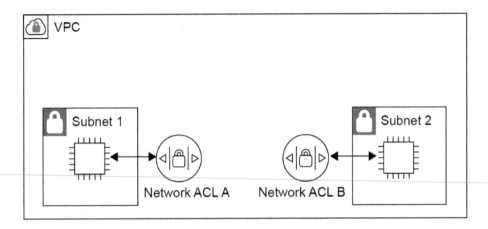

Figure 2.6: NACLs

NACLs and SGs serve different purposes and have distinct characteristics for securing your VPC. *Table 2.3* shows an explanation of the key differences:

Category	SGs	NACLs
Scope of operation	Operate at the instance level, associated with individual EC2 instances within a VPC. Control inbound and outbound traffic at the instance level	Operate at the subnet level, associated with subnets within a VPC. Control traffic entering and exiting entire subnets, affecting all instances within that subnet
Rule evaluation	Stateful: Rules are evaluated based on the state of the connection. If you allow inbound traffic from a specific IP, the corresponding outbound traffic is automatically allowed. Rules are evaluated independently for each instance	Stateless: Rules are evaluated based on defined criteria, separately for inbound and outbound. Rules must be defined for both directions and are evaluated in a sequential order
Rule types	Allow specifying which IP addresses or other SGs can communicate with the instances. Rules focus on allowing or denying specific traffic sources and destinations	Provide fine-grained control, allowing rules based on IP addresses, port ranges, and protocols. Used for detailed network security requirements
Default behavior	All inbound traffic is denied by default, unless explicitly allowed. Outbound traffic is allowed by default	Both inbound and outbound traffic are allowed by default. Custom rules must be created to restrict traffic as needed

Table 2.3: SGs versus NACLs

In this section, you have learned about the main security controls within a VPC and how they differ. You can now take a look at how you can connect to your VPC via the internet, private connections, and how you can get VPCs to communicate with each other if required.

VPC Connectivity

Ensuring effective connectivity within your AWS VPC is a foundational aspect of designing a functional and secure cloud network. To achieve this, you need to configure various essential components and settings that work together seamlessly to enable communication while maintaining security and control. Imagine trying to design the road layout for an entire city to ensure traffic can flow freely, but only certain types of traffic (such as buses or taxis) can use certain roads. AWS provides tools to help users access your services via the internet, as well as allowing operational and development staff backend access to your applications and databases. It also allows you to set up cross-VPC communications using VPC peering. You can now start by looking at how you can enable internet access in your public subnets within your VPC to allow users to connect and to allow your services to communicate with the internet themselves to get updates or to pull in real-time data from external sources.

As the following diagram shows, VPC connectivity can get very complex very quickly, so it is important to spend time planning your VPC design and connections before you start building:

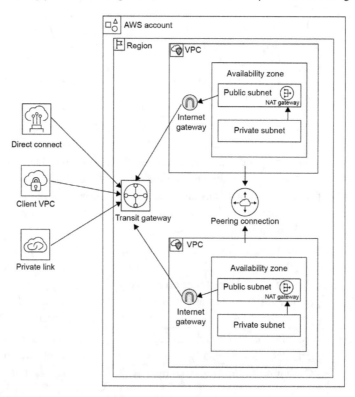

Figure 2.7: VPC connectivity

Internet Gateways

Internet gateways serve as the entry and exit points for internet-bound traffic within your VPC. They enable resources in public subnets to connect to the internet securely. With internet gateways, your resources can access external services hosted on the internet, ensuring seamless connectivity.

For example, web servers located in public subnets require an internet gateway to respond to user requests over the internet securely.

Network Address Translation (NAT) Gateways

NAT gateways act as intermediaries between private subnets and the internet. They facilitate outbound connections initiated by resources within private subnets while masking their private IP addresses. NAT gateways provide a secure way for your resources to access external services without exposing their internal IP addresses directly to the internet.

NAT gateways themselves do not offer direct internet connections. To do that, you need to use them in conjunction with an internet gateway that sits in a public subnet.

Key differences between NAT and internet gateways

NAT and internet gateways initially seem very similar, but they have several differences, both in the way they work and the way you use them, as shown in *Table 2.4*:

Aspect	Internet Gateways	NAT Gateways
Purpose	Provide direct internet access to resources in public subnets. Enable inbound and outbound internet traffic for these resources	Allow outbound internet access for resources in private subnets. Block unsolicited inbound traffic
Use cases	Stateful: Rules are evaluated based on the state of the connection. If you allow inbound traffic from a specific IP, the corresponding outbound traffic is automatically allowed. Rules are evaluated independently for each instance	Used when resources in private subnets need to initiate outbound connections to the internet, for example, software updates or accessing external APIs
Security	Expose resources in public subnets to the internet, making them accessible from anywhere	Enhance security by ensuring that resources in private subnets can communicate with the internet while keeping their private IP addresses hidden from external sources

Aspect	Internet Gateways	NAT Gateways
Traffic direction	Handle both inbound and outbound traffic, allowing public subnet resources to accept incoming connections and initiate outbound connections	Primarily handle outbound traffic initiated by resources in private subnets

Table 2.4: NAT versus internet gateways

Continuing the example, if you had a VPC with web servers in public subnets that need to accept incoming requests from users over the internet, you would configure an internet gateway. For your private database servers in a private subnet, you would configure a NAT gateway to allow them to initiate outbound connections securely.

Once you have set the gateways up, you need to tell your VPC to use them. This is done via route tables.

Route Tables

Route tables in AWS VPCs play a vital role in directing network traffic. By associating subnets with specific route tables, you gain precise control over how traffic flows within your VPC. You can define rules to route traffic locally within the VPC, direct it to internet gateways for external access, or even send it to other VPCs through VPC peering connections.

To illustrate, you can configure a custom route table to route traffic from application servers to a network firewall appliance within your VPC, adding an extra layer of security to your network.

Virtual Private Network (VPN) Connections

VPN connections establish secure communication links between your AWS VPC and on-premises networks. These encrypted tunnels allow data to traverse between your VPC and your on-premises data center or remote offices. VPN connections are crucial when you need to extend your network infrastructure securely to the cloud.

For instance, if your company has an on-premises data center with sensitive data, VPN connections provide a secure bridge to migrate workloads to AWS while maintaining security and compliance.

There are several types of VPNs that you can use with AWS:

- **AWS Direct Connect**: Provides dedicated, private network connections between your on-premises data center or corporate network and AWS resources. It offers high-speed, low-latency connections for mission-critical workloads. This would typically be used when you have a large volume of data that needs to be transferred between your on-premises data center and AWS resources regularly, and you require high-speed, low-latency connections – for example, if you need to keep some data on-premises while moving the application to AWS.

- **AWS Site-to-Site VPN**: Allows you to create encrypted VPN connections between your on-premises network and your Amazon VPCs. This enables secure communication between your data center and AWS resources over the internet. You would pick a Site-to-Site VPN when you want to securely extend your on-premises network into AWS to access resources hosted in Amazon VPCs.

- **AWS Client VPN**: A managed VPN service that enables remote users to securely access AWS resources and on-premises networks from anywhere using OpenVPN-compatible client software. It simplifies remote access and user authentication. Client VPNs work well when you have remote employees, contractors, or partners who need secure access to AWS resources and your on-premises network from remote locations or while traveling.

- **AWS PrivateLink**: Allows you to access AWS services over a private connection without using public IPs. It is a secure and efficient way to connect to AWS services from your VPCs or on-premises environments. If you want to securely access AWS services over a private connection without exposing your data to the public internet, then PrivateLink should meet your needs.

- AWS also offers solutions to help manage connections and VPNs by handling inbound and outbound connections and forwarding them to the correct VPC or endpoint:

- **AWS Transit Gateway**: Simplifies network connectivity and routing by acting as a hub that connects multiple Amazon VPCs, VPN connections, and Direct Connect gateways. It streamlines network architecture, making it easier to scale and manage. Transit Gateway is commonly used when you have a large number of VPCs and need to manage the data flow between them, but it also works well when connected to a small number of VPNs.

- **AWS VPN CloudHub**: Enables multiple on-premises networks to connect to multiple Amazon VPCs using a hub-and-spoke model. It simplifies network connectivity for organizations with complex network topologies. It is designed for companies that have multiple remote branch offices or partner networks that need to connect to multiple Amazon VPCs via a centralized hub-and-spoke network design.

As you can see, there are a lot of different ways to connect to a VPC from outside of the AWS network. This is tested within the exam so you should be able to explain the different VPN options and when to use them.

You can now look at how you would connect multiple VPCs together via VPC peering and AWS Transit Gateway.

VPC Peering

VPC peering simplifies network architecture by establishing connections between multiple VPCs. This enables seamless communication between resources in different virtual networks without the need for complex VPN setups or exposing resources to the public internet.

Imagine your organization maintains separate VPCs for development, testing, and production environments. VPC peering allows data sharing and communication while keeping these environments logically isolated, facilitating efficient development and testing before deployment to production.

However, successful VPC peering requires careful planning, including correct IP allocation and addressing potential IP range overlap.

Proper IP address allocation is fundamental to setting up VPC peering effectively. Each VPC in a peering relationship must have a unique and non-overlapping IP address range. This ensures that there is no ambiguity in routing traffic between VPCs, and it prevents potential conflicts that could disrupt communication.

Consider a scenario where two VPCs have overlapping IP address ranges. This overlap can lead to routing issues and unintended consequences, such as traffic being directed to the wrong VPC or instances with conflicting IP addresses. To avoid such complications, meticulous IP address planning and allocation are crucial.

If you discover that your VPCs have overlapping IP address ranges or you need to resolve such a conflict, there are several approaches you can consider:

- **Re-define the IP ranges of one of the VPCs**: One option is to reconfigure the IP address range of one of the VPCs to eliminate the overlap. This may involve updating the IP addresses of instances, subnets, and route tables in the affected VPC. While effective, this approach can be disruptive and time-consuming, particularly in production environments.

- **VPC peering with a transit VPC**: Another approach is to introduce a transit VPC with unique IP address ranges that acts as an intermediary between the conflicting VPCs. The transit VPC can route traffic between the peered VPCs without IP conflicts. This method is suitable when redefining the IP range of the VPCs is not feasible or practical.

- **VPC peering with Network Address Translation (NAT)**: You can set up VPC peering with NAT instances or NAT gateways in one of the conflicting VPCs. NAT can translate the source or destination IP addresses of packets to ensure that they do not overlap with the other VPC's address range. While this can resolve IP conflicts, it introduces some complexity in routing and network configuration.

- **AWS PrivateLink**: AWS PrivateLink allows you to access services over a private connection. Instead of directly connecting VPCs with overlapping IP ranges, you can leverage AWS PrivateLink to route traffic through AWS services using unique IP addresses, preventing conflicts.

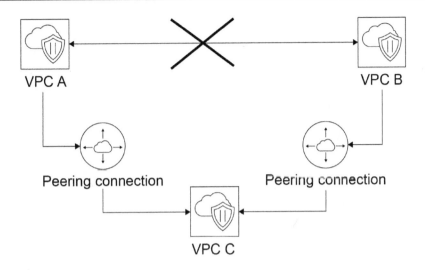

Figure 2.8: VPC peering

If you have multiple VPCs in your account, you may find that setting up peering connections between all of them gets very complicated and difficult to scale efficiently. As you can see in the previous diagram, VPCs do not have transitive connectivity. That means that if you have defined a peering relationship between VPC A and VPC C, and between VPC B and VPC C, there is still no route between VPC A and VPC B. Using AWS Transit Gateway can assist in the management or this type of routing.

AWS Transit Gateway

AWS Transit Gateway acts as a central hub that controls the flow of traffic between all the connected networks, which can include VPCs, AWS Direct Connect gateways, and VPNs. The main advantage of AWS Transit Gateway is its ability to consolidate and manage the interconnectivity of multiple VPCs and on-premises networks through a central hub. This setup significantly simplifies network management and reduces operational complexity. It enables scalable connectivity and centralized management, making it easier for users to manage their entire AWS network with just a few clicks.

Unlike VPC peering, Transit Gateway can support transitive routing by functioning as a centralized network hub. This hub connects multiple VPCs, on-premises networks, and other services, allowing them to communicate with each other seamlessly. Transit Gateway simplifies network architecture by enabling all connected networks to route traffic through this central point, eliminating the need for multiple, direct peering connections between each network. Therefore, while VPC peering is suitable for simpler or fewer connectivity requirements, AWS Transit Gateway is preferred for more complex and scalable network architectures.

Now you have learned enough about the theory of VPCs, let us go ahead and build one.

Hands-on Lab

You are now going to build two VPCs, both with two private and two public subnets, which follow AWS best practices for VPC design. This is a typical VPC architecture where you could create and run an application. Throughout this book, you will add more features to this VPC, including creating servers and simple code to run a small application. Once the VPCs are created, you are going to add internet connectivity to them and then connect the two VPCs together using VPC peering. Make sure you do not end up with overlapping IP ranges.

You have two options to create these VPCs, depending on personal preference. You can use the AWS Management Console, or you can use the **AWS Command Line Interface** (**AWS CLI**).

First, we will look at the console steps.

Creating the First VPC

The first step is to create a VPC. Rather than using the default VPC, creating one manually will help you to turn the theory you have learned in this chapter into real-world knowledge:

1. Log in to the AWS Management Console: `http://console.aws.amazon.com/`.

2. Navigate to the VPC dashboard by going to `Services` and selecting `VPC`.

3. Click `Create VPC`. Name your VPC (e.g., `AWSExamVPC1`). Set the IPv4 CIDR block (e.g., `10.0.0.0/16`). Leave the `IPv6 CIDR block` and `Tenancy` settings as the default. Click `Create`.

Creating Subnets for the First VPC

Now you have created the VPC, you will need to create the subnets so that you can split the traffic into public and private. This will keep your private information, such as databases, secure while allowing internet access to the public subnets:

1. Firstly, you need to create public subnets. In the VPC dashboard, go to `Subnets`, then click `Create Subnet`. Select `AWSExamVPC1`. Name the subnet (e.g., `Public-Subnet-1A`). Choose an AZ. Set the IPv4 CIDR block (e.g., `10.0.1.0/24`).

    Repeat this to create a second public subnet in a different AZ.

2. Now, to create private subnets, repeat the subnet creation steps, naming them (e.g., `Private-Subnet-1A`, `Private-Subnet-1B`) and using different CIDR blocks (e.g., `10.0.2.0/24`, `10.0.3.0/24`).

Setting up an Internet Gateway for the First VPC

An internet gateway will allow your VPC to connect to the internet, allowing both inbound and outbound internet traffic. Follow the given steps to set up an internet gateway for the first VPC:

1. To create an internet gateway, go to `Internet Gateways` and click `Create Internet Gateway`. Name it (e.g., `AWSExamIGW1`) and click `Create`. Attach it to `AWSExamVPC1`.

Setting up a NAT Gateway for the First VPC

A NAT gateway allows your private subnets to connect to the internet for outbound-only traffic. This allows them to obtain patches or updates from the internet without letting traffic from the internet reach them:

1. To create a NAT gateway, go to `NAT Gateways` and click `Create NAT Gateway`. Enter a name (e.g., `AWSExamNAT1`). Select one of the public subnets. Click `Allocate Elastic IP`.
2. Click `Create NAT Gateway`.

Configuring Route Tables for the First VPC

The route tables control how traffic flows around your AWS account and between VPCs. Setting this up correctly ensures any servers you create can communicate with each other as well as with the internet if required:

1. To set up a public route table, go to `Route tables` and select the default route table for `AWSExamVPC1`.
2. Edit routes to add a route to the internet gateway (`Destination: 0.0.0.0/0`, `Target: AWSExamIGW1`).
3. Associate it with the public subnets.
4. To set up a private route table, create a new route table in `AWSExamVPC1`.
5. Add a route to the NAT gateway (`Destination: 0.0.0.0/0`, `Target: NAT Gateway`).
6. Associate it with the private subnets.

Repeating the Previous Steps for the Second VPC

Now, you will create another VPC so that you can set up VPC peering in the next section. Follow the given steps to create the same:

1. To create the second VPC, name the resources appropriately (e.g., `AWSExamVPC2`, `Public-Subnet-2A`, `Private-Subnet-2A`, `AWSExamIGW2`).

2. Use a different IPv4 CIDR block for `AWSExamVPC2` (e.g., `10.1.0.0/16`).

Setting up VPC Peering

VPC peering allows you to connect two VPCs together. This is very useful as your applications start to grow or you need to share data between applications. VPC peering allows you to use the AWS internal network rather than sending data over the internet:

1. To initiate VPC peering, go to the VPC dashboard, under `Peering Connections`, and click `Create Peering Connection`.

2. Name the peering connection and select `AWSExamVPC1` as the requester and `AWSExamVPC2` as the accepter.

3. Click `Create Peering Connection` and then `Accept Request` on the following screen.

4. To update route tables for VPC peering, for each VPC, add a route in both the public and private route tables for the CIDR block of the other VPC, targeting the VPC peering connection.

After completing these steps, you will have two VPCs, each with two public and two private subnets, an internet gateway for public subnets, a NAT gateway for private subnets, and route tables configured for both local routing and VPC peering.

For beginners, using the console offers more interactive feedback and visual assistance. Using the API allows you to create AWS resources using code. This allows you to repeat the same creation steps repeatedly with minimal extra work. In the AWS exam, you will be tested on some common API commands, so this offers a good opportunity to learn and practice. The following steps are optional if you have created two VPCs using the console, but are recommended.

Creating the First VPC

Firstly, you need to create an empty VPC. The following code is run using the AWS CLI on your machine. Create VPC the VPC:

```
aws ec2 create-vpc --cidr-block 10.0.0.0/16
```

Here is the output:

```
{
    "Vpc": {
        "CidrBlock": "10.0.0.0/16",
        "DhcpOptionsId": "dopt-07980fce8249c9b48",
        "State": "pending",
        "VpcId": "vpc-0f8495d89c6eb252f",
        "OwnerId": "797714106169",
        "InstanceTenancy": "default",
        "Ipv6CidrBlockAssociationSet": [],
        "CidrBlockAssociationSet": [
            {
                "AssociationId": "vpc-cidr-assoc-0d13d08c281f360b7",
                "CidrBlock": "10.0.0.0/16",
                "CidrBlockState": {
                    "State": "associated"
                }
            }
        ],
        "IsDefault": false
    }
}
```

Use the VpcId for the next steps.

Creating Subnets for the First VPC

Once the VPC has been created, you need to create the subnets.

Create public subnets:

```
aws ec2 create-subnet --vpc-id <VpcId> --cidr-block 10.0.1.0/24
--availability-zone us-east-1b
aws ec2 create-subnet --vpc-id <VpcId> --cidr-block 10.0.2.0/24
--availability-zone us-east-1c
```

Here's the output:

```
{
    "Subnet": {
        "AvailabilityZone": "us-east-1b",
        "AvailabilityZoneId": "use1-az2",
        "AvailableIpAddressCount": 251,
        "CidrBlock": "10.0.1.0/24",
```

```
        "DefaultForAz": false,
        "MapPublicIpOnLaunch": false,
        "State": "available",
        "SubnetId": "subnet-0d1bb9d5b6c08836b",
        "VpcId": "vpc-0f8495d89c6eb252f",
        "OwnerId": "797714106169",
        "AssignIpv6AddressOnCreation": false,
        "Ipv6CidrBlockAssociationSet": [],
        "SubnetArn": "arn:aws:ec2:eu-west-1:797714106169:subnet/
subnet-0d1bb9d5b6c08836b",
        "EnableDns64": false,
        "Ipv6Native": false,
        "PrivateDnsNameOptionsOnLaunch": {
            "HostnameType": "ip-name",
            "EnableResourceNameDnsARecord": false,
            "EnableResourceNameDnsAAAARecord": false
        }
    }
}
```

To create private subnets, run the following commands:

```
aws ec2 create-subnet --vpc-id <VpcId> --cidr-block 10.0.3.0/24
--availability-zone us-east-1b
aws ec2 create-subnet --vpc-id <VpcId> --cidr-block 10.0.4.0/24
--availability-zone us-east-1c
```

Setting up an Internet Gateway for the First VPC

Now, create the internet gateway so that our VPC can communicate with the internet.

Create and attach the internet gateway:

```
aws ec2 create-internet-gateway
```

Here's the output:

```
{
    "InternetGateway": {
        "Attachments": [],
        "InternetGatewayId": "igw-0dd580e1b1f0567c2",
        "OwnerId": "797714106169",
        "Tags": []
    }
}
```

Use the `InternetGatewayId` in the next step:

```
aws ec2 attach-internet-gateway --vpc-id <VpcId> --internet-gateway-id
<InternetGatewayId>
```

Setting up a NAT Gateway for the First VPC

Create a NAT gateway to allow our private subnets to receive updates from the internet as required.

Allocate an elastic IP:

```
aws ec2 allocate-address
```

Here's the output:

```
{
    "PublicIp": "54.195.13.168",
    "AllocationId": "eipalloc-0d06d6efa559ff463",
    "PublicIpv4Pool": "amazon",
    "NetworkBorderGroup": "us-east-1",
    "Domain": "vpc"
}
```

Use the highlighted allocation ID for the next step.

Create a NAT gateway:

```
aws ec2 create-nat-gateway --subnet-id <SubnetId> --allocation-id
<AllocationId>
```

Here's the output:

```
{
    "NatGateway": {
        "CreateTime": "2023-10-05T22:22:38.000Z",
        "NatGatewayAddresses": [
            {
                "AllocationId": "eipalloc-0d06d6efa559ff463"
            }
        ],
        "NatGatewayId": "nat-0c61bf8a12",
        "State": "pending",
        "SubnetId": "subnet-0d1bb9d5b6c08836b",
        "VpcId": "vpc-0f8495d89c6eb252f",
        "ConnectivityType": "public"
    }
}
```

Configuring Route Tables for the First VPC

Set up the route tables to allow traffic to flow to the internet. Find the public route table ID. You can find the public route table by looking for `"Main":` `true` in the output:

```
aws ec2 describe-route-tables --filters "Name=vpc-id,Values=<VpcId>"
```

Here's the output:

```
{
    "RouteTables": [
        {
            "Associations": [
                {
                    "Main": true,
                    "RouteTableAssociationId": "rtbassoc-
08682f95b51aa3509",
                    "RouteTableId": "rtb-06f2f33305f9e915c",
                    "AssociationState": {
                        "State": "associated"
                    }
                }
            ],
            "PropagatingVgws": [],
            "RouteTableId": "rtb-06f2f33305f9e915c",
            "Routes": [
                {
                    "DestinationCidrBlock": "10.0.0.0/16",
                    "GatewayId": "local",
                    "Origin": "CreateRouteTable",
                    "State": "active"
                }
            ],
            "Tags": [],
            "VpcId": "vpc-0f8495d89c6eb252f",
            "OwnerId": "797714106169"
        }
    ]
}
```

Public route table

Add a route to the internet gateway:

```
aws ec2 create-route --route-table-id <RouteTableId> --destination-
cidr-block 0.0.0.0/0 --gateway-id <InternetGatewayId>
```

Private route table

Create and add a route to the NAT gateway:

```
aws ec2 create-route-table --vpc-id <VpcId>
```

Here's the output:

```
{
    "RouteTable": {
        "Associations": [],
        "PropagatingVgws": [],
        "RouteTableId": "rtb-08ad44d166feb3e6f",
        "Routes": [
            {
                "DestinationCidrBlock": "10.0.0.0/16",
                "GatewayId": "local",
                "Origin": "CreateRouteTable",
                "State": "active"
            }
        ],
        "Tags": [],
        "VpcId": "vpc-0f8495d89c6eb252f",
        "OwnerId": "797714106169"
    }
}
```

```
aws ec2 create-route --route-table-id <RouteTableId> --destination-
cidr-block 0.0.0.0/0 --gateway-id <NatGatewayId>
```

Repeating the Previous Steps for the Second VPC

Now you need to create a second VPC so that you can configure VPC peering in the next section.

Use different CIDR blocks (e.g., 10.1.0.0/16 for AWSEXAMVPC2).

Setting up VPC Peering

You want to enable communication between these two VPCs, so you need to set up VPC peering.

Initiate and accept VPC peering:

```
aws ec2 create-vpc-peering-connection --vpc-id <VpcId> --peer-vpc-id
<VpcId>
```

Here's the output:

```
{
    "VpcPeeringConnection": {
        "Status": {
            "Message": "Initiating Request to 9999999999999",
            "Code": "initiating-request"
        },
        "Tags": [],
        "RequesterVpcInfo": {
            "OwnerId": "999999999999",
            "VpcId": " vpc-00d3d458f4 ",
            "CidrBlock": "10.0.0.0/28"
        },
        "VpcPeeringConnectionId": "pcx-111ddd555",
        "ExpirationTime": "2024-03-12T12:00:00.000Z",
        "AccepterVpcInfo": {
            "OwnerId": "999999999999",
            "VpcId": " vpc-0f8495d89c6eb252f "
        }
    }
}
```

Now accept the request from the peer VPC using the following command:

```
aws ec2 accept-vpc-peering-connection --vpc-peering-connection-id
<VpcPeeringConnectionId>
```

Now, you can update the route tables for VPC peering.

Add routes in the route tables of both VPCs for peering:

```
aws ec2 create-route --route-table-id <RouteTableId>
--destination-cidr-block 10.1.0.0/16 --vpc-peering-connection-id
<VpcPeeringConnectionId>
aws ec2 create-route --route-table-id <RouteTableId>
--destination-cidr-block 10.0.0.0/16 --vpc-peering-connection-id
<VpcPeeringConnectionId>
```

Replace placeholders such as <VpcId> with actual IDs from your AWS environment. This CLI approach automates the process, enabling efficient replication and deployment of network configurations in AWS.

You will be using this VPC setup throughout this book, so it is a requirement for future labs. If you do not want to manually create it, you can download the CloudFormation template for it via the GitHub link in the *Technical Requirements* section in the *Preface*. CloudFormation will be covered in *Chapter 11, Management and Governance*.

Summary

In this chapter, you have explored AWS VPCs from the ground up, covering fundamental concepts, essential components, and crucial security and connectivity features. AWS VPCs serve as the foundation for constructing secure, scalable, and resilient cloud environments, empowering you to design and manage networks tailored to your specific requirements. You have looked into external connectivity, as well as routing between different VPCs. You finished the chapter with a hands-on lab where you built two VPCs, both with private and public subnets, and created a peering connection between them.

Exam Readiness Drill – Chapter Review Questions

Apart from mastering key concepts, strong test-taking skills under time pressure are essential for acing your certification exam. That's why developing these abilities early in your learning journey is critical.

Exam readiness drills, using the free online practice resources provided with this book, help you progressively improve your time management and test-taking skills while reinforcing the key concepts you've learned.

HOW TO GET STARTED

- Open the link or scan the QR code at the bottom of this page

- If you have unlocked the practice resources already, log in to your registered account. If you haven't, follow the instructions in *Chapter 16* and come back to this page.

- Once you log in, click the START button to start a quiz

- We recommend attempting a quiz multiple times till you're able to answer most of the questions correctly and well within the time limit.

- You can use the following practice template to help you plan your attempts:

Working On Accuracy		
Attempt	Target	Time Limit
Attempt 1	40% or more	Till the timer runs out
Attempt 2	60% or more	Till the timer runs out
Attempt 3	75% or more	Till the timer runs out
Working On Timing		
Attempt 4	75% or more	1 minute before time limit
Attempt 5	75% or more	2 minutes before time limit
Attempt 6	75% or more	3 minutes before time limit

The above drill is just an example. Design your drills based on your own goals and make the most out of the online quizzes accompanying this book.

First time accessing the online resources? 🔓

You'll need to unlock them through a one-time process. **Head to *Chapter 16* for instructions**.

Open Quiz	
https://packt.link/SAAC03Ch02	
OR scan this QR code →	

3

Identity and Access Management

In this chapter, you will delve deep into the world of **identity and access management** (IAM), where we will provide you with a comprehensive understanding of its capabilities and mechanisms. You will discover how IAM enables controlled access to **Amazon Web Services** (AWS) services and resources, offering a framework to manage user identities, permissions, and security settings. You will be guided through creating and managing IAM users, groups, roles, and policies, with the best practices focused on securing your AWS environment. From understanding the principle of least privilege to implementing effective user access strategies, this chapter will provide you with the essential knowledge and skills required to master IAM and enhance the security posture of your AWS infrastructure.

The chapter will finish with a hands-on lab, allowing you to practice setting up IAM users and policies.

In this chapter, we will cover the following main topics:

- An IAM overview
- Users, roles, and policies
- Identity providers
- IAM access analysis
- IAM policy simulator

Let's begin.

An IAM Overview

Imagine IAM as a security system for an office building. In this analogy, the office building represents your AWS environment, and each room inside it is an AWS resource, such as an **Elastic Compute Cloud (EC2)** instance, a **Simple Storage Solution (S3)** bucket, or a database. Here's how IAM applies:

- **IAM users as employees**: Each employee (IAM user) has a unique ID badge (credentials) that allows them access to the building (AWS environment). Depending on their role in the company, some might have access to many rooms (resources), while others may only have access to a few. This can be mapped to the user permissions granted by IAM.

- **IAM groups as departments**: Different departments in the company (IAM groups) have common access needs. For example, the engineering team might need access to the server room and the development labs, much like an IAM group has specific permissions for its members.

- **IAM roles as temporary passes**: Sometimes, a visitor or a contractor (an external AWS service or a user from another AWS account) might need temporary access to certain parts of the building. They are given a temporary pass (an IAM role) that grants them specific access for a limited time.

- **IAM policies as access rules**: The security protocols (IAM policies) are the rules that determine who is allowed to enter which room and what they are allowed to do there. These rules are carefully crafted and regularly updated to ensure that everyone has access to the places they need for their job, but no more.

- **Permissions boundaries as restricted area clearances**: Some high-ranking employees have a master key that potentially gives them access to all rooms. However, their ID badges are programmed (permissions boundaries) to prevent them from using their master key in certain high-security areas, ensuring that even the most privileged users have checks on their access. This can be used to ensure that even if you accidentally gave permissions to someone who shouldn't have them, the permissions boundary would still restrict access.

- **Multi-Factor Authentication (MFA) as additional security checks**: For particularly sensitive areas, an employee might need to go through an extra security checkpoint (MFA), such as a fingerprint scan or a retinal scan, to ensure an added layer of security.

IAM plays a key role in AWS security, as it enables fine-grained access control to AWS resources. This control ensures that only authenticated and authorized users and services can access your AWS resources. It is a fundamental aspect of cloud security to comply with various security protocols and requirements. Using IAM, you create specific policies to grant permissions to users and actively deny them permissions too. In addition, IAM can grant permissions to AWS services, allowing them access to other AWS services and resources.

Next, we will learn about the core components of IAM, including users, groups, roles, and policies.

Users, Roles, and Policies

IAM operates much like a highly detailed and customizable security system, organizing users, roles, groups, and policies to ensure that the right individuals and services have the appropriate access to resources.

Figure 3.1 shows how IAM users, roles, groups, and policies interact:

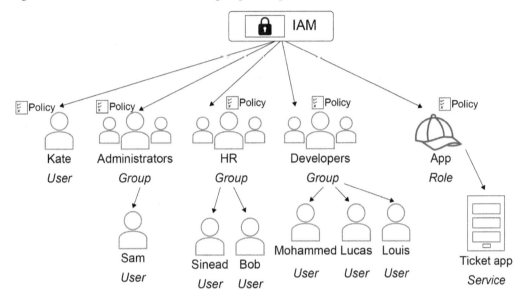

Figure 3.1 – IAM users, groups, and roles

You can now take a detailed look at IAM Users.

Users

IAM users are akin to individual employees in a company. Each user has a unique identity within AWS, and you can grant them access to various AWS services and resources. Users can be human users (such as developers or administrators) or can represent applications or services. When you create an IAM user, you define their access level, ranging from administrative access to limited, read-only access. Users can be assigned long-term credentials, such as a password for AWS Management Console access or access keys for programmatic access (an API or CLI). The principle of least privilege should be applied. This philosophy ensures that users have only the permissions they need to perform their tasks.

Managing user permissions involves assigning and adjusting the access rights of IAM users. This is typically done through IAM policies, which define what actions a user can perform and on which resources. Regularly reviewing and updating these permissions ensures that users have access only to the resources they need, helping to maintain a secure AWS environment.

Best practices for IAM user security include using strong passwords, enabling MFA, regularly rotating credentials, and following the principle of least privilege. These practices help in safeguarding user accounts from unauthorized access and potential security breaches.

IAM users within the same department or needing the same permissions can be grouped together to make administration easier.

Groups

IAM groups are like departments within a company, where each department has a certain set of permissions based on the job function. Groups in IAM are a way of managing multiple users who need the same set of permissions. For example, you could have a group named "developers" and assign permissions that all developers need, such as access to code development tools and development databases. Any user added to this group automatically inherits these permissions. This is a best practice for managing large numbers of users, as it simplifies the task of assigning and revoking permissions.

Roles

IAM roles are similar to job positions within a company, equipped with specific permission sets necessary to perform a certain role. IAM roles in AWS are used for flexible, secure access management, differing significantly from users and groups. They are designed not to represent an individual user but to provide a set of permissions to make AWS service requests.

Roles are distinguished primarily by their use of temporary security credentials. Unlike IAM users, roles do not have permanent, long-term credentials such as a username and password or access keys. Instead, when a role is assumed, AWS issues temporary security credentials for a specific session. These credentials are dynamically generated and come with an expiration time, enhancing the security profile by reducing the risk of credential compromise.

Roles are often used to grant permissions to AWS services to act on your behalf. For example, you might assign a role to an Amazon EC2 instance, allowing it to access an S3 bucket. Roles are also used for cross-account access, enabling users from one AWS account to access resources in another account securely. This feature is particularly useful in large organizations with multiple AWS accounts.

Roles are also routinely used in scenarios involving identity federation. They can be used to grant access to users who already have identities outside of AWS, such as corporate users or users authenticated by a mobile or web application. By assuming a role, these external users temporarily gain permission to act in the AWS environment without the need for IAM user credentials.

IAM roles can be assumed by anyone or anything that needs them, as long as permission is granted. This makes them a flexible tool for managing permissions. When a role is assumed, the entity (user, service, or application) gets permissions defined in the role's policy. This policy dictates what the entity can and cannot do in AWS.

We will now take a look at how you define the access for each user, group, or role using IAM policies.

Policies

Policies in IAM are the rulebooks that define who is allowed to do what. They are **JavaScript Object Notation (JSON)** documents that explicitly list permissions and stipulate what actions are allowed or denied on which AWS resources. There are two types of policies – managed policies (created and managed by AWS or by a user) and inline policies (directly attached to an IAM user, group, or role). Policies are incredibly flexible, allowing you to define permissions with great specificity. For example, a policy can allow a user to start but not stop a particular EC2 instance, or it can allow access to an S3 bucket only if the request comes from a specific IP address range. *Figure 3.1* shows how the two different policies are attached to users and roles:

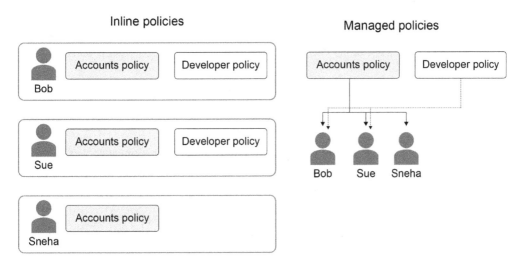

Figure 3.2 – IAM policy types

An AWS policy is a set of instructions that defines who has what permissions in AWS. Policies are written in the JSON format. The following is a simple example of an AWS policy. This policy allows the user to list all buckets in Amazon S3 and to read objects from a specific bucket, named AWSExamBucket:

```
{
    "Version": "2012-10-17",
    "Statement": [
        {
            "Effect": "Allow",
            "Action": "s3:ListAllMyBuckets",
            "Resource": "arn:aws:s3:::*"
        },
```

```
        {
            "Effect": "Allow",
            "Action": "s3:GetObject",
            "Resource": "arn:aws:s3:::AWSExamBucket/*"
        }
    ]
}
```

Let's break down the fields in this policy:

- The `Version` field specifies the policy language version. `2012-10-17` is the most recent version. This should not be changed without AWS guidance.

- The `Statement` field is an array of individual statements (you can have more than one).

- Each statement includes the following:

- `Effect`, which can be either `"Allow"` or `"Deny"`, indicating whether actions are allowed or denied.

- `Action`, which specifies the action or actions that will be allowed or denied. Here, `s3:ListAllMyBuckets` allows the user to list all S3 buckets, and `s3:GetObject` allows them to read objects from `AWSExamBucket`.

- `Resource`, which defines the specific AWS resources that the statement applies to. The first statement applies to all S3 buckets (as denoted by the `*`), while the second applies only to objects in `AWSExamBucket`.

This policy is a basic example of using just one AWS Service, S3. AWS policies can get much more complex and cover unlimited services, allowing very granular control over who can do what within your AWS environment.

IAM policies can also contain a permission boundary. Permission boundaries in IAM serve as a method to set the maximum permissions that an IAM user or role can have, acting like guardrails within an organization's permissions structure. They allow the delegation of permissions management while preventing users or roles from exceeding a predefined level of access. When an IAM entity has a permission boundary, it can only perform actions allowed by both its IAM policies and the boundary. This ensures that the entity's permissions do not exceed those defined in the boundary, even if its own policies would allow more extensive actions.

These boundaries are especially useful in scenarios of delegated administration. For instance, they enable certain users to create new IAM roles or users but restrict the level of access these new entities can have. Let's say you want to delegate the management of S3 buckets in your AWS account to a specific IAM user or group without giving them full administrative access to your entire AWS account. Delegated administration would let you do this simply and easily. It is important to note that permission boundaries do not themselves grant permissions. Rather, they limit the maximum permissions that can be granted by IAM policies attached to a user or role. If you have granted someone permission to access your account, you want to make absolutely sure they cannot do anything malicious.

Permission boundaries are used in organizational structures with varying levels of administrators and are helpful in situations that require controlled delegation of IAM management. They enhance security by preventing privilege escalation and provide a safe way to empower users to manage IAM entities within controlled limits. Imagine you work for a large organization with multiple teams of developers, who are responsible for deploying and managing applications in AWS. Each team can create and manage their own resources, such as EC2 instances, S3 buckets, and Lambda functions. However, you want to ensure that no developer or team can grant themselves excessive permissions, such as administrative access, that could potentially lead to security risks or unintentional costs. Using permission boundaries would block their ability to grant additional privileges that they should not have.

Identity Providers (IdPs)

Federated access in AWS allows users to access AWS resources using existing credentials from an external IdP, such as a corporate directory. This eliminates the need to create separate IAM users for each identity, streamlining the login process and enhancing security.

Configuring federated access in AWS involves setting up trust between AWS and the external identity provider, using IAM roles and **Security Assertion Markup Language** (**SAML**) 2.0. This configuration allows users authenticated by an external IdP to assume an IAM role and access AWS resources, in accordance with the permissions associated with that role.

First, you start by setting up an external IdP, such as Active Directory, Google, or any other service that supports SAML 2.0. This IdP handles user logins and manages their identities outside of AWS. Next, in the AWS Management Console, you create an IAM identity provider that connects to this external IdP. You'll need to provide some details about the IdP and upload a metadata file to establish a connection between AWS and your external IdP.

After this, you create IAM roles in AWS that users will assume when they log in. These roles define what actions users are allowed to perform in AWS. You also set up a trust policy for each role, specifying that only users authenticated by your IdP can use these roles. When users want to access AWS, they log in through the external IdP using their existing credentials. Once the user is authenticated, the IdP provides a SAML assertion, a security token that contains information about the user.

AWS uses this SAML assertion to determine which IAM role the user can assume. The user then exchanges this assertion for temporary AWS credentials, allowing them to access AWS services or the Management Console with the permissions defined by the role they assumed.

Finally, it's important to remember that these temporary credentials will eventually expire. When that happens, the user must log in again through the IdP to continue accessing AWS.

The preceding process is represented in *Figure 3.3*:

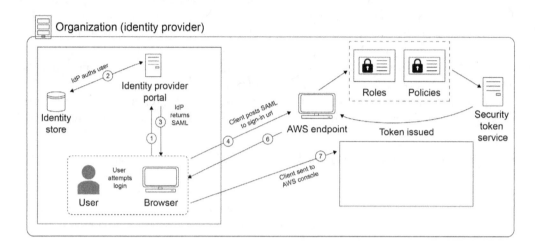

Figure 3.3 – A federated login flow

In this process, AWS IAM effectively leverages the existing identity management system of an organization, simplifying user management and maintaining security by using federated identities to access AWS resources. This way, users do not need separate AWS credentials and permissions are centrally managed, aligning with the organization's security and access policies.

Security considerations for using federated access include ensuring secure communication channels, regularly auditing access and activities, and applying the principle of least privilege in assigning roles. It is also essential to manage the IdP securely, as it plays a critical role in the authentication process.

Setting up a federation login requires you to have a third-party provider, which typically is outside of AWS; therefore, you will not test this in the hands-on lab in this chapter. However, you can follow the previous steps if you wish to do this yourself for further learning.

IAM Access Analyzer

IAM Access Analyzer is a tool within AWS that helps to identify the resources in your AWS account that are shared with an external entity or that are not in use and, therefore, do not follow the **principle of least privilege**. It does this by analyzing policies and reporting on any that grant public or cross-account access. This tool is vital for maintaining a secure AWS environment by ensuring that only intended users have access to your resources, especially with external entities that you do not have full control or governance over.

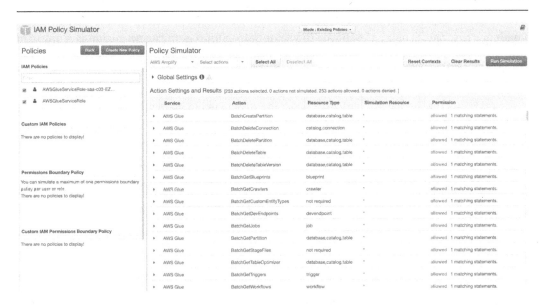

Figure 3.4 – IAM Access Analyzer

Setting up IAM Access Analyzer involves enabling it in the IAM console and reviewing the output. Once enabled, it automatically analyzes policies and generates comprehensive findings. IAM Access Analyzer is regional, so you need to create an audit run for each region in which you operate. It is also worthwhile running it for *all* regions that you have access to, even if you do not use them for deployments, as hackers or bad actors can exploit these unused regions to operate unseen.

It is recommended to add tags to all IAM roles and policies as a best practice. This makes it much easier to find IAM components that have been added outside of your approved processes. Most hackers will not follow any tagging requirements, as they need to operate as quickly as possible, and using tagging allows those roles and policies to be found and removed more quickly.

As well as using IAM Access Analyzer, you can also check your policies to ensure that they do not grant too many or too few permissions. You can use the IAM Policy Simulator to do this, which you will learn about next.

The IAM Policy Simulator

The IAM policy simulator is a tool that is designed to help AWS users understand, test, and validate the effects of access control policies. This tool is particularly useful for administrators and security professionals who need to manage complex IAM policies across a variety of users, groups, and roles within an AWS environment. The policy simulator allows users to simulate how their IAM policies will actually work in practice, without needing to apply them in a live environment. This enables a more proactive approach to security and access control, allowing the identification and correction of unintended permissions or denials before they impact an operational environment.

One of the key features of the IAM policy simulator is its ability to simulate permissions for any IAM user, group, or role within an organization's AWS account. Users can select specific IAM entities and actions, and then they simulate how those entities would interact with various AWS resources based on existing policies. The simulator provides detailed results for each simulation, indicating whether a given action would be allowed or denied under the current policy configurations. This is invaluable for testing the effects of new policies or changes to existing policies, ensuring that they perform as expected and adhere to the organization's security standards.

The tool can be accessed via an external link, not directly via the AWS Management Console: `https://policysim.aws.amazon.com/`.

You will now put into practice some of the key areas you have learned about in this chapter.

Hands-on Lab

In this lab, you will practice using IAM users, groups, policies, and permission boundaries to securely create a user with only a subset of permissions, following the principle of least privilege. This will give you hands-on knowledge that will help you in the AWS exam by being able to understand this complex subject in practice, as well as theory. In this scenario, you have a user called David who is new to the infrastructure team. He will need access to certain AWS services, but he should be restricted to make sure that he can't accidentally launch services with high costs.

First, you will see how to do this in the AWS Management Console.

Creating an IAM Group

First, you will create an IAM group. Creating a group allows you to logically link users that need the same permissions to help make admin tasks easier:

1. Log in to the AWS Management Console: `http://console.aws.amazon.com/`.
2. Navigate to the IAM dashboard. Go to `Services` and select `IAM`.
3. Click `Create New Group`.
4. Name your group (e.g., `Operators`).
5. Skip adding policies and click `Create Group`.

Creating an IAM User

Once you have created a group, you need to create a user who will be able to log in and operate AWS services:

1. Click Add user. Enter a username (e.g., David). Tick the box to allow AWS Management Console access.

2. Click Next.

3. In the Set permissions section, add David to the new group by selecting Add user to group and choosing the Operators group.

4. Click Next.

5. Click Create User.

6. Make a note of David's password so that you can log in as that user for testing.

Creating a Custom Policy

You will now create a custom policy so that David can be granted specific permissions for his role:

1. Stay on the IAM dashboard.

2. Go to the Policies section and click Create policy.

3. In the visual editor, choose EC2 and S3 services, and specify Allow all actions. Add a new permission for EC2 and set it to Deny. Select RunInstances and TerminateInstances.

4. Review and name the policy (e.g., EC2_S3_OperatorsPolicy).

5. Click Create policy. Go back to Groups and select Operators.

6. Go to the Permissions tab and click Attach Policy.

7. Find and select EC2_S3_OperatorsPolicy, and then attach it to the group.

Setting a Permissions Boundary for a User

To restrict David's access to only the precise services he is allowed to use, you will create a permission boundary to stop him from being able to override the permissions he has:

1. Stay on the IAM dashboard.

2. Go to Policies.

3. Click on Create Policy.

4. Click on JSON and replace the placeholder code with the following JSON:

```
{
    "Version": "2012-10-17",
    "Statement": [
        {
            "Effect": "Allow",
            "Action": "ec2:*",
            "Resource": "*"
        },
        {
            "Effect": "Deny",
            "Action": "*",
            "NotResource": "arn:aws:ec2:*:*:instance/*"
        }
    ]
}
```

5. Click Next.

6. Name the policy UserBoundary.

7. Click Create policy.

8. Go to Users and select David.

9. In the User details, navigate to Permissions boundaries.

10. Click Add permission boundary.

11. Select UserBoundary and Set boundary.

Testing

The combination of policies you have created should only allow David to work with EC2 instances and not create or shut them down. Can you understand why this is the case, even though you granted him specific permissions for S3?

You can now test this to make sure it works:

1. Navigate to the IAM policy simulator: https://policysim.aws.amazon.com/home/index.jsp.

2. Select David from the list of users on the left.

3. Select S3 from the Services dropdown and click Select All.

4. Click Run Simulation.

5. You can see that all S3 actions are denied. This is due to the permissions boundary that you set, which only allows EC2 actions.

6. Untick `UserBoundary` from the list on the left and click `Run Simulation` again. Review the difference to understand what the permission boundary has done.

In this lab, you created an IAM group, created a user called `David`, and added him to the group. You then granted permissions to the group and David individually. A permissions boundary was added that restricted the services David could access so that when you tested the permissions, he was unable to access S3, even though he had an inline policy attached that gave those permissions. You should now feel confident in answering IAM-based questions in the exam, having gained some practical experience in working with IAM policies, users, and roles.

Summary

This chapter provided a comprehensive overview of IAM, an essential service in AWS for securely controlling access to AWS resources. You explored the key components of IAM, users, roles, groups, and policies, each of which serves a distinct yet interconnected function. IAM users, akin to individual identities within AWS, can be granted varying levels of access to AWS services and resources. IAM groups simplify permission management by categorizing users with similar access needs, while IAM roles offer a flexible approach to assigning temporary permissions, especially useful in scenarios such as cross-account access and identity federation. IAM policies, written in JSON format, are the core mechanism for defining and regulating access permissions. We also delved into advanced features such as permission boundaries and IAM Access Analyzer, which add layers of security and compliance. The chapter emphasized the importance of best practices, such as the principle of least privilege and regular monitoring, to maintain a secure AWS environment. This comprehensive understanding of IAM is crucial for effectively managing identity and access in the AWS cloud, ensuring that only authenticated and authorized users and services can access specific resources, in line with an organization's security and operational policies.

In the next chapter, you will learn about the different compute options on AWS, including servers and containers, and some fast-start options using AWS Elastic Beanstalk.

Exam Readiness Drill - Chapter Review Questions

Apart from mastering key concepts, strong test-taking skills under time pressure are essential for acing your certification exam. That's why developing these abilities early in your learning journey is critical.

Exam readiness drills, using the free online practice resources provided with this book, help you progressively improve your time management and test-taking skills while reinforcing the key concepts you've learned.

HOW TO GET STARTED

- Open the link or scan the QR code at the bottom of this page

- If you have unlocked the practice resources already, log in to your registered account. If you haven't, follow the instructions in *Chapter 16* and come back to this page.

- Once you log in, click the START button to start a quiz

- We recommend attempting a quiz multiple times till you're able to answer most of the questions correctly and well within the time limit.

- You can use the following practice template to help you plan your attempts:

Working On Accuracy		
Attempt	Target	Time Limit
Attempt 1	40% or more	Till the timer runs out
Attempt 2	60% or more	Till the timer runs out
Attempt 3	75% or more	Till the timer runs out
Working On Timing		
Attempt 4	75% or more	1 minute before time limit
Attempt 5	75% or more	2 minutes before time limit
Attempt 6	75% or more	3 minutes before time limit

The above drill is just an example. Design your drills based on your own goals and make the most out of the online quizzes accompanying this book.

First time accessing the online resources? 🔒

You'll need to unlock them through a one-time process. **Head to** *Chapter 16* **for instructions**.

Open Quiz

https://packt.link/SAAC03Ch03

OR scan this QR code →

4

Compute

Understanding compute resources on **Amazon Web Services** (**AWS**) is fundamental for anyone seeking success in the AWS certification exams. In this chapter, you will explore the diverse compute options available, ranging from traditional instances to modern container services. You will learn about the intricacies of launching, monitoring, and optimizing compute resources, gaining the confidence to tackle exam questions related to compute on AWS.

In this chapter, you are going to cover the following main topics:

- Introduction to compute on AWS

- **Elastic Compute Cloud** (**EC2**) instances

- Elastic Beanstalk for rapid application deployment

- Containers such as Elastic Container Service, Elastic Kubernetes Service, and Fargate and using AWS Batch to run jobs

- Instance security and access methods

- Let's dive in!

Introduction to Compute on AWS

Compute on AWS refers to the ability to process and execute tasks using virtual servers and services provided by the AWS cloud infrastructure. AWS offers a versatile range of compute options to cater to a diverse set of application and workload requirements. **Traditional virtual servers**, known as EC2 instances, form the foundation, allowing users to launch and manage virtual machines with various operating systems and configurations. Many companies are currently running a wide range of operating systems across their IT estate. Many end users will be running macOS or Windows on their laptops, many of the application servers will be running Unix, and it is likely that a lot of the login and security permissions are being stored on a Windows server using Active Directory. As a result, being able to move all of these different server types to EC2 and reduce the need to manage these physical servers on-premises is a massive benefit and offers a large cost saving to many customers. Additionally, AWS provides serverless computing with services such as AWS Lambda, enabling users to run code without provisioning or managing servers (you will learn about the serverless options in *Chapter 9, Serverless and Application Integration*).

Containerization (containerization is a process that packages an application and its dependencies into a single unit called a container, which can run identically across different computing environments) is another key aspect, with services such as Amazon **Elastic Container Service** (**ECS**) for container orchestration and **Elastic Kubernetes Service** (**EKS**) for managing Kubernetes clusters. AWS Elastic Beanstalk simplifies application deployment by handling infrastructure management tasks, making compute resources more accessible for developers.

You can first learn about the differences between a traditional virtual machine and a container.

Virtual Machines (VMs)

A VM is a software emulation of a physical computer that runs an entire **operating system** (**OS**) and applications within it.

VMs are isolated environments that encapsulate an entire OS stack, including the kernel, libraries, and binaries, and allocate dedicated resources (CPU, memory, and storage) from the host machine.

Each VM requires its own separate OS installation, which consumes more resources and incurs overhead due to the duplication of OS components.

VMs provide strong isolation between applications but may suffer from performance overhead due to the emulation of hardware and the duplication of OS resources. Isolation is important for both security and performance. Isolation stops one application from being able to access another even if they run on the same shared server. It also stops one application from taking too much of the resources available, causing performance issues for all who share the server. This is known as "noisy neighbor" syndrome and is a problem for all shared systems.

Containers

A container is a lightweight, portable, and self-sufficient runtime environment that packages an application and its dependencies together. Containers share the host OS kernel and runtime libraries, allowing them to run in isolated user-space environments without the need for a separate OS installation.

Containers use a layered file system to efficiently share resources and dependencies while isolating the application's runtime environment. A layered file system organizes data in layers, where each layer builds upon the previous one, allowing for modularity, easier updates, and the ability to roll back changes without affecting the entire system. For example, you would have a core boot or operating system layer at the top that all of the smaller programs running would inherit. However, each program would have its own layer with parameters set specifically for its own area without impacting any other system.

Containers are more lightweight and resource-efficient compared to VMs as they eliminate the overhead of running multiple OS instances and share resources with the host OS.

Containers provide fast startup times, efficient resource utilization, and scalability, making them ideal for microservices architectures, **continuous integration/continuous deployment (CI/CD)**, and cloud-native applications.

Figure 4.1 shows the difference in the architecture of the two options:

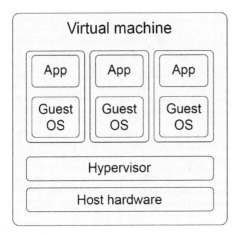 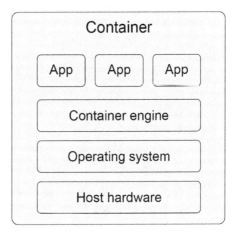

Figure 4.1: Virtual machines versus containers

In summary, while both containers and VMs provide isolation and encapsulation for running applications, containers are more lightweight, efficient, and portable compared to VMs, making them well-suited for modern application deployment and orchestration in cloud environments.

Now that you have learned the key differences between containers and virtual servers, you can take a look at the different compute options that AWS offers:

- **Amazon EC2**: Amazon EC2 provides resizable virtual servers (instances) in the cloud, allowing you to quickly deploy and scale compute capacity as needed.

- For example, choose Amazon EC2 for hosting web applications, running backend services, or running batch processing jobs. For instance, you can launch EC2 instances to host a WordPress website, deploy a microservices architecture, or run data analytics workloads.

- **AWS Elastic Beanstalk**: AWS Elastic Beanstalk is an easy-to-use service for deploying and managing applications in the cloud without worrying about infrastructure provisioning and management.

- Choose Elastic Beanstalk for deploying and managing web applications, APIs, or backend services without having to manage the servers. For instance, you can use Elastic Beanstalk to deploy a scalable web application written in Java, Python, Node.js, or PHP without managing servers or infrastructure.

- **Amazon Elastic Container Service (ECS)**: Amazon ECS is a managed container orchestration service that allows you to run Docker containers at scale. Choose Amazon ECS for containerized applications, microservices, or batch-processing workloads. If you are using Docker containers, then ECS will be your best option.

- **Amazon Elastic Kubernetes Service (EKS)**: Amazon EKS is a managed Kubernetes service that simplifies the deployment, management, and scaling of containerized applications that are using Kubernetes, an open source container orchestration platform. Choose Amazon EKS for deploying and managing Kubernetes clusters to run containerized applications, microservices, or batch-processing workloads. If you are using Kubernetes, then EKS will be your best choice.

- **AWS Fargate**: AWS Fargate is a serverless compute engine for containers that allows you to run containers without managing the underlying infrastructure. Choose AWS Fargate for deploying containerized applications without worrying about server provisioning, scaling, or patching, if you are looking to run any containers without having to provision your own EC2 instances, and when you need rapid, simple scaling.

- **AWS Batch**: AWS Batch is a fully managed batch processing service provided by **AWS** that enables you to efficiently run batch computing workloads in the cloud without the need to manage the underlying infrastructure. With AWS Batch, you can dynamically provision compute resources, automatically scale resources to meet workload demands, and efficiently schedule and execute batch jobs.

  Opt for AWS Batch when you need to process large volumes of data or perform compute-intensive tasks in a scalable and cost-effective manner. For instance, you can leverage AWS Batch to process data analytics pipelines, perform image and video rendering, or execute simulations and modeling tasks without the overhead of managing server infrastructure.

- Each compute option on AWS offers distinct advantages and is suitable for different types of workloads. Understanding your application requirements and workload characteristics will help you choose the most appropriate compute option to meet your needs. There will be questions in the exam where you will need to decide the best service to use for a specific type of workload, so understanding the key differences between them is critical.

You can start by learning about the first-ever service AWS released – EC2.

Elastic Compute Cloud (EC2)

This is where AWS began. Amazon EC2 is a foundational service within AWS that provides resizable compute capacity in the cloud. EC2 instances are virtual servers that allow you to run applications and workloads, ranging from simple to complex, with flexibility and scalability. In this chapter, you will explore the key aspects of EC2 instances, covering various topics that are relevant to the *AWS Certified Solutions Architect - Associate (SAA-C03)* exam.

When choosing an EC2 instance, you will need to decide between different instance sizes, operating systems, storage persistence, CPU scaling abilities, as well as cost optimizations. It is a lot to consider. You can start by looking at the different types of EC2 instances you can provision and when you should use them.

Understanding EC2 Instance Types

EC2 instance types are optimized to meet specific performance, storage, and networking requirements. These instance types are grouped into families, each tailored to different use cases such as general-purpose computing, memory-intensive applications, compute-intensive workloads, storage-optimized tasks, accelerated computing needs, and **high-performance computing** (**HPC**) requirements. The different instance types available are as follows:

- **General Purpose**: General purpose instances provide a balance of compute, memory, and networking resources. They are suitable for a wide range of applications, including web servers, development environments, and small to medium-sized databases.

- **Compute Optimized**: Compute-optimized instances deliver high-performance compute capabilities, making them ideal for CPU-bound applications such as HPC, batch processing, and media transcoding.

- **Memory Optimized**: Memory-optimized instances are designed to handle memory-intensive workloads such as in-memory databases, real-time analytics, and large-scale caching. They offer a high ratio of memory to vCPUs, enabling efficient processing of large datasets.

- **Storage Optimized**: Storage-optimized instances are optimized for applications that require high-performance, low-latency access to local storage. They are well-suited for data-intensive workloads such as NoSQL databases, data warehousing, and log processing.

- **Accelerated Computing**: Accelerated computing instances are equipped with specialized hardware accelerators such as **graphics processing unit** (**GPU**) to accelerate specific types of computational tasks such as machine learning inference, graphics rendering, and video processing.

- **HPC Optimized**: HPC instances are designed for demanding computational workloads that require high compute power, low-latency networking, and parallel processing capabilities. They are commonly used in scientific research, financial modeling, and engineering simulations.

One significant distinction among EC2 instance types is between burstable instance sizes and standard instance sizes. Burstable instances, represented by instance types with the t prefix (e.g., t3.micro, t3.small), offer a unique pricing and performance model compared to standard instances:

- **Burstable Instances**: Burstable instances are designed for workloads with variable CPU utilization patterns. They accumulate CPU credits during periods of low activity, which can then be used during bursts of higher demand. Burstable instances are ideal for applications that experience periodic spikes in CPU usage, such as web servers, development environments, and small databases. It is essential to monitor CPU credits to ensure consistent performance during sustained high workloads because when your credits run out, you will see performance degradation (standard mode) or increased costs (unlimited mode).

- **Standard Instances**: Standard instances, such as those in the M, C, R, and other families, provide a fixed level of CPU performance based on the instance size selected. Unlike burstable instances, standard instances offer consistent CPU performance without the need to manage CPU credits. They are suitable for applications with steady-state workloads or those requiring predictable performance levels, such as enterprise applications, databases, and data processing tasks.

Once you have decided which instance class and size you need, you will also need to decide which operating system and software you want to run on it. You do this by choosing an **Amazon Machine Image (AMI)**.

Amazon Machine Images (AMIs)

When launching an EC2 instance, you select an AMI that defines the initial software configuration and operating system for the instance. AWS offers a broad range of pre-configured AMIs for various operating systems, including Amazon Linux, Ubuntu, Windows Server, and more. Additionally, you can create custom AMIs tailored to your specific application requirements, including pre-installed software, configurations, and security settings. AWS-provided AMIs are included in the price of the instance and the cost depends on the instance class and size you select as well as the storage. AWS AMIs typically install only a base operating system, leaving any software installations and server configuration up to the user. However, there are community and Marketplace AMIs you can use that contain pre-installed software and have OS parameters configured to optimize the software you will be using. The community AMIs are free and tend to feature open source software, whereas the Marketplace AMIs are chargeable (typically per hour of usage) but tend to have licensed software or additional features such as a hardened instance (an instance that is highly secure).

Figure 4.2 shows AWS AMI Marketplace offerings for pre-installed WordPress:

Figure 4.2: AWS AMI Marketplace offerings for pre-installed WordPress

Instance Store Versus Amazon Elastic Block Store (EBS)

You will be learning about storage options in more depth in *Chapter 5, Storage*, but there is an important choice to be made when you first provision an EC2 instance. EC2 instances can utilize either instance store volumes or EBS volumes for storage. Instance store volumes provide temporary block-level storage that is physically attached to the host server, offering high I/O performance but limited durability. Instance storage is *only* available when you provision an EC2 instance. In contrast, EBS volumes are network-attached storage volumes that persist independently of the EC2 instance, providing durability, availability, and the ability to be detached and reattached to other instances. You can create an EBS volume at any time and they are not directly linked to EC2 provisioning.

There are often exam questions that will ask about the best storage type for the workload you will be running. It is important to remember that any data stored on an instance store volume is lost when the instance is stopped, whereas data on an EBS volume persists even if the instance it is attached to is stopped or deleted.

In general, an EC2 instance is available on a schedule you decide, which can be 24/7 too. These are known as **On-Demand Instances**. These work well for user-based workloads that need the service to be available during specific times. However, some workloads that do processing tasks rather than support a user-facing application could use AWS Spot Instances instead.

Spot Instances

Spot Instances are a cost-effective purchasing option offered by Amazon EC2 that allows users to bid on spare EC2 compute capacity. These instances can significantly reduce costs compared to On-Demand Instances, often offering discounts of up to 90%. Spot Instances are ideal for workloads that are flexible in terms of timing and can tolerate interruptions, such as batch processing, data analysis, and test/development environments.

However, it is important to note that Spot Instances can be reclaimed by AWS with little notice if the current Spot price exceeds your bid or if the capacity is needed by On-Demand or Reserved Instances. Therefore, they are not suitable for mission-critical or time-sensitive applications. To mitigate interruptions, users can utilize features like Spot Fleet, which diversifies instance types and Availability Zones, or implement application checkpointing and retries. Despite the potential interruptions, Spot Instances offer significant cost savings and are an excellent choice for workloads with flexible requirements.

If your requirements are more static and unlikely to change considerably in a fixed time period, then **Reserved Instances** can work better.

Reserved Instances (RIs)

EC2 RIs are a purchasing option for EC2 instances at discounted rates compared to On-Demand Instances. When you purchase an EC2 Reserved Instance, you commit to a one-year or three-year term in exchange for a significant discount on the hourly usage rate of the instance. RIs provide a capacity reservation, ensuring that the specified instance type is available to you when needed, which can be particularly beneficial for applications with steady-state or predictable usage patterns.

There are three types of EC2 RIs:

- **Standard RIs**: These offer the biggest discounts compared to On-Demand Instances and provide capacity reservation in a specific Availability Zone within a region.

- **Convertible RIs**: With Convertible RIs, you have the flexibility to change the instance type, operating system, or tenancy of the reservation if your needs evolve over time. While they offer slightly lower discounts compared to Standard RIs, Convertible RIs provide greater flexibility.

- **Scheduled RIs**: Scheduled RIs allow you to reserve capacity for specific time periods, enabling you to match your capacity reservation to a recurring schedule, such as daily, weekly, or monthly workloads.

EC2 RIs are ideal for applications with predictable usage patterns, steady-state workloads, or long-term commitments. By purchasing RIs, you can achieve significant cost savings compared to running On-Demand Instances, making it a cost-effective option for organizations looking to optimize their cloud infrastructure spending.

It is possible to combine RIs, On-Demand Instances, and EC2 Spot Instances to support one application with different needs. You can purchase RIs to cover the baseline requirements of your application, use On-Demand Instances for scaling, and Spot Instances for ad hoc tasks such as analytics requests. On top of that, you can look to leverage Auto Scaling to allow the compute required to support the application to grow and shrink when needed.

Auto Scaling

Auto Scaling is a feature of Amazon EC2 that automatically adjusts the number of instances in a fleet based on demand. It helps maintain application availability and optimize costs by scaling capacity up or down in response to changing traffic patterns. Auto Scaling enables you to define scaling policies based on metrics such as CPU utilization, network traffic, or custom application metrics, ensuring your application can handle varying workload demands efficiently. You can now take a look at how it works in more depth.

Auto Scaling Groups (ASGs)

At the core of Auto Scaling are **Auto Scaling Groups** (**ASGs**), which are collections of EC2 instances that share similar characteristics and serve a common purpose. ASGs enable you to specify minimum, maximum, and desired capacities for your fleet of instances. They provide the foundation for scaling policies and serve as the mechanism through which instances are launched or terminated in response to scaling events. To understand this better, take a look at *Figure 4.3*:

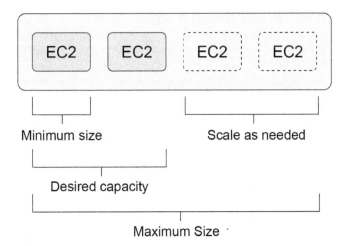

Figure 4.3: EC2 Auto Scaling Group

Scaling Policies

Scaling policies define the rules and conditions under which Auto Scaling adjusts the number of instances within an ASG. These policies are based on scaling metrics that measure the performance and utilization of your application. Some common scaling metrics include the following:

- **CPU utilization**: Scaling based on CPU utilization allows Auto Scaling to add or remove instances as CPU usage surpasses or falls below predefined thresholds. This metric is particularly useful for CPU-bound applications or those with fluctuating compute demands.

- **Network traffic**: Scaling based on network traffic metrics enables Auto Scaling to dynamically adjust capacity in response to changes in inbound or outbound network traffic. This is crucial for applications with variable network activity, such as web servers or API endpoints.

- **Custom application metrics**: In addition to built-in metrics such as CPU utilization and network traffic, Auto Scaling allows you to define custom application metrics tailored to your specific workload requirements. These metrics could include application response time, queue length, or any other metric indicative of application performance.

Once you have defined your scaling group and your scaling metrics, you need to decide what actions you want the ASG to take.

Scaling Actions

When scaling events occur—triggered by the conditions defined in scaling policies—Auto Scaling takes specific actions to adjust the capacity of the ASG:

- **Launching new instances**: In response to increased demand, Auto Scaling launches new instances based on the AMI and configuration specified in the ASG. These instances are automatically added to the fleet and start serving incoming requests.

- **Terminating instances**: Conversely, when demand decreases, Auto Scaling terminates instances to reduce costs and maintain optimal resource utilization. Instances are terminated based on configurable criteria, such as oldest launch configuration or least active instance.

Scaling actions can be configured with a timeout parameter to avoid constant scaling up and down on sudden spikes. For example, you might want to only scale up or down when the CPU spike is above your threshold for 1 minute rather than instantly. This helps stop the ASG from trying to provision an instance when the CPU spike only exists for a few seconds. There is no point in provisioning a new instance if, by the time it comes online, the traffic metrics are back below the threshold.

You can also use cooldown policies to make sure that instances are not being constantly provisioned and terminated if your load is inconsistent. For example, you can set a cooldown to stop any further scaling from taking place for 5 minutes. Rather than using fixed timeouts or cooldowns, you can also use predictive scaling.

Predictive Scaling

Predictive scaling is an advanced feature of Auto Scaling that leverages machine learning algorithms to forecast future demand based on historical patterns. By analyzing past usage data, predictive scaling can anticipate upcoming traffic spikes or lulls and proactively adjust capacity accordingly, minimizing the impact of sudden changes in workload. For example, an accountancy firm is busier on the last few days of each month than in the middle of the month. Predictive scaling can learn this pattern and start to autoscale before demand grows so there is no loss of performance.

Lifecycle Hooks

Lifecycle hooks provide a mechanism for performing custom actions during the launch or termination of instances in an ASG. By attaching lifecycle hooks to scaling events, you can orchestrate additional tasks such as configuring instance settings, initializing application components, or performing cleanup operations. Some examples of good use cases are the following:

- Before terminating instances, you may want to ensure that applications gracefully shut down to avoid data loss or service disruption.

- Before allowing traffic to be routed to newly launched instances, you may want to perform health checks or readiness validations to ensure they are fully operational.

- Before an instance is placed into service, you may need to initialize application settings or configurations to ensure it operates correctly. For example, you might want to read in parameters from AWS Parameter Store or AWS Secrets Manager to configure the application as it loads.

As you can see, ASGs can be extremely powerful to help scale your compute to be both cost-optimized and grow to handle the needs of your application.

You have now learned about all the critical elements of how to provision an EC2 instance, the differences between the instance classes, storage types, and how to scale optimally using ASGs. You can now look at another compute option that you can use when you want to deploy and manage applications without worrying about the underlying infrastructure – **AWS Elastic Beanstalk**.

AWS Elastic Beanstalk

Elastic Beanstalk allows you to deploy and manage web applications and services without needing to create your own compute or infrastructure. It provides developers with a platform to quickly deploy applications without worrying about the underlying infrastructure setup. It offers less control than using an EC2 instance, but as it is much faster and simpler to launch, it works well for many standard applications.

Here are some of the main features of Elastic Beanstalk:

- **Ease of deployment**: The deployment process is automated and managed for you. This makes it easy for developers to upload their application code and let the platform handle the deployment, provisioning, and scaling of the underlying resources.

- **Automatic scaling**: It automatically scales the application environment based on traffic levels, ensuring optimal performance and cost efficiency. Elastic Beanstalk can scale resources up or down based on predefined triggers or policies.

- **Managed infrastructure**: AWS manages the underlying infrastructure, including servers, load balancers, and auto-scaling groups, allowing developers to focus on building and improving their applications rather than managing infrastructure.

- **Multiple programming languages and platforms**: Elastic Beanstalk supports various programming languages and platforms, including Java, Python, Node.js, Ruby, PHP, .NET, and Docker containers, providing flexibility for developers to choose the technology stack that best fits their needs.

- **Integrated monitoring**: It offers built-in monitoring and logging features that provide insights into application performance, resource utilization, and errors. Administrators and developers can easily view metrics, logs, and events through the AWS Management Console.

- **Limited customization and control**: While Elastic Beanstalk manages many aspects of the infrastructure, developers have the flexibility to customize the environment configuration, including instance types, security settings, and networking options, to meet specific requirements. This does not give you the same level of customization as an EC2 self-managed environment.

- **Cost-effective pricing**: Pricing for Elastic Beanstalk is based on the underlying AWS resources consumed by the application, making it a cost-effective option for many use cases.

Elastic Beanstalk works well when you want to prioritize ease of deployment, scalability, automation, and cost-effectiveness for your web applications and services and are willing to sacrifice some ability to highly customize your environment.

Let's now take a deeper look into how Elastic Beanstalk works and its main components.

Elastic Beanstalk Architecture

Under the hood, Elastic Beanstalk works as a **Platform as a Service (PaaS)** offering. PaaS is a model that allows developers to create and build their own applications without ever having to worry about provisioning servers, networks, or infrastructure. This allows developers to create a managed environment for deploying and scaling web applications and services. Elastic Beanstalk is designed to hide or abstract away the complexity of choosing and provisioning the infrastructure such as load balancing, auto-scaling, and application management, allowing you to focus on developing and optimizing your application code.

When deploying an application to Elastic Beanstalk, developers upload their code or container images, along with a configuration file specifying their application's requirements and dependencies. Elastic Beanstalk then automatically provisions the necessary compute resources, such as EC2 instances or containers, based on the specified configuration. It manages these resources, handles load balancing across instances, and scales the environment dynamically in response to changes in traffic or workload demands. Additionally, Elastic Beanstalk integrates with other AWS services for logging, monitoring, and deployment automation, providing you with a complete platform for building and managing scalable web applications with ease.

Take a look at the main components of an Elastic Beanstalk deployment:

- **Application**: At the core of Elastic Beanstalk is your application code. This can be a web application, a microservice, or any other application that you want to deploy to AWS. Elastic Beanstalk supports various programming languages, frameworks, and platforms, including Java, Python, Node.js, Ruby, Docker, and others.

- **Environment**: An environment in Elastic Beanstalk represents a collection of AWS resources (e.g., EC2 instances, load balancers, databases) that run your application. Each environment is associated with a specific application version and configuration settings. You can create multiple environments (e.g., development, staging, production) for different stages of your application lifecycle.

- **Application version**: Before deploying your application to an environment, you must create an application version. An application version is a snapshot of your application code and its dependencies at a specific point in time. It includes your source code, configuration files, and any other resources required to run your application.

- **ASG**: Elastic Beanstalk automatically manages the underlying infrastructure by using AWS ASGs. An ASG dynamically adjusts the number of EC2 instances in your environment based on traffic demand and resource utilization. This ensures that your application can scale seamlessly to handle varying workloads.

- **Load Balancer**: Elastic Beanstalk includes a load balancer (either Classic Load Balancer or Application Load Balancer) to distribute incoming traffic across multiple EC2 instances running your application. This improves availability, fault tolerance, and scalability by evenly distributing requests and offloading SSL termination.

- **EC2 instances**: Your application runs on one or more EC2 instances within the environment. These instances are automatically provisioned and managed by Elastic Beanstalk. You can customize the instance type, operating system, and other configuration settings based on your application requirements.

- **Configuration settings**: Elastic Beanstalk provides a set of configuration options that allow you to customize various aspects of your environment, such as instance type, environment variables, scaling policies, logging settings, and security configurations. You can configure these settings using the Elastic Beanstalk management console, CLI, or API.

- **Database integration**: Elastic Beanstalk seamlessly integrates with AWS database services such as Amazon RDS, Amazon Aurora, Amazon DynamoDB, and Amazon ElastiCache. You can provision and manage databases directly from the Elastic Beanstalk console and connect them to your application for data storage and retrieval.

You need to be careful when using a database embedded with your Elastic Beanstalk environment because when you remove or modify the application, the database can also be deleted. It is recommended that you store the database outside of the Elastic Beanstalk deployment if you need that data to be persistent.

To summarize, Elastic Beanstalk serves as a PaaS solution, abstracting away the complexities of infrastructure management and allowing developers to focus solely on their application code. Key components include the application, environment, application version, ASG, load balancer, EC2 instances, and configuration settings. Each of these elements plays a vital role in deploying and scaling applications effectively. Pay close attention to the relationship between environments and application versions, as well as the integration with AWS services such as Auto Scaling, load balancing, and database management.

At the end of this chapter, there is a *Hands-On Labs* section where you can create an Elastic Beanstalk environment that will help turn the theory into practice.

You can now read about the second main group of compute options on AWS – containers.

AWS Containers

AWS offers two types of container services, AWS **Elastic Container Service (ECS)** and AWS **Elastic Kubernetes Service (EKS)**. ECS is a fully managed container orchestration service offered by AWS. It simplifies the process of deploying, managing, and scaling containerized applications, allowing developers to focus on building and running their applications rather than managing the underlying infrastructure. While EKS offers a similar functionality, it leverages an open source container platform orchestration system called Kubernetes.

Containers are a lightweight form of virtualization that package an application or code and its dependencies together. Unlike traditional VMs, containers share the host operating system kernel and only contain the application and its dependencies, making them more efficient and portable.

An analogy for a container on AWS is akin to a shipping container in the logistics industry. Just as a shipping container is a standardized, portable unit used for transporting goods across different modes of transportation such as ships, trains, and trucks, a container in AWS encapsulates an application and its dependencies into a standardized, portable unit that can run consistently across different environments. Like how a shipping container provides a self-contained environment for goods, a container on AWS provides a self-contained environment for an application, ensuring that it runs reliably regardless of the underlying infrastructure. Additionally, just as shipping containers can be easily loaded, unloaded, and moved between different transportation vehicles, containers on AWS can be easily deployed, scaled, and managed across various AWS services and environments, making them highly versatile and efficient for application deployment and operations.

In traditional EC2 deployments, applications are deployed onto VMs (EC2 instances), each running its own operating system. This approach provides isolation but can lead to resource inefficiencies and management overhead. In contrast, containers encapsulate applications and their dependencies into a single package that can run consistently across different environments. Containers share the host operating system kernel, resulting in faster startup times, improved resource utilization, and greater portability compared to VMs.

> **Note**
>
> You do not need to know Docker or Kubernetes for the exam. However, you will need to know the differences between the AWS services that support each. Now, take a look at ECS architecture and optimization techniques before moving on to EKS.

ECS Architecture

ECS contains several components that will look very different if you are used to running VMs. The main concept for containers is to think of them as running a specific function rather than an application. While they can run applications as well, they are often used to host microservices that are subsets of a bigger application, and they get created and removed as and when required:

- **Dockerfile**: A Dockerfile is a script containing a list of instructions that Docker uses to build a container image.

- **Task definition**: A task definition is a blueprint for running containers on ECS. It defines the container images, CPU and memory requirements, networking configuration, and other parameters needed to run a task. Task definitions are versioned and can be updated to deploy new versions of applications. You can create a maximum of 10 containers using one task definition.

- **Task**: A task is an instance of a task definition running on ECS. It represents one or more containers that are deployed together to perform a specific function. Tasks can be run on ECS clusters and are managed by ECS services.

- **Cluster**: A cluster is a logical grouping of ECS container instances that run tasks and services. It provides the infrastructure for running containerized applications and manages the placement of tasks across container instances.

- **Service**: A service is a long-running task that ensures that a specified number of task instances are running and automatically replaces any failed tasks. It allows you to define the desired state of your application and ensures that it remains running and healthy.

- **Container instance**: A container instance is an EC2 instance that is registered with an ECS cluster and runs the ECS container agent. It provides the compute capacity for running tasks and services and is managed by ECS.

- **Container registry**: A container registry is a repository for storing and managing container images. ECS integrates with container registries such as Amazon **Elastic Container Registry (ECR)** to store and deploy container images.

- When you create an ECS cluster, you need to define how the tasks will be run and whether they should auto scale or be distributed across multiple containers if needed. Getting this wrong can end up being either very costly for little benefit or having an application that cannot meet its performance requirements. Therefore, it is important to understand the best practices around ECS optimization.

ECS Optimization

One of the best reasons for using ECS is its flexibility and ability to optimize for both cost and performance. ECS can be used to offer powerful scaling and minimal operational overheads. Some recommendations on how to use ECS include the following:

- **Optimize task definitions**: Ensure your task definitions are as lightweight and efficient as possible. The best architecture for ECS is for each container to do one job well and efficiently rather than trying to do too many things. Strategies to keep the definitions lightweight ensure you only use the smallest base images and do not add functionality that is not needed.

- **Use task placement strategies**: ECS task placement strategies allow you to optimize resource utilization and distribute tasks evenly across your cluster instances. We will discuss task placement in more depth in the next section, *Task Placement Strategies*.

- **Implement auto scaling**: If you need to maintain a certain performance level and throughput, you can implement auto scaling policies for ECS to automatically change the number of running tasks based on workload demand. Use Amazon EC2 Auto Scaling or Amazon ECS capacity providers to dynamically scale resources up or down to maintain desired performance levels.

- **Leverage service discovery**: Use AWS Cloud Map or Amazon Route 53 for service discovery to dynamically register and discover ECS services and tasks. Implement service discovery to simplify communication between microservices and enable seamless integration with other AWS services.

- **Secure container images**: Ensure that container images are scanned for vulnerabilities and security risks before deployment. Use tools such as Amazon ECR image scanning or third-party solutions to identify and remediate security issues in container images.

- Now you can take a look at task placement strategies as these often feature in the *AWS SAA-C03* exam.

Task Placement Strategies

Task placement involves determining where tasks that are instances of containers should be placed within an ECS cluster. ECS offers several options for task placement, including **spread**, **binpack**, and **random** strategies. Spread placement spreads tasks across Availability Zones to enhance availability and fault tolerance. Binpack placement maximizes resource utilization by packing tasks onto the fewest number of instances, thus optimizing cost. Random lets ECS decide where to run the task using randomized placement to try to minimize overloaded nodes. Additionally, task placement constraints allow users to specify rules regarding where tasks can or cannot be placed based on factors such as instance attributes, platform constraints, or custom attributes. This gives you fine-grained control over task placement to maximize cost efficiency and performance. *Figure 4.4* shows how task placement strategies work:

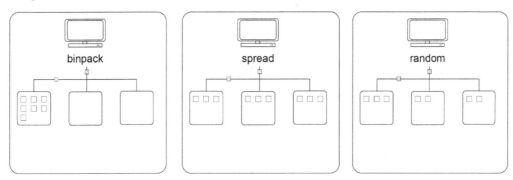

Figure 4.4: Task placement strategies

To summarize, ECS uses Docker containers to run your code or application. You have fine-grained control over where the task is run, allowing you to optimize the cluster for cost or performance.

Now that you have learned about the key components and management techniques for ECS, you can take a similar look at EKS to see how it differs.

EKS Architecture

EKS has a similar structure and purpose as ECS. Containers in EKS are designed to encapsulate specific functions rather than entire applications. Often utilized for hosting microservices within larger applications, containers are dynamically created and removed as needed, adapting to fluctuating demands efficiently. The naming of the components differs in EKS. There are often exam questions with a mixture of EKS and ECS terms to try to confuse students, so be aware. Here are some of the key terms used in EKS:

- **Pod**: In EKS, a Pod represents a unit of deployment, comprising one or more containers sharing networking and storage resources. Pods are the basic building blocks for running applications in Kubernetes.

- **Deployment**: A Deployment in EKS manages the lifecycle of pods, ensuring that a specified number of replicas are running and handling updates and rollbacks. Deployments provide mechanisms for controlling the rollout and scaling of applications in Kubernetes.

- **Service**: Kubernetes Services provide a stable endpoint for accessing a set of pods. They enable load balancing and service discovery within the cluster, allowing applications to communicate with each other reliably.

- **Node**: Nodes are the underlying compute instances in an EKS cluster where Pods are scheduled to run. Each node runs a Kubernetes kubelet, which manages the Pod lifecycle on that node. A kubelet is a small agent that controls how the Pod operates.

- **Control Plane**: The control plane in EKS encompasses various Kubernetes control plane components, including the API server, scheduler, and controller manager. These components collectively manage the state of the cluster and orchestrate tasks such as scheduling, scaling, and monitoring.

EKS Optimization

EKS optimization is handled very similarly to ECS. You want to make sure your Dockerfiles contain only the minimum instructions to run the code required and do not have libraries that are not used. You also want to make sure your compute is not over-resourced. EKS allows you to use auto-scaling mechanisms to ensure your workloads always have enough resources to run effectively without having to provision compute that sits idle. The main difference from ECS is how tasks or pods are placed.

Pod Scheduling

Pod scheduling in Kubernetes is the process of determining where to place Pods within the cluster's nodes based on various constraints and requirements. The Kubernetes scheduler is responsible for making these placement decisions, taking into account factors such as resource availability, node characteristics, affinity/anti-affinity rules, and pod specifications. The scheduler takes the following into account:

- **Node selection:** When a new pod is created, the scheduler selects an appropriate node from the cluster to run the pod. The selection process considers factors such as node capacity, resource availability (CPU, memory), and node labels or attributes.

- **Resource requests and limits:** Pods can specify resource requests and limits for CPU and memory. Resource requests indicate the amount of resources a pod requires to run, while limits define the maximum amount of resources a pod can consume. The scheduler considers these resource requirements when selecting nodes to ensure that pods have sufficient resources to run without causing resource contention.

- **Node affinity and anti-affinity**: Node affinity and anti-affinity rules allow you to influence pod placement based on node labels or attributes. Node affinity specifies preferences for pod placement on nodes with specific labels, while anti-affinity rules prevent pods from being scheduled on nodes that have certain labels. This allows you to distribute pods across nodes based on node characteristics or workload requirements.

- **Pod affinity and anti-affinity**: Pod affinity and anti-affinity rules allow you to influence pod placement based on the presence or absence of other pods. Pod affinity specifies preferences for co-locating pods with certain labels or attributes, while anti-affinity rules prevent pods from being scheduled on nodes that already have pods with specific labels. This can be useful for workload isolation, spreading related pods across different nodes, or co-locating pods that require communication.

- **Taints and tolerations**: Nodes can be tainted to repel certain pods unless they have specific tolerations. Taints are used to mark nodes with certain characteristics (e.g., hardware features, environment constraints) that may affect pod placement. Pods can specify tolerations to indicate that they are willing to tolerate taints on nodes.

Overall, pod scheduling in Kubernetes can be complex, but when configured correctly, it can allow a dynamic process that considers various factors to ensure efficient resource utilization, workload distribution, and fault tolerance within the cluster. By understanding and leveraging these scheduling mechanisms, you can optimize pod placement to meet your application's requirements while maximizing cluster efficiency and resilience.

If you need another method to help optimize and control your costs using either ECS or EKS, you can consider using serverless solutions. Containers can run on an EC2 instance or you can leverage a serverless solution that does not require you to provision or configure your own instances. Now, take a look at AWS Fargate.

AWS Fargate

AWS Fargate is a serverless compute engine for containers that allows you to run containers without having to manage the underlying infrastructure. With Fargate, you can focus on designing and deploying your containerized applications without worrying about provisioning, managing, or scaling EC2 instances. You can define your containerized application and specify the CPU and memory requirements, and AWS handles the rest, including provisioning and scaling the infrastructure needed to run your containers. Fargate will automatically scale up and down to meet your workload needs without you having to create auto scaling groups yourself.

In terms of pricing differences, Fargate follows a pay-per-use pricing model, where you only pay for the vCPU and memory resources consumed by your containers, rounded up to the nearest second. This allows you to optimize costs by only paying for the resources you actually use, without the overhead of managing and maintaining EC2 instances. However, per vCPU, Fargate is more expensive than EC2, so if you can accurately provision your EC2 instances to run your workload without waste, then this would be more cost-optimal. Fargate works well when you have a spiky or unknown workload that would be hard to correctly provision EC2 instances to handle.

Now that you have learned what containers are and how to use them to create and support an application, take a look at how you can use them to support scheduled jobs that require high levels of coordination.

AWS Batch

AWS Batch simplifies the process of running batch computing workloads in the cloud by automating the provisioning and scaling of compute resources. With AWS Batch, users can submit batch jobs, define job execution parameters, and let the service handle the rest. It uses container technologies and rapid scaling capabilities. AWS Batch ensures efficient resource utilization, cost optimization, and reliable job execution.

Typically, AWS Batch is extremely useful when you need many tasks to be run simultaneously, when you have dependencies that may control the order that the tasks are run, or if you require a centralized scheduling service that can coordinate jobs across a wide range of AWS services. Some typical use cases include the following:

- **Data processing**: AWS Batch is ideal for processing large volumes of data, such as ETL jobs, data validation, and log analysis. AWS Batch can control the provisioning of spot instances to ensure your jobs are run cost-efficiently.

- **Scientific computing**: It is well-suited for running scientific simulations, computational chemistry, bioinformatics, and other compute-intensive workloads.

- **Media processing**: It can handle media transcoding, image processing, and video rendering tasks efficiently and cost-effectively.

- **CI/CD**: Organizations can leverage AWS Batch for executing build and test jobs as part of CI/CD pipelines, ensuring rapid and reliable software delivery.

Now that you understand when AWS Batch can be useful, you can learn how to configure and set it up.

Working with AWS Batch

AWS Batch works with jobs that contain both a definition of what needs to be done and a schedule. AWS Batch uses a combination of job queues and compute resources to manage and run jobs. The main components of AWS Batch are as follows:

- **Jobs**: In AWS Batch, a job represents a unit of work submitted by a user to be executed within a compute environment.

- **Job Definitions**: They define how jobs are executed, including Docker container image specifications, command line arguments, and resource requirements.

- **Job Queues**: They act as a buffer between job submissions and execution, prioritizing and scheduling jobs based on parameters such as priority and dependencies.

- **Compute Environments**: These are managed compute resources provisioned by AWS Batch to run jobs, configurable with various instance types, sizes, and EC2 Spot Instances.

Figure 4.5 shows how all these components fit together:

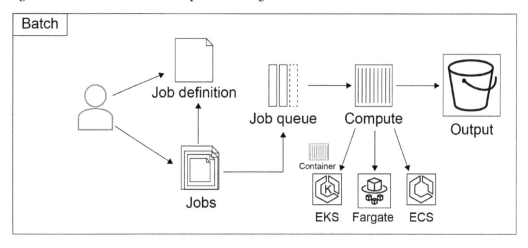

Figure 4.5: AWS Batch architecture

To run AWS Batch, you need to create and upload a container image that contains the code you need to run. Once you have the container image uploaded, you create a script to define the job, and finally, you run it. The basic steps to set this up are as follows:

1. Build a Docker image with the required code.
2. Create an Amazon ECR repository for the Docker image you just created.
3. Send/push the built image to ECR for storage.

4.   Create your job script and upload it to S3 so it can be read by the container during runtime.

5.   Create or modify an IAM role that will allow the jobs to read from an S3 bucket.

6.   Create a job definition that uses the image you created.

7.   Submit and run a job that executes the job script from the S3 bucket.

Once the job is created, it can be run with any schedule you wish and AWS Batch will auto scale the compute needed to run it, making it extremely cost-efficient and easy to manage.

The final area to cover in this topic is perhaps the most important – security. Now, you can learn how to access compute resources in the most secure manner, following AWS best practices.

Instance and Container Security

Securing and accessing EC2 instances as well as ECS or EKS clusters within AWS requires a strategic approach to ensure both robust security measures and efficient accessibility. Here are some best practices, starting with EC2.

EC2 Security

EC2 instances reside within a VPC (*Chapter 2, Virtual Private Cloud*), so they are able to benefit from VPC security measures such as security groups and **network access control lists** (**NACLs**) to limit access. You can also use IAM roles to further control what other AWS services can be used from within the EC2 instance and to grant access to users. You should also consider using encryption of the data that is held on the EC2 instances to ensure it cannot be accessed without authorization. Now take a look at the main areas of security you have available:

- **Security groups**: Implement security groups to control inbound and outbound traffic to EC2 instances. Define rules based on IP addresses, ports, and protocols to restrict access to only necessary resources and services.

- **NACLs**: Employ NACLs to further control traffic at the subnet level. Configure rules to allow or deny specific IP addresses or ranges, providing an additional layer of security for EC2 instances.

- **IAM roles**: Leverage IAM roles to grant temporary permissions to EC2 instances instead of storing long-term credentials on the instances themselves. This enhances security and simplifies access management, especially for applications running on EC2 instances.

- **Data encryption**: Utilize AWS **Key Management Service** (**KMS**) to encrypt data at rest and in transit. Encrypt sensitive data stored on EC2 instances and implement SSL/TLS for securing communication between instances and other services.

- **Patch management**: Regularly update and patch EC2 instances to address security vulnerabilities and ensure the latest security fixes are applied. Utilize AWS Systems Manager or third-party tools for automated patch management.

Access to an EC2 instance can also be secured. In the past, you would typically use a username and password to gain access, but the passwords could be breached so different methods such as using a **Secure Shell (SSH)** key were introduced. Other methods that do not involve any keys or passwords are now also available via AWS. This also means that you do not necessarily need to open any ports on your EC2 instances, which reduces the routes open to any potential hackers. You can access an EC2 instance using the following methods:

- **SSH**: SSH is a widely used protocol for securely accessing remote servers, including EC2 instances. Users typically use an SSH client to connect to the instance using its public IP address or DNS name and the associated private key pair.

- **Remote Desktop Protocol (RDP)**: RDP is used for accessing Windows-based EC2 instances. Users can connect to the instance using an RDP client such as Remote Desktop Connection on Windows or a third-party RDP client. They need to provide the instance's public IP address or DNS name along with the username and password configured for the instance.

- **Bastion hosts**: Bastion hosts, also known as jump hosts, are intermediary servers deployed in a public subnet of a VPC. They act as a single entry point for accessing private instances located in private subnets securely. Users first access the bastion host using SSH and then SSH from the bastion host to the target EC2 instance. Using a bastion is seen as a more secure option as the bastion could be **hardened** and have very high levels of logging. A hardened server is one specifically designed to be highly secure with advanced security and logging. The bastion can also be quickly shut down if a breach happens, whereas this would be more difficult if a hacker gained direct access to an application server.

- **AWS Systems Manager Session Manager**: AWS Systems Manager provides a Session Manager feature that allows users to securely connect to EC2 instances without requiring inbound SSH or RDP ports to be open. Users can access instances directly from the AWS Management Console or **command-line interface (CLI)**, eliminating the need for bastion hosts and managing SSH keys.

- **Virtual private network (VPN)**: Organizations can set up VPN connections to their VPCs to establish secure access to EC2 instances. Users connect to the VPN server using VPN client software and then access the instances within the VPC as if they were on the same network.

Now, take a look at how you can secure an ECS and an EKS cluster.

ECS or EKS Cluster Security

Container security differs from an EC2 instance as you would not typically access the underlying instance. Rather, you would connect to the container or pod. However, if you are using EC2 instances for your compute in ECS or EKS, then those instances sit within a VPC, allowing you to follow similar rules to a non-container EC2 instance. Now, you can focus on the specific security enhancements offered to containers:

- **IAM Roles for Service Accounts (IRSA)**: Use IRSA to associate IAM roles directly with Kubernetes or Docker service accounts in EKS and ECS clusters. This enables fine-grained access control to AWS services and resources from within Kubernetes pods or Docker containers.

- **Role-Based Access Control (RBAC)**: Configure RBAC to define granular permissions within clusters and containers, ensuring that only authorized users and services have access to specific resources and operations.

- **Network policies**: Utilize Kubernetes network policies to restrict traffic between pods and namespaces within ECS or EKS clusters. Define rules based on pod labels, IP addresses, or ports to enforce segmentation and isolate workloads. These differ from using security groups or NACLs as these operate at the pod or container layer, not the server layer.

- **Container image security**: Implement best practices for securing container images, such as scanning for vulnerabilities, signing images with trusted keys, and restricting image sources to trusted registries. Use AWS **ECR** or third-party registries integrated with EKS or ECS.

- **Audit logging and monitoring**: Enable audit logging and monitoring within ECS or EKS clusters to detect and respond to security incidents in real time. Utilize AWS CloudTrail, Amazon CloudWatch, and third-party logging solutions for comprehensive visibility into cluster activities.

It is important to remember that when using containers running on EC2 instances, you have both the EC2-level security rules, such as NACLs and security groups, and the container layer security. Using both together can create extremely secure policies, but it can become complex quickly with rules that can clash with each other.

Hands-on Lab

Throughout this chapter, you have learned about the theory of EC2 instances and ECS/EKS clusters. You can now practice creating these in our AWS account, starting with EC2.

EC2 Lab

The objective of this hands-on lab is to provide you with practical experience in deploying and managing EC2 instances and creating an ASG to ensure high availability and scalability:

1. Log in to the AWS Management Console.

2. Navigate to the EC2 dashboard. Click on `Launch Instance` to begin the instance creation process.

3. Choose the latest Amazon Linux AMI (at the time of writing, this was Amazon Linux 2023). Feel free to launch other AMIs, but they may not be covered under the Free tier, so remember to delete them when done.

4. Select an instance type based on your requirements. If you choose `t2.micro`, you generally will be covered under the Free tier.

5. Create a new key pair and store the key safely. If you are using a Mac or a Linux-based computer, then save the key as `.pem`. If you using a Windows computer and are using PuTTY, then save it as `.ppk`.

6. Under `Network settings`, select `Create security group`. Check the `Allow SSH traffic from` button and choose `My IP` from the dropdown. This allows you to SSH into the instance.

7. Review and launch the instance.

8. Once the instance is launched, note down its public IP address or DNS name.

9. Open an SSH client (e.g., PuTTY for Windows, Terminal for macOS/Linux).

10. Use the SSH client to connect to the EC2 instance using the key pair chosen during instance creation. The username for an EC2 instance is typically `ec2-user`.

11. Navigate to the EC2 dashboard.

12. Click on `Auto Scaling Groups` in the left navigation pane.

13. Click on `Create Auto Scaling group`.

14. Click `Create Launch template`.

15. Give the Launch Template a name and select the Amazon Linux AMI that you used to launch the original EC2 instance.

16. Select an instance class of `t2.micro` to use the Free tier and make sure it uses the key pair you created earlier.

17. Leave everything else as the defaults and create the launch template.

18. Return to the previous screen and choose the launch template just created. Give the ASG a name and click `Next`.

19. Choose the network details for the instance location. Select a VPC and subnets. You need at least one subnet.

20. Configure scaling policies for the ASG, setting the minimum node count to 1 and the maximum node count to 2. Select `Target tracking scaling policy` and change `Average CPU utilization` to 1. You will set it this low to ensure that the scaling policy is met for demonstration purposes.

21. Leave everything else as the default, clicking `Next` as needed. Click `Create Auto Scaling Group`.

22. Monitor the ASG on the EC2 dashboard to observe its current instance count and status.

23. Observe how the ASG automatically scales out to accommodate the load based on the configured scaling policy of 1% CPU. You should see the number of nodes hit 2, which was the maximum you configured. As you set a warm-up condition of 300 seconds, it will take around 5 minutes for the scaling to complete.

24. Terminate the EC2 instances and delete the Auto Scaling Group to avoid incurring unnecessary charges.

In this hands-on lab, you learned how to create and manage EC2 instances, connect to them using SSH, and set up an ASG to ensure the high availability and scalability of your application.

Let's now look at creating a sample application using ECS.

ECS Lab

You will now create a small test website using a Docker image that uses nginx. Nginx is a simple web hosting service, and it will be used to create a basic website:

1. Log in to the AWS Management Console.

2. Navigate to the ECS dashboard.

3. Click on `Clusters` in the left navigation pane.

4. Click on `Create Cluster` and give it a name. Leave `Default namespace` as the default. Select `AWS Fargate (serverless)` for `Infrastructure`.

5. Review other settings in the `Monitoring and Advanced` section if you wish and create the cluster. This creates and runs a CloudFormation template, so if you wish to see what is run under the hood, you can navigate to CloudFormation and watch the stack be created.

6. Navigate to `Task definitions` in the left-hand menu and select `Create task definition`.

7. Give it a name and make sure the deployment type is AWS Fargate. Select `None` for `Task roles` and `Create new role` for `Task execution role`.

8. Under the `Container - 1` section, define the settings you need for your specific container. This is where you give the details of the image to be used. For this example application, you need to give it a name and for the image URI, use `nginx:latest` – `nginx` is the name of the image we want to use and `latest` means to use the most recent version. You can select a specific version if you want and this can be useful when testing different versions of your own code. This image is already hosted in ECR. You can explore that too if you wish. If the deployment takes more than five minutes to deploy, then check the `Events` tab under the service to see any error messages that may need to be resolved before trying again.

9. Under `Container port`, check the following:

    - Port: `80`

    - Protocol: `TCP`

    - `Port name`: Give it any name you want to identify it

    - `App protocol`: `HTTP`

10. Leave all other settings as the defaults but expand the sections to understand the advanced settings you can change.

11. Click `Create` at the bottom of the page.

12. Navigate back to the `Task Definitions` page and select the definition you just created. You can see that it has created a revision or a version. Select `revision-1`.

13. To use the task you have created, it needs to be deployed. This means provisioning this container within the ECS cluster. Click the `Deploy` dropdown from the top right and select `Create Service`.

14. Review all the options on this page to understand them. You need to make two changes. Firstly, under the `Deployment configuration` section, you need to give a service name. Secondly, to allow you to have access to the website that this will create, enable `Public IP`. Check that `Public IP` is turned on.

15. As you are creating a very simple demo application, there is no need for load balancing (load balancing is covered in more depth in *Chapter 7, Data and Analytics*), so you will leave the load balancing option as `None`. If you were creating an application that needed to scale beyond a single container, you would want to enable load balancing.

16. Click `Create` at the bottom to deploy the container image to your ECS cluster. Again, this uses CloudFormation in the background so you can watch or review the stack there.

17. After a few minutes, review that the service has been successfully created.

18. Once the service is successfully deployed, navigate to the ECS dashboard.

19. Click on the cluster name you created, then select the `Tasks` tab. Click on the task that is running.

20. Go to the `Configuration` tab and locate `Public IP`. Click on `Open address`.

21. You should see the nginx configuration page.

22. Delete the ECS service and task definition to avoid incurring unnecessary charges.

23. Delete the ECS cluster, container registry, and any associated resources.

In this hands-on lab, you learned how to create and manage an Amazon ECS cluster, deploy a demo nginx application using ECS, and access the application via a load balancer. ECS provides a flexible and scalable platform for running containerized applications, enabling efficient container orchestration and management in the AWS cloud environment.

Summary

In this chapter, you learned about the various ways to run computations on AWS, which gives you the flexibility to process and execute tasks using AWS's cloud infrastructure. You found out that AWS offers a range of compute options tailored to different application needs, including traditional virtual servers with EC2 and container-based solutions using Amazon ECS and EKS for orchestrating Docker containers and Kubernetes clusters, respectively.

You read about the differences between virtual machines and containers, where virtual machines provide a complete emulation of a physical computer, offering strong isolation by running an entire operating system, while containers offer a more lightweight and efficient approach by sharing the host's operating system and isolating applications in user space. This makes containers ideal for modern application deployment due to their fast startup times, resource efficiency, and scalability.

You learned about the importance of choosing the right EC2 instance types, how to scale your applications effectively using ASGs, and best practices for securing your instances and containerized deployments. This includes using security groups, network access control lists, IAM roles for granting permissions, and ensuring data encryption, as well as adopting strategies for secure access and audit logging to maintain a secure and efficient AWS environment.

Through the compute services provided by AWS, such as EC2 for resizable cloud servers, Elastic Beanstalk for easy application deployment without managing the infrastructure, ECS for managing Docker containers, EKS for Kubernetes management, AWS Fargate for running containers without managing servers, and AWS Batch for efficient batch processing, you learned that AWS has a solution for nearly any computational need. These services allow you to deploy everything from simple web applications to complex, scalable microservices architectures and batch processing jobs, providing the tools needed to select the best compute option for your specific workload requirements.

In the next chapter, you will learn about AWS storage options, including S3, EBS, and FSx.

Exam Readiness Drill - Chapter Review Questions

Apart from mastering key concepts, strong test-taking skills under time pressure are essential for acing your certification exam. That's why developing these abilities early in your learning journey is critical.

Exam readiness drills, using the free online practice resources provided with this book, help you progressively improve your time management and test-taking skills while reinforcing the key concepts you've learned.

HOW TO GET STARTED

- Open the link or scan the QR code at the bottom of this page

- If you have unlocked the practice resources already, log in to your registered account. If you haven't, follow the instructions in *Chapter 16* and come back to this page.

- Once you log in, click the START button to start a quiz

- We recommend attempting a quiz multiple times till you're able to answer most of the questions correctly and well within the time limit.

- You can use the following practice template to help you plan your attempts:

Working On Accuracy		
Attempt	Target	Time Limit
Attempt 1	40% or more	Till the timer runs out
Attempt 2	60% or more	Till the timer runs out
Attempt 3	75% or more	Till the timer runs out
Working On Timing		
Attempt 4	75% or more	1 minute before time limit
Attempt 5	75% or more	2 minutes before time limit
Attempt 6	75% or more	3 minutes before time limit

The above drill is just an example. Design your drills based on your own goals and make the most out of the online quizzes accompanying this book.

First time accessing the online resources? 🔒

You'll need to unlock them through a one-time process. **Head to** *Chapter 16* **for instructions**.

Open Quiz	
https://packt.link/SAAC03Ch04 OR scan this QR code →	

5
Storage

AWS offers many different storage services designed to address a wide array of storage needs, from high-throughput applications to long-term archiving. This chapter delves deeper into the specifics of AWS's storage options, ensuring you have the knowledge to choose the most appropriate solution for your needs. This chapter helps you understand the different storage solutions you can choose and how and when to choose them.

Whether you are looking to store application data, serve website content, back up databases, or archive critical information, AWS provides scalable, secure, and high-performing storage options. From the simplicity of **Simple Storage Service (S3)** for object storage to the robust and scalable file systems provided by **Elastic Block Store (EBS)**, **Elastic File System (EFS)**, and Amazon **File Server (FSx)**, this chapter will equip you with the knowledge to choose and implement the right AWS storage solutions for your applications. Additionally, we'll explore how AWS Backup can simplify the backup and restore process across AWS services.

In this chapter, the following topics will be covered:

- Amazon S3
- Amazon EBS
- Amazon EFS
- Amazon FSx
- AWS Backup

Now, you can start with an overview and introduction to the different types of storage needs a business may have.

Introduction to AWS Storage

Before you learn about the different AWS storage services that are available, it is important to understand the different types of storage needs you may have. At the most basic level, storage types can be categorized into object storage, block storage, and file storage, each serving distinct purposes and offering unique advantages.

Object Storage

Object storage is the simplest and most scalable form of storage available. It manages data as distinct units, or objects, each stored in an environment generally with no folder hierarchy. Every object consists of the data itself, a variable amount of metadata, and a globally unique identifier. It is ideal for storing photos, videos, documents, and backup files, especially when accessibility from anywhere on the web is required. Object storage excels at managing massive amounts of unstructured data because it is highly scalable and designed for durability, availability, and security.

Block Storage

Block storage divides data into fixed-sized blocks, each with a unique identifier but without encompassing metadata (as object storage does). This type of storage is similar to traditional hard drives and is used where performance and efficiency are critical, such as with databases or enterprise applications. Block storage allows for individual blocks to be mounted as a hard drive by a server. The key advantage of block storage is its ability to support transaction-intensive applications with low latency. Some applications that are transaction-intensive include online e-commerce platforms, online gaming systems, and financial trading platforms.

File Storage

File storage organizes data into files and folders, similar to the file systems on most computers and servers. It is accessible through established protocols such as the **Network File System** (**NFS**) or the **Server Message Block** (**SMB**), allowing multiple users or applications to share the stored files across a network. File storage is particularly beneficial for applications requiring a shared file system, collaboration on documents, or where directory hierarchies are necessary. When working with file storage, you need to make sure that the data you use is readable by the operating system you are using. Not all operating systems use the same formats and there can be significant cost and performance implications for using the wrong one.

File Systems and Formatting

Within file storage, different file systems can be used depending on the requirements of the application or the operating system. File systems also involve formatting, which is the process of preparing the storage device for data storage, and organizing the files in a way that the operating system can read and write. Formatting includes setting up the file system structure, such as **New Technology File System (NTFS)** for Windows environments or Ext4 for Linux systems. The choice of file system and format depends on compatibility with the operating system, performance requirements, and specific features such as encryption or journaling.

Understanding the distinctions between object, block, and file storage, along with the various file systems and formatting options, is crucial for making informed decisions on data storage in the cloud. The *AWS Certified Solutions Architect – Associate (SAA-C03) Certification* often tests a student's knowledge of the differing storage types, so it is important to be able to explain when you would use each type of storage and its key characteristics. The right choice depends on the specific application requirements, performance needs, and scalability considerations.

Now that you have learned about the different storage types available, you can look at AWS's offerings and services.

Amazon S3

Amazon S3 is one of the first and most critical services AWS offers. Launched in 2006, it provides a robust platform for storing and retrieving any amount of data. Its key features, such as scalability, high durability, fine-grained security measures, and performance, make it an ideal solution for a wide range of applications. From static website hosting and content distribution to backup and archival solutions, S3 offers an efficient and cost-effective storage solution. Its integration with other AWS services and third-party applications further enhances its versatility, enabling organizations to build complex, scalable applications with ease.

The main organizational unit of S3 is called a **bucket**. Bucket names must be totally unique globally, so you may have to be a bit creative with the names as the name `audit-logs` has probably already been used. Within a bucket, you can create folders and objects. Folders can be used to logically control where the objects reside.

The main features of S3 are as follows:

- **Scalability**: Stores and retrieves any amount of data at any time. S3 can handle massive amounts of data, making it ideal for applications requiring unlimited storage space. You can store an unlimited number of objects with a maximum size of 5 TB per object.

- **Durability and availability**: S3 provides comprehensive durability and availability guarantees. Your data is redundantly stored across multiple facilities and is designed to offer a standard 99.999999999% durability (in some situations, the durability is lower than this, as you will learn later in this section). This durability means that if you had 1 million objects in S3, you could expect to go 10 million years before you lost one. That is good odds.

- **Security**: Features such as bucket policies and **Access Control Lists** (**ACLs**) help manage access to your data. S3 also integrates with AWS **Identity and Access Management** (**IAM**) for secure data handling.

- **Performance**: S3 is optimized for high performance, with capabilities such as S3 Transfer Acceleration for faster data uploads and downloads globally.

- **Version controls**: S3 offers the ability to create new versions of your objects rather than overwriting them. This allows you to recover data or revert to an earlier version if it is accidentally overwritten.

- **Data tiering**: Not all data needs to be stored with very high durability or needs to be accessed quickly. Data tiering allows some objects to be saved in archival storage for less cost but with a longer read time.

As you can see, even something seemingly as simple as an object store has many configuration options that can influence both your costs and your performance. Now, you can look at some of the main features of S3, starting with the most important topic of security.

Security Controls in Amazon S3

Like any service in AWS, security is an extremely important area to get right. The internet is full of stories of customers leaving S3 buckets open to the world. In fact, there is a website that constantly searches for open buckets. If you or your company is using S3 already, perhaps check the website to make sure you are not on it (`https://buckets.grayhatwarfare.com/buckets?type=aws`). As a result, by default, all S3 buckets are created without public access, and you would need to manually override this if needed.

Take a look at some of the main methods to secure and control access on your S3 buckets:

- **Bucket policies**: These **JavaScript Object Notation** (**JSON**)-based policies allow you to define permissions at the bucket level, specifying what actions are allowed or denied.

- **ACLs**: ACLs provide a more granular level of control, allowing you to manage access to individual objects. ACLs have been generally phased out and replaced by IAM access controls instead.

- **AWS IAM**: With IAM, you can create users, groups, and roles with specific permissions to access S3 resources, enabling secure access control. These are the newer versions of ACLs and can be applied at the bucket or object level to give fine-grained controls.

You can see how you can use a combination of bucket and object policies to control access to specific users and actions. For example, you can create a bucket policy to only allow a certain IAM group to access it, but then you can create an additional IAM policy to only let certain superusers modify or delete any object or folder.

In addition to access controls, S3 also allows you to use encryption to keep the data secure, even if the AWS backend servers are hacked. S3 offers both **server-side encryption (SSE)** for data at rest and SSL/TLS for data in transit. For SSE, you can choose between AWS-managed keys (S3-SSE), **customer master keys (CMKs)** managed in AWS **Key Management Service (SSE-KMS)**, or a customer-provided key (SSE-C).

It also has highly customizable logging and monitoring to quickly alert you if a bucket has been accessed inappropriately.

S3 provides access logs that can be analyzed for security and access patterns. Integration with AWS CloudTrail further enhances monitoring by logging API calls.

Versioning in Amazon S3

Versioning is a powerful feature of Amazon S3 that keeps multiple variants of an object in the same bucket. This feature is designed to protect your data from being overwritten or deleted, providing a clear way to recover from unintended user actions and application failures. Versioning can also be used to ensure compliance with regulations that may apply to your organization. Some compliance frameworks such as the **Payment Card Industry Data Security Standard (PCI-DSS)** and **Health Insurance Portability and Accountability Act (HIPAA)** require that files cannot be edited or deleted for a certain amount of time to guarantee their consistency and credibility. S3 offers features that can help in maintaining that consistency ensuring you remain compliant. Some of these features are as follows:

- **Data preservation**: Once you enable versioning for a bucket, S3 preserves, retrieves, and restores every version of every object stored in that bucket. This includes all writes and even deletions of objects.

- **Recovery**: Versioning makes it easier to recover from both accidental deletion and application logic failures. You can also use it as a part of your backup strategy.

- **Multi-factor authenticated deletes**: To provide an additional layer of security, you can configure a bucket to require **multi-factor authentication (MFA)** for the deletion of object versions.

- **Object locking**: S3 supports object locking to stop any object from being modified or deleted either indefinitely or within a certain timeframe. S3 can be run in governance mode, where some users may be granted permission to make modifications, or in compliance mode, where no users are granted permission to make changes.

Using versioning can come at a significant cost as older versions of your objects may not be deleted, and therefore, storage requirements can grow rapidly. You can manually or programmatically delete older versions when no longer required. For example, you could create a Lambda function to delete all versions except the current and one previous version. However, this requires manual work and monitoring and may struggle to scale. Instead, S3 offers a function called **lifecycle policies**, which can be used to automate this.

You can now learn about lifecycle policies and storage classes.

Lifecycle Policies and Storage Classes

Lifecycle policies in S3 allow you to create rules that control where and in which **storage class** data is stored and when that data is ultimately removed. S3 offers a variety of storage classes designed to meet the diverse needs of data storage in terms of access frequency, cost-effectiveness, and durability. For example, if you have data that is highly critical for your business but is accessed very rarely, you will want to store that in a different storage class to data that is accessed every second.

The classes S3 offers currently are as follows:

- **Standard**: Ideal for frequently accessed data, offering high durability, availability, and performance. As the name suggests, this is the default.

- **Standard-Infrequent Access (Standard-IA)**: Suitable for data that is less frequently accessed but requires rapid access when needed. Offers a lower storage price than S3 Standard, with a retrieval fee. You would use this if you needed to store data, perhaps for compliance reasons, but you would need to access it occasionally without having to wait a long time for it to be retrieved.

- **One Zone-IA**: Similar to Standard-IA, but stores data in a single Availability Zone, offering lower costs at the expense of reduced availability. You would choose this option if your data was less critical and could be rebuilt from elsewhere if the consequences of loss would be minimal.

- **Glacier and S3 Glacier Deep Archive**: Designed for long-term archiving with very low storage costs. Data retrieval times range from minutes to hours. Glacier and Deep Archive should be used if you need to store data for a long time for compliance purposes, but that data would rarely if ever be read and you would be happy to wait potentially a few hours to retrieve it. This most closely maps with the offsite storage many companies use for their data centers. Each retrieval is charged.

- **S3 Outposts**: For data requiring AWS storage on-premises for latency-sensitive applications. Again, this is not technically a storage class, but this may feature in the exam. Instead of storing your objects on AWS servers, you can implement S3 features on your own servers allowing you to use the same API calls as if you were running in S3 but with minimal latency.

In addition to these specific tiers, AWS offers **Intelligent Tiering**. Intelligent Tiering automatically moves your data between four different storage classes to trade costs versus access speed based on how often you access the data. The four different tiers are as follows:

- **Frequent access**: For data that is regularly accessed, more often than once every 30 days. Storage costs are high but retrieval costs are low. Retrieval times are in milliseconds.

- **Infrequent access**: For data that is less regularly accessed but needs to be available almost instantly when needed. Storage costs are lower than frequent access but retrieval costs are higher. Retrieval times are the same as frequent access.

- **Archive access**: For data that is rarely accessed but needs to be retained. Data retrieval can be slow. Storage costs are low but retrieval costs are high. Retrieval times can take 3–5 hours.

- **Deep archive access**: For data that is not expected to be accessed unless in exceptional circumstances. Storage costs are very low but retrieval costs are very high. Retrieval times can be 12 hours.

For some customers who may have specific compliance or data storage requirements, Intelligent Tiering is insufficient for their needs. These customers can use lifecycle policies instead to manage which tier their data is stored in based on their own rules. It can be hard to understand the different storage options, so take a look at *Figure 5.1*, which shows a common scenario for a bank that is legally required to keep all customer data for a minimum of five years:

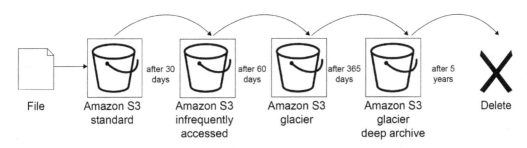

Figure 5.1: S3 lifecycle policy

In this diagram, you can see that a policy has been created to move all objects from S3 Standard to S3 IA after 30 days of its creation, then after 60 days, they would move to Glacier storage, and after a year (or 365 days), they would move to Glacier Deep Archive, and after five years, they would finally be deleted. This would allow the newer files that are likely being accessed more frequently to be charged only for their storage costs and allow unlimited free access, and then, as the files age and are less likely to be regularly accessed, they are moved to storage classes with much lower storage fees but higher retrieval fees. This is the trade-off. You need to understand how often a file will be accessed versus the cost of storing it.

In some cases, the data in your S3 bucket is so critical to the business that even a **Service Level Agreement (SLA)** of 99.9999999% is not enough or you need to guarantee that the S3 bucket can still be accessed even if an AWS Region went offline. You may also want to automatically share files with another bucket or another account. If this is the case, you can use S3 replication.

S3 Replication

Amazon S3 replication automatically copies objects between S3 buckets for backup, disaster recovery, or to decrease latency for users in different locations. Setting up replication requires enabling versioning on both the source and destination buckets, configuring permissions, and creating a replication rule to filter which objects are replicated.

When dealing with sensitive data that is encrypted, you will need to also make sure the encryption keys are accessible by the target bucket, particularly when sharing cross-region or cross-account. S3 supports SSE with either S3-managed keys (SSE-S3) or AWS Key Management Service keys (SSE-KMS), and client-side encryption. For SSE-KMS, you will need to specify the KMS keys for both source and destination buckets in the replication setup. If your buckets are across different AWS accounts, make sure the KMS key policies allow access from the source account.

You have now learned about all the critical features of S3 that will be tested in the exam. You will create a simple website using S3 and implement versioning in the hands-on lab at the end of this chapter.

Now, take a look at a second type of AWS storage that can be compared to using a hard drive on your own computer. This is called Amazon EBS.

Amazon EBS

Amazon EBS is a high-performance block storage service designed for use with EC2 for all types of workloads at any scale. A broad range of workloads, such as database applications, containerized applications, and big data analytics engines, can benefit from EBS's reliable, scalable, and secure storage solutions. EBS volumes are automatically replicated within their Availability Zone to protect your data from component failure, offering high availability and durability. Unlike S3, EBS stores data in blocks rather than files, allowing it to be used to host an operating system that runs your EC2 instance. You can consider EBS to be like a hard disk drive within your own computer.

> **Note**
>
> It is important to note that EBS is not shared storage. You cannot simultaneously attach an EBS volume to more than one EC2 instance. If you need to do this for shared files, you will need to use Amazon EFS, which is discussed in the *Amazon EFS* section later in this chapter. This detail is often tested in the exam.

EBS storage is created as a volume and each volume can be configured differently to meet your needs. Look at the main options and choices you have when creating a new EBS volume.

Storage Options

Amazon EBS provides a variety of volume types to meet the diverse performance and cost requirements of applications. Each EBS volume type is optimized for a specific use case and can be categorized into two main types: **solid-state drive (SSD)**-backed volumes for transactional workloads, such as databases and boot volumes, and **hard disk drive (HDD)**-backed volumes for throughput-intensive workloads, such as big data and data warehouses. The different types of EBS storage are as follows:

- **General Purpose SSD (gp2 and gp3)**: gp2 and gp3 are cost-effective storage options that balance price and performance for a wide variety of transactional workloads. gp3, the latest generation, offers customers the ability to independently scale **input/output operations per second (IOPS)** and throughput without having to provision additional block storage capacity, making it a more flexible and cost-efficient option. gp storage is the most commonly used storage option. Most customers would use gp storage unless they hit a specific performance restriction that forces them into using provisioned IOPS.

- **Provisioned IOPS SSD (io1 and io2)**: Designed for I/O-intensive workloads, especially databases, that require consistent and low-latency performance. io2 volumes offer higher durability and IOPS per GiB than io1, making them suitable for critical business applications that need sustained IOPS performance or more than 16,000 IOPS or 250 MiB/s of throughput per volume.

- **Throughput optimized HDD (st1)**: These magnetic storage options are ideal for frequently accessed, throughput-intensive workloads such as big data, data warehouses, and log processing. st1 volumes are designed to deliver low-cost storage with high throughput, making them unsuitable for boot volumes. Examples of customers using st1 storage would be companies running large analytics processing jobs, such as a lab processing huge volumes of data. These customers need huge throughput to the storage layer but they are less time-conscious than a production system would be.

- **Cold HDD (sc1)**: Optimized for less frequently accessed data, sc1 provides the lowest cost per gigabyte of all EBS volume types. It is best used for large, cold datasets where minimizing storage cost is crucial, but access speed is less critical. sc1 storage would be a good fit for companies needing to store archive information on an EBS volume.

EBS does not have a lifecycle policy or storage classes as with S3. If you need to archive data for compliance reasons, then you would need to copy that data to a different storage system such as S3 or Amazon EFS (you will learn about this later in this chapter, in the *Amazon EFS* section).

Data Persistence

One of the critical features of Amazon EBS is data persistence. Unlike instance store volumes (see *Chapter 4, Compute*), the data on an EBS volume persists independently of the life of the associated EC2 instance. When an EC2 instance is shut down, the data on its attached EBS volumes remains intact and can be accessed the next time the instance is started. This characteristic makes EBS volumes suitable for use as primary storage for databases, file systems, or any application that requires access to persistent storage. It also allows you to detach an EBS volume and move it to a different EC2 instance. This can be useful when you want to change an EC2 instance to a different type or location without losing your data.

EBS Snapshots

EBS snapshots provide a durable, block-level backup of your EBS volumes. Snapshots are incremental, meaning only the blocks on the volume that have changed after your most recent snapshot are saved, minimizing the time required to create the snapshot and saving on storage costs. Snapshots can be used to instantiate new EBS volumes, move volumes across Availability Zones, and safeguard your data for long-term durability. You can also share snapshots with different accounts, allowing you to recreate a test scenario away from your production or even share application data with a third party for debugging. In a hands-on lab at the end of the chapter, we will create a snapshot and learn how to share it.

Now you have learned about EBS and how it works as a storage option alongside an EC2 instance, it is time to understand the other main storage option that has been mentioned several times in this section: Amazon EFS.

Amazon EFS

Amazon EFS is a cloud-native, scalable file storage service that provides a simple elastic file system that can be used simultaneously by multiple EC2 instances. With EFS, you can scale your storage up or down as your files grow or shrink, without directly managing capacity. EFS is designed to be highly durable and available, making it ideal for a wide range of applications and use cases, from serving web content and media files to supporting data analytics, containerized applications, and much more. EFS can support thousands of concurrent **NFS** connections, providing your applications with a common data source that can be accessed securely from multiple Amazon EC2 instances or other AWS services. NFS lets you access and use files on a remote computer as if they were on your own computer. It is very commonly used to create shared drives and files that staff within a company can all use together.

EFS can be considered as a network drive you access from your computer but one that is not directly attached to it. EFS can also be used with **on-premises computers**, so you do not need to use EC2 to access it, unlike with EBS. As you go through this section, you will see that EFS has many more similarities with S3 than EBS.

> **Note**
>
> EFS can be used by any operating system that can currently run on EC2. However, it is designed for and performs best with Linux operating systems. If you are running Windows, then you should consider Amazon FSx for Windows instead. This is covered in the next section. This can come up in the exam and catch students out!

Lifecycle Policies and Storage Classes

Unlike EBS, Amazon EFS offers lifecycle policies similar to S3, which you learned about earlier in this chapter. However, EFS only offers two different storage classes, which is far fewer than S3. You can create a lifecycle policy to move files between the two classes automatically based on how often the files are accessed. The two different storage tiers are as follows:

- **Standard**: This is the default storage class for all files in EFS. It is designed for files that are accessed frequently and offers the lowest latency. It is suitable for performance-sensitive use cases where data needs to be readily accessible.

- **Infrequent Access (IA)**: The IA storage class is designed for files that are not accessed frequently, offering a cost-effective storage solution.

Data Persistence

One of the key features of Amazon EFS is that the data on the file system persists independently of any EC2 instance's life. This means that if an EC2 instance is shut down or terminated, the data stored in EFS remains intact and is continuously accessible from other EC2 instances or AWS services that have permission to access the file system. This persistent and shared storage feature is particularly beneficial for applications that need to access and share the same set of data across multiple instances or services, providing a highly available and durable storage solution. This shared access is also critical for containerized applications running on Amazon **Elastic Container Service** (**ECS**) or **Elastic Kubernetes Service** (**EKS**), where containers need to access and share the same data.

Performance

As well as choosing between different lifecycle policies, EFS also supports different storage classes. These differ from EBS to cater to the different use cases. You need to choose between two different modes to control the IOPs available and you also need to choose between three different throughput options. If you recall, IOPs is the number of operations per second and throughput is the total amount of data being read and written to disk.

Performance Modes

EFS offers two performance modes:

- **General Purpose**: This is the standard setting for EFS, making it well-suited for applications that are sensitive to delays, such as those requiring quick responses to user interactions. For example, consider a website hosting scenario where EFS is used to store and serve web content. In this case, low latency is crucial to ensure that web pages load quickly for visitors. Similarly, for a **content management system** (**CMS**) where users frequently access and update content, or for home directories accessed by various users, maintaining swift and responsive file operations is key. This mode ensures that each operation, such as opening or saving a file, happens almost instantly, providing a smooth user experience.

- **Max I/O**: This is designed for situations requiring high levels of data read and write operations, capable of supporting intense workloads from many EC2 instances simultaneously. Imagine a large-scale data processing application where hundreds of servers are analyzing large datasets stored on EFS. Here, the priority shifts toward handling a massive volume of operations over the need to minimize delay in each operation. While operations might take a bit longer to complete compared to General Purpose mode, Max I/O allows the system to conduct many more operations in parallel, significantly increasing the overall data processing capacity. This mode is essential for applications such as big data analysis or machine learning, where throughput—the amount of data processed per second—takes precedence over the speed of individual file operations.

Throughput Modes

EFS also provides two throughput modes:

- **Bursting Throughput**: Throughput on EFS scales with the size of the file system in this mode. The larger the file system, the higher the throughput it can burst to when needed. This mode suits many workloads by offering a baseline performance level with the ability to burst to higher throughputs for periods of high demand.

- **Provisioned Throughput**: In cases where your application's throughput requirements exceed the Bursting Throughput mode's capabilities, you can opt for Provisioned Throughput mode. This mode allows you to specify the file system's throughput independently of the amount of data stored, ensuring that your application can achieve the required performance.

EFS does not support snapshots for sharing data or for backup purposes. Instead, you can back up your EFS drives using AWS Backup, which you will cover in the *AWS Backup* section later in this chapter.

In summary, Amazon EFS offers a highly flexible, durable, and scalable file storage solution that meets a wide range of application needs. With its simple configuration, automatic scaling, and cost-optimized storage classes, EFS provides a robust solution for shared file storage in the cloud.

Amazon FSx

The final AWS storage service that you will learn about in this chapter is called **Amazon File Server x (FSx)**. FSx offers managed service support for third-party file systems that work well with Windows operating systems or if you need an extremely performant system that exceeds the limitations of EFS. FSx is a file store so it behaves in a similar manner to EFS. First, you can explore the two different versions of FSx that exist today: FSx for Windows File Server and FSx for Lustre.

Amazon FSx for Windows File Server

Many customers running Windows-based applications on-premises struggle to migrate to AWS as they rely on native Windows features for handling their storage. FSx for Windows File Server offers a fully managed native Microsoft Windows file system so that you can easily run and operate your Windows-based applications that require file storage on AWS. It is built on Windows Server and provides a rich set of features such as SMB protocol access, Active Directory integration, and NTFS, making it ideal for a wide range of applications that require Windows-based file storage.

FSx for Lustre

This is another type of application that needs specialized storage options, particularly for **high-performance computing (HPC)**. HPC often involves machine learning or advanced AI applications that require processing huge amounts of data quickly. These applications commonly use a storage solution called Lustre. FSx for Lustre is a fully managed Lustre-compliant storage system allowing those applications to run in AWS with the demanding performance standards they require. FSx for Lustre integrates with Amazon S3, allowing you to link your file system with an S3 bucket for automatic data import/export, which is particularly beneficial for workloads that need to process and analyze large datasets.

Both offerings are fully managed, which means AWS takes care of the underlying infrastructure, software patching, and maintenance, enabling you to focus on your applications rather than the complexities of file system deployment and management. Amazon FSx is designed to integrate with other AWS services, providing flexible access to compute resources such as Amazon EC2 instances, S3, and container services.

AWS Backup

AWS Backup is designed to offer a simple and cost-effective solution to back up your data across the AWS ecosystem, including Amazon EC2 instances, EBS volumes, RDS databases, DynamoDB tables, EFS file systems, and more. It automates backup processes, enabling businesses to meet their backup requirements without the need for custom scripts or manual processes. AWS Backup is also useful to ensure that your backup policies are being kept. If you legally require customer data to be held for five years, you can use AWS Backup to enforce that rule across all of your AWS services. The main AWS Backup features are as follows:

- **Automated backup schedules**: AWS Backup allows you to define backup policies, known as backup plans, that automate the backup process based on schedules and retention rules. This ensures that your data is backed up regularly without manual intervention.

- **Cross-service coverage**: With AWS Backup, you can protect data across multiple AWS services from a single console, streamlining the management of backup activities and recovery processes.

- **Encryption and compliance**: AWS Backup ensures that all backups are encrypted using AWS KMS keys, providing secure data protection. Additionally, it helps businesses comply with regulatory requirements by offering backup activity logging and audit capabilities.

- **Lifecycle management**: You can manage the lifecycle of your backups by setting policies that automatically transition backups to colder storage for cost savings and delete old backups that are no longer required.

- **Restoration**: AWS Backup facilitates quick and reliable data restoration from backups, minimizing downtime and data loss in case of accidental deletions, data corruption, or disasters.

To use AWS Backup, you first create a backup plan. This would include the frequency of the backups, the retention period, or any lifecycle policies that apply. You would then assign the resources to the plan. You can do this manually or by using tagging on the resources. Once done, the resources will be automatically added to the backup plan without needing to make any further changes at the resource level.

In this chapter, you have learned about the different types of storage that exist (object, file, or block) and how those storage options align with AWS services. You have also learned how to secure the data by using AWS Backup to organize your backups across a wide range of AWS services.

You can now try some hands-on labs to practice using these storage services in the real world, starting with creating a website that runs from an S3 bucket.

Hands-on Lab

You can now start with the hands-on lab section of the chapter. This will give you a practical understanding of the concepts at hand.

S3 Website

Hosting a website on Amazon S3 is a cost-effective and simple way to deliver your content without the need for a web server. Amazon S3 can serve static content directly to web browsers. In this lab, you will create some simple website files and then upload these to a new S3 bucket that has policies to allow public access:

1. Create a file in an editor with the following code (you don't need to understand this for the exam):

```
<html>
<head>
</head>
<body>
<h1>Hello World</h1>
<p>This is my first website</p>
</body>
</html>
```

2. Save it in a file called `index.html`.

3. Log in to the AWS Management Console and navigate to the S3 service.

4. Click `Create bucket`. Give your bucket a unique name. Remember that an S3 bucket name needs to be unique globally!

5. Select the AWS Region closest to you for better performance.

6. Uncheck `Block all public access` settings and acknowledge that the bucket will be publicly accessible. This is required to serve your website to visitors:

7. Click `Create bucket`.

8. Open your newly created bucket and click `Upload`:

9. Add your `index.html` file and click `Upload`.

10. Once your files are uploaded, click on your bucket name and navigate to the `Properties` tab.

11. Scroll down and click `Edit` under `Static website hosting`:

12. Choose `Use this bucket to host a website` and enter `index.html` as the `Index document` value:

13. Click `Save`. Scroll back down to the `Static website hosting` section. Take note of the endpoint URL provided; this is your website's URL hosted on S3,

14. If you try to access the endpoint at this point, you will receive an error saying `Permission Denied`. This is because while we have said that this bucket can have public access, we haven't granted that access yes.

15. Navigate to the `Permissions` tab of your bucket.

16. Scroll to the `Bucket policy` section and click `Edit`.

17. Enter a policy that grants public read access to your website files. Here's an example policy (replace the highlighted bucket name with the name of your S3 bucket). Leave the `/*` characters at the end:

```
{
  "Version": "2012-10-17",
  "Statement": [{
    "Sid": "PublicReadGetObject",
    "Effect": "Allow",
    "Principal": "*",
    "Action": "s3:GetObject",
    "Resource": "arn:aws:s3:::saa-c003-kg/*"
  }]
}
```

18. Click `Save changes`.

19. Open a web browser and navigate to your S3 endpoint URL. Your static website should now be accessible to anyone on the internet.

20. Note that in some editors, if you save the file as HTML, it will create a website based on the code; your file will show as the text you entered and will not be formatted as you would expect. This shows the website is working correctly and it's just a file formatting issue.

21. Remove the file and delete the bucket as needed.

In this lab, you created a simple website just using a text file and an S3 bucket. In the next lab, you are going to create an AWS Backup plan.

AWS Backup Plan

In this lab, you are going to create an AWS Backup plan and then apply that to any resources in your account that have a tag called `Production`. Let's start by creating a simple backup plan:

1. Log in to the AWS console and navigate to AWS Backup.

2. In the AWS Backup dashboard, click on `Backup plans` on the left sidebar and then click `Create backup plan`.

3. You have the option to create a new plan from a template or build a new one. For this tutorial, you will choose `Build a new plan`.

4. Name your backup plan `Production`.

5. Under `Backup rules`, click on `Add rule`.

6. Provide a rule name: `DailyBackup`.

7. Set `Backup frequency` to `Daily`.

8. For `Backup window`, choose `Use backup window defaults`.

9. In `Transition to cold storage`, enter `30` days and set `Expire` to `365` days.

10. Click `Create a new backup vault` and call it `ProductionVault`.

11. Click `Create plan`.

12. With the backup plan created, the next step is to assign AWS resources to be backed up. AWS Backup allows you to do this using resource tags, which is a powerful way to automate backups for resources across your account.

13. Navigate to the `Resource assignments` tab within your backup plan.

14. Click `Assign resources`.

15. Provide an `Assignment name` value.

16. Under `IAM role`, choose `AWSBackupDefaultServiceRole`, which is the default IAM role.

17. In the `Resource type` dropdown, select the AWS resource type you want to back up. Select EC2. It does not matter whether you have any EC2 instances in your account at the moment.

18. Use the `Tag-based assignment` option to specify tags. To pick up all EC2 instances tagged as `Production`, set Key as `Environment` and `Value` as `Production`.

19. Click `Assign resources` to complete the setup. If you have any EC2 instances tagged, these will now be automatically backed up daily, so be aware of any additional costs in your account.

In these labs, you learned how to use S3 to create a static website, which demonstrates the power of a simple storage system. You then created a backup policy using AWS Backup to learn how to enforce backup standards across your AWS account.

Summary

In this chapter, you delved into the array of AWS storage options, looking at a thorough examination of services including Amazon S3, EBS, EFS, FSx, and AWS Backup. Each service is designed to meet different storage needs, from highly durable object storage to block and file storage solutions optimized for a variety of use cases. You explored how S3 serves as a robust and scalable object storage platform, ideal for a wide range of data storage scenarios from web applications to backup and restore operations. EBS's block storage capabilities offer the high performance and low latency required for EC2 instances, whereas EFS provides scalable file storage perfect for use with cloud and on-premises servers. FSx brings fully managed third-party file systems to the AWS cloud, catering to specific needs such as HPC and Windows-based applications. Lastly, you covered how AWS Backup integrates these storage services, offering a unified solution for backing up and protecting your data across AWS.

You finished up with hands-on exercises where you put theory into practice by building a static website, utilizing S3's storage capabilities, and establishing an AWS Backup plan that leverages tagging to automate and streamline the backup process for various AWS resources.

Exam Readiness Drill - Chapter Review Questions

Apart from mastering key concepts, strong test-taking skills under time pressure are essential for acing your certification exam. That's why developing these abilities early in your learning journey is critical.

Exam readiness drills, using the free online practice resources provided with this book, help you progressively improve your time management and test-taking skills while reinforcing the key concepts you've learned.

HOW TO GET STARTED

- Open the link or scan the QR code at the bottom of this page
- If you have unlocked the practice resources already, log in to your registered account. If you haven't, follow the instructions in *Chapter 16* and come back to this page.
- Once you log in, click the START button to start a quiz
- We recommend attempting a quiz multiple times till you're able to answer most of the questions correctly and well within the time limit.
- You can use the following practice template to help you plan your attempts:

Working On Accuracy		
Attempt	Target	Time Limit
Attempt 1	40% or more	Till the timer runs out
Attempt 2	60% or more	Till the timer runs out
Attempt 3	75% or more	Till the timer runs out
Working On Timing		
Attempt 4	75% or more	1 minute before time limit
Attempt 5	75% or more	2 minutes before time limit
Attempt 6	75% or more	3 minutes before time limit

The above drill is just an example. Design your drills based on your own goals and make the most out of the online quizzes accompanying this book.

First time accessing the online resources? 🔒
You'll need to unlock them through a one-time process. **Head to** *Chapter 16* **for instructions**.

Open Quiz

https://packt.link/SAAC03Ch05

OR scan this QR code →

DNS and Load Balancing

Domain Name System (**DNS**) and load balancing are critical components of designing highly available and scalable cloud architectures. DNS allows domain names to be mapped to IP addresses so that computers can find each other on the internet. It functions as the address book of the internet. Amazon Route 53 is the AWS service for managing DNS and supports various routing policies and health checks to direct traffic. Load balancers distribute incoming requests across multiple servers/endpoints to prevent overloading any single resource. They ensure traffic is routed to healthy endpoints. **Elastic Load Balancing** (**ELB**) is the AWS-managed load balancing service and offers Classic, Application, Network, and Gateway load balancers to suit different traffic types and routing requirements. Choosing the right DNS routing policies and load balancer is key to building resilient, scalable systems on AWS. This overview covers core concepts of DNS, Route 53, load balancing, and ELB to provide knowledge for making optimal design decisions when architecting highly available applications on AWS.

In this chapter, you are going to look at the following main topics:

- A general overview of DNS and load balancing
- Amazon Route 53
- AWS Elastic Load Balancing
- Amazon CloudFront

We will start with an overview of DNS.

Overview of DNS

DNS allows computers or servers to find each other across the internet. Before you try to understand DNS, you first need to understand domain names.

Domain Names

Consider your mobile phone. Your mobile phone has a unique 11-digit number that allows people to contact you. If someone would like to contact you, they either type in the 11-digit number or search through their contacts list to find you by name. How often do you type in the mobile number when you try to contact someone? These days, most people just memorize their own mobile number and simply can't remember the phone numbers of their entire contact list. Instead, they rely on the name-to-number mapping in their phone's Contacts app.

Domain names are essentially the same. Every computer or server that wants to connect to the internet must have an IP address, and it is these IP addresses that we use to send information to when trying to communicate with another server. IP addresses are easy for computers to use and interpret but are far less easy for humans to remember. Therefore, domain names were created as human-readable addresses for servers.

However, while domain names may be easy for humans to read and remember, they mean very little to a server and, as such, a mapping needs to exist between the domain name and the corresponding IP address. This is where DNS comes in. It is the address book of the internet: look up a domain name and get the corresponding IP address.

Anatomy of a DNS Name

A DNS name looks like the address you can see in *Figure 6.1*.

Figure 6.1: A DNS name

On the right-hand side there is the **top-level domain** (**TLD**). In this case, the TLD is `.com`, but you might see other TLDs, such as `.org` or `.io`. The next important part of the DNS name is the domain or subdomain component, in this case, `amazon`. `amazon` is a subdomain of `.com`, and `www.` is a subdomain of `amazon`. Understanding the name is only a small part of the problem. You also need to understand how IP addresses are mapped to domain names. This is called DNS resolution.

DNS Resolution

While the address book analogy explains DNS at a high level, naturally, the process is more complicated than that. DNS mapping information is stored on DNS servers and a request to map a domain name to an IP address may need to query several DNS servers to get the answer. Now you can explore this process with an example.

You have just bought a brand-new laptop and you are visiting amazon.com for the first time. *Figure 6.2* shows how the DNS resolution works at a high level:

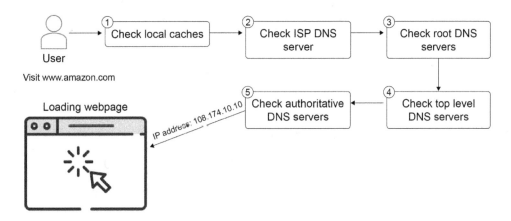

Figure 6.2: DNS resolution pathway

1. The first step in the DNS resolution pathway is to check the local caches on the laptop. If the laptop has visited amazon.com before, then the IP address may be stored in one of these caches. The main caches that exist are the browser cache, DNS cache, and host file. Cache information is temporary, so the IP information may not be present. In this example, the laptop is new and has never visited a web page, so no information is present in the cache. You can now proceed to *step 2*.

2. Next, you check the DNS server for the **internet service provider** (**ISP**). In all honesty, given how popular amazon.com is, it is likely that your ISP DNS server has the corresponding IP address, but for the sake of the argument, you can pretend that it does not.

3. The next place you check is the root DNS server. This returns the correct top-level domain server (.com).

4. When your request is routed to the top-level domain server for the .com domain, the records are checked for the correct authoritative name server.

5. Finally, when the request reaches the correct authoritative nameserver, the correct IP address is found and returned to the client.

Now that your browser has the IP address for amazon.com, it initiates a TCP connection to the IP address and you get to browse your favorite shopping items! With the basics of DNS covered, let's look at load balancing.

Amazon Route 53

Amazon Route 53 is the AWS managed service for managing DNS for your AWS cloud platform. As a global service, Route 53 has servers all over the world, making it highly available and fully managed by AWS.

> **Note**
> The 53 in Route 53 refers to the port that DNS operates on!

Route 53 provides three main functions for your DNS requirements:

- **DNS resolution**: Route internet traffic to your AWS resources
- **Domain name registration**: Purchase a domain name for use with your web applications
- **Monitor the health of your resources**: Route 53 will automatically send requests to your resources to ensure it can forward requests to them

You will learn more about each of these features in the coming sections. You will begin with DNS resolution.

Route 53 DNS Resolution

For Route 53 to route internet traffic to your resources, you need to have created a hosted zone. A hosted zone is a concept that's unique to Route 53 and is essentially a collection of records that belong to a particular domain name. There are two types of hosted zone – public hosted zones and private hosted zones:

- **Public hosted zones**: Routes traffic from the internet to your internet-facing resources
- **Private hosted zones:** Routes DNS requests that originate from within your VPC

No matter whether a hosted zone is public or private, it contains a collection of DNS records for your resources. When a hosted zone is first created, two types of records are created by default:

- **Name server (NS)**: This identifies the DNS servers for a given hosted zone. Four of these will be configured automatically, pointing to name servers that have already been provisioned for your use.
- **Start of authority (SOA)**: This identifies the authoritative DNS server and is already provisioned for your use.

Route 53 also supports the common record types that you may have come across before:

- **A record**: Maps a hostname to an IPv4 address.

- **AAAA record**: Maps a hostname to an IPv6 address.

- **Mail exchange (MX) record**: Lists the mail exchange servers for a domain (if you are hosting a mail server).

- **Text (TXT) record**: Allows human-readable text in a domain.

- **Canonical name (CNAME) record**: Maps a hostname to another hostname. For example, you might want to direct `www.example.com` and `example.com` to the same web application. If `example.com` is already configured with an A record, you can create a CNAME record pointing `www.example.com` at `example.com`.

There is one record type that is unique to Route 53. This is the `Alias` record.

Alias record maps a custom hostname to an AWS resource that ordinarily has its own internal AWS name (i.e., CloudFront distributions or load balancers).

For all records, you specify a value called **time to live (TTL)**. TTL is essentially how long that record can remain cached and reused before DNS has to query for the latest information again.

Health Checks

Route 53 can perform health checks for most routing policies to ensure that they route traffic to healthy resources. Health checks can be configured to check an endpoint that can be defined as either an IP address or a domain using TCP, HTTP, or HTTPS. When a health check has been configured, Route 53 will send a request every 30 seconds and will determine whether the resource is healthy or unhealthy based on the response. It can also assess the outcome of other health checks or CloudWatch alarms. When monitoring CloudWatch alarms, Route 53 will consider a resource healthy if the alarm is in the OK state. If the alarm is in the ALARM state, it will be considered unhealthy. You can customize how Route 53 will handle an alarm in the INSUFFICIENT state with the healthy, unhealthy, or last known status options.

Finally, by default, Route 53 uses a fleet of recommended health checkers across the world but you can customize this list if you choose to by removing regions that you don't think are relevant to your platform.

Routing Policies

When creating records in Route 53, you have to define which routing policy you would like this record to use, in addition to the record type. The following routing policies are supported in Route 53:

- Simple routing
- Failover routing
- Multivalue answer routing
- Weighted routing
- Latency-based routing
- Geolocation routing
- Geoproximity routing
- IP-based routing

For each routing policy, you will learn what the criteria are for routing, as well as whether the routing policies support health checks and private hosted zones. It's unlikely that you'll need to understand the distinction for the SAA C03 exam, but it's worth trying to remember them if you can.

Simple Routing

- **Health checks supported**: No
- **Private hosted zones supported**: Yes

This policy is what it says on the tin. It simply routes traffic to the IP address associated with your domain with no weighting or latency considerations. If the record has multiple IP addresses, they are returned to the client in a random order and the client chooses one of the values and resubmits the request.

Failover Routing

- **Health checks supported**: Yes
- **Private hosted zones supported**: Yes

Failover routing will route a request to a healthy resource and if that resource becomes unhealthy, will route the request to an alternative resource. This is useful when architecting for redundancy.

Geolocation Routing

- **Health checks supported**: Yes
- **Private hosted zones supported**: Yes

Geolocation routing is useful for global web applications, or any platform that is spread across the world. It allows you to determine where requests are routed based on where they originated. For example, you may want all requests from Australia and New Zealand to be routed to a server or load balancer in the Sydney region to minimize latency for your users. Locations can be defined at the continent or country level.

Weighted Routing

- **Health checks supported**: Yes
- **Private hosted zones supported**: Yes

This policy allows you to associate multiple resources to a record and then determine how much traffic should be routed to each resource. This is particularly useful when performing A/B testing of new application features. You can begin by sending a small amount of traffic to the resource with the new feature, then, as your confidence grows in its stability, you can change the weighting until all traffic is directed to the resource with the new feature.

Latency-Based Routing

- **Health checks supported**: Yes
- **Private hosted zones supported**: Yes

This is similar to geolocation routing but, instead of defining geographical locations, latency-based routing determines the best resource to route a request to by choosing the Region with the lowest latency.

Multivalue Routing

- **Health checks supported**: Yes
- **Private hosted zones supported**: Yes

If you need a simple routing policy that performs health checks, then multivalue routing may be the policy you need. It will return multiple values that can be health-checked. Health checks need to be configured or Route 53 will assume the resource is healthy.

IP-Based Routing

- **Health checks supported**: Yes
- **Private hosted zones supported**: No

IP-based routing gives you control over where requests should be routed when they originate from a particular CIDR range. For example, an on-demand streaming service may want to ensure that all requests from a particular ISP are routed to a particular load balancer endpoint because it will provide a better experience for the end users. While this is similar to geolocation and latency-based routing, in those policies, AWS determines the best option for the end users. In IP-based routing, you determine the best option for the end users.

Geoproximity Routing

- **Health checks supported**: No
- **Private hosted zones supported**: Yes

While geolocation routing selects the best location based on where the user is located, geoproximity routing selects the best location based on where your resource is located. This is defined using the Route 53 Traffic Flow feature and requires you to create traffic policies that define how requests will be routed based on where your resources are located. By setting a bias value, you are able to control the size of the geographical region.

That covers what you need to know about DNS and Amazon Route 53 for the SAA-CO3 exam. Next, you will look at load balancing and ELB.

Overview of Load Balancing

In the DNS overview, you learned what happens when one client tries to connect to a website. amazon. com is a very popular website, however, and at any one time, it might have to handle thousands, if not hundreds of thousands, of requests. A single server cannot handle that many requests, and so large, busy websites are often served on multiple servers. To accomplish this, you need a way to make sure the requests are spread evenly across the servers that serve the website. This is where load balancing comes in.

A load balancer sits in front of your servers and routes requests across the servers that it manages according to its configuration. It ensures that requests are only routed to healthy servers and that those healthy servers are not overloaded. As such, load balancers are key items of infrastructure to ensure high availability, redundancy, and flexibility.

High Availability and Redundancy

A lot of the design decisions you make in the cloud come down to how resilient and highly available you want your infrastructure to be. First, you must understand what each of these terms means.

High Availability

A highly available architecture is one that remains available most of the time (i.e., has the maximum uptime). When looking at AWS services, some will have claims attached to them regarding their availability. For example, Amazon S3 has an availability SLA of 99.9%. This means that in a billing cycle, they commit to the S3 service being available to use 99.9% of the time, and if they fail to meet this SLA, you get service credits in return. You achieve high availability by removing single points of failure.

Redundancy

Redundancy is how you achieve high availability. In its basic form, redundancy means provisioning extra copies of your infrastructure so that if the first set fails, you can switch to using the second set with minimal impact on your users. In the case of a web application, you may provision two servers so that if the first fails, you can switch DNS to the second. Designing for redundancy should take into account not only how available you want your application to be but also how much money you want to spend. We'll talk more about designing resilient architectures in *Chapter 13, Design Resilient Architectures*.

ELB

ELB is the load-balancing service in AWS. It can load balance not just EC2 instances but also containers and Lambda functions. Consider a simple web application hosted on a single instance, as shown in *Figure 6.3*:

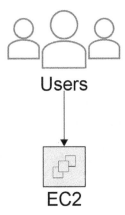

Figure 6.3: Simple web application with one instance

In the scenario in *Figure 6.3*, if there was a spike in traffic larger than the instance could handle, it is likely the website would crash because there are not enough servers to handle the traffic. So, you need extra servers and the ability to manage the load across these servers. This is where ELB becomes useful.

In *Figure 6.4*, you can see that the load balancer becomes the entry point for user requests and manages the distribution of user requests across the several instances you have serving your web application:

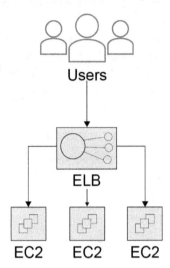

Figure 6.4: ELB distributing the load across several instances

ELB is, by default, an elastic service managed by AWS. This means that it has built-in redundancy and high availability that is abstracted away from you so that you do not need to worry about it. Under the hood, ELB is actually several instances that AWS manages, and the number of these instances will scale up and down according to the amount of traffic your ELB has to handle. It is not the single point of failure that it seems to be at first.

Load balancers in AWS work using two components that you may not be familiar with: target groups and listeners.

Target Groups

To use an elastic load balancer, you must configure a **target group**. A target group is a group of targets (i.e., instances or Lambda functions) that you would like the load balancer to send traffic to. The target group also defines what health checks should be performed. To check that an instance is healthy, by default, the ELB will send a request to each target in the target group every 30 seconds. If the target is healthy, it will continue to send user requests to that target. If the target is unhealthy, that is, the instance or Lambda function cannot be reached, the ELB will mark the target as unhealthy, and user requests will be sent to one of the remaining healthy targets in the target group.

Listeners

In order for the ELB to direct user requests correctly, you also need to configure a listener. A listener will route your user's requests according to the rules it has configured. A listener may have multiple rules, and each rule will have a priority. The lower the number, the higher the priority. For your simple web application, you would want to forward all HTTP requests that come in on port 80 to your web application target group. So, you would create a listener with a default rule that requests on port 80 are forwarded to the web application target group. If you have multiple target groups, you can have different rules to forward traffic to each one.

Load Balancer Types

There are four types of load balancer: Classic, Application, Network, and Gateway. Regardless of the type, listeners and target groups are required. You will now read about each one in more detail.

Classic (Legacy)

This load balancer is the previous generation of load balancer for use with the previous generation of EC2, EC2 Classic. It is able to operate at both layer 7 and layer 4 of the **Open Systems Interconnection (OSI)** model, thus it is able to handle HTTP, HTTPS, and TCP requests. Unless you are working with EC2 Classic, you should avoid using a Classic load balancer.

Application

The **Application Load Balancer (ALB)** operates at layer 7 of the OSI model and handles HTTP and HTTPS traffic as well as WebSocket traffic. It can handle path-based routing, which means it can direct traffic to particular servers based on the URL passed in the request (*Figure 6.5*).

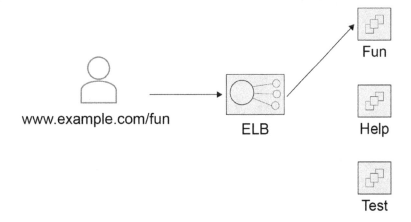

Figure 6.5: Path-based routing

The ALB also supports TLS termination (with the appropriate certificates), sticky sessions (where a request from a user will be directed to the same target it had previously been directed to), and Lambda functions as targets.

Sticky sessions are a useful feature of the ALB that ensures a user who has visited a target previously always has their requests sent to the same server on subsequent visits. This is useful for shopping applications where you might have a basket of items that you'd like to go away and think about, and then come back to later. This works using a cookie that is stored in the user's browser and passed to the application on a return visit.

TLS termination means that the load balancer handles the process of encrypting and decrypting SSL and TLS connections, removing the need for your application to handle the logic to do so.

Network

The **Network Load Balancer (NLB)** operates at layer 4 of the OSI model at the connection level. NLB supports **Transmission Control Protocol (TCP)**, **User Datagram Protocol (UDP)**, and **Transport Layer Security (TLS)** traffic but does not have the same rich routing options that the ALB offers, such as path-based routing. This is the perfect load balancer when you want to handle extremely high loads while keeping latency low.

Gateway

The **Gateway Load Balancer (GWLB)** allows users to forward traffic to a fleet of third-party virtual appliances for traffic inspection before forwarding traffic to your application. The load balancer is provisioned in the VPC that contains the inspection appliances, and traffic from the internet is routed to this load balancer via a GWLB endpoint in the application VPC. The inspection appliances will assess the traffic and either drop the traffic or forward it to the application targets, as shown in *Figure 6.6*:

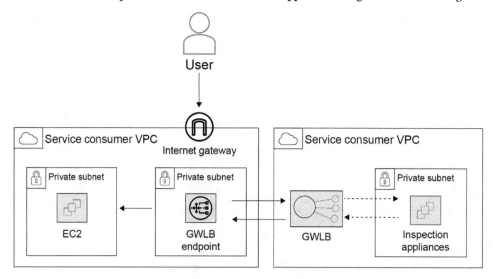

Figure 6.6: Architecture of a GWLB

For a quick comparison of load balancers, see *Table 6.1*:

Feature	Classic	Application	Network	Gateway
Load balancer type	Layers 4 and 7	Layer 7	Layer 4	Layers 3 and 4
Target type	-	IP, instance, Lambda	IP, instance, ALB	IP, instance
Protocol listeners	TCP, SSL/TLS, HTTP, HTTPS	HTTP, HTTPS, gRPC	TCP, UDP, TLS	IP
Static IP address	No	No	Yes	No
Health checks	TCP, SSL/TLS, HTTP, HTTPS	HTTP, HTTPS, gRPC	TCP, HTTP, HTTPS	TCP, HTTP, HTTPS

Table 6.1: Comparison of load balancers

Load balancing is an essential component of highly available and resilient architectures. When assessing which load balancer is required, make sure you take into account the requirements needed of the load balancer.

While load balancing helps distribute traffic across multiple servers, content delivery networks such as Amazon CloudFront improve performance even further by caching content at edge locations closer to users. Let's explore Amazon CloudFront.

Overview of Amazon CloudFront

Amazon CloudFront is a globally distributed **content delivery network** (**CDN**) provided by AWS. CDNs help to speed up the distribution of your content by storing it closer to your users. Think of your favorite pizza takeaway chain. When you order a pizza, instead of the order going all the way back to the main restaurant location across town to make it, the order is fulfilled by the takeaway nearest to you.

The takeaways around the city are like edge locations in a CDN. They keep popular pizzas ready-made and available for quick delivery when orders come in. The main takeaway is like the origin server where the original food is made. When you order pizza online, the order goes to the nearest takeaway instead of the main shop. This allows much faster delivery times since the pizza does not have to be made from scratch and driven across town. Similarly, a CDN has edge locations around the world that cache popular content. When a user requests that content, it is served from the nearest edge location, providing low latency and fast delivery instead of being served from the distant origin server. In both cases, distributing resources closer to the user provides faster and more efficient delivery!

CloudFront can cache content from origins such as Amazon S3 buckets, EC2 instances, ELB, or Route 53. It uses distributions to manage how content is delivered, with web distributions for HTTP/HTTPS traffic and RTMP distributions for media streaming. With over 200 edge locations worldwide and regional edge caches in each AWS region, CloudFront is a key service for delivering high-performance web applications with low latency. It integrates seamlessly with other AWS services, such as S3, EC2, and Lambda@Edge, to optimize content delivery.

Caching Rules

Configuring caching rules and policies in Amazon CloudFront is important for optimizing the performance and cost of your content delivery. At its core, CloudFront allows you to control how long content gets cached at the edge locations before expiring and having to fetch new copies from your origin web servers.

The default cache behavior defines the default caching rules that apply across all files in your distribution unless overridden. Here, you specify settings such as minimum, maximum, and default cache expiry times for your files from one second to one full year. Longer expiry periods, like one week, allow more reuse for static assets, whereas dynamic web pages may need a shorter expiry period of one day. You also configure whether CloudFront will consider headers, cookies, and query strings when caching content. Factoring these in leads to more cache misses. Additional custom cache behaviors can be created to apply different caching rules to specific paths and file types. For example, you may want one-week caching for JPEG images but one-day caching for API results JSON.

Invalidations provide a way to proactively expire content when you make updates instead of having to wait out the cache period. Monitoring cache hit ratios (i.e., how often your cache content is served rather than the stored content) in the CloudFront dashboard helps fine-tune behaviors for optimal delivery cost and performance. Getting the caching strategies right is crucial for taking full advantage of CloudFront's global edge locations and minimizing requests to the origin infrastructure. Testing with different policies can determine the right harmonization between keeping content up to date and maximizing efficiency through long-lived caching close to your end users for lightning-fast response times.

While CloudFront is primarily used for content delivery, it also has some very useful security features that you should be aware of for the exam.

Security

Amazon CloudFront provides a set of security capabilities to help protect sensitive content delivered through its content delivery network. By integrating natively with various AWS services, CloudFront can enable encrypted, authenticated, and monitored content flows from origin to viewer.

CloudFront distributions support serving content exclusively over HTTPS by integrating with AWS Certificate Manager to procure SSL/TLS certificates automatically. This ensures encrypted in-transit flows between CloudFront edge caches and end users, preventing eavesdropping on communication.

Signed URL and signed cookie capabilities add a layer of authentication requiring viewers to present valid tokens issued by the content owner, preventing unauthorized hotlinking even for public objects. Geo-restriction features can whitelist or blacklist access from certain countries at the CloudFront edge, enabling the implementation of region-specific business rules.

For origin protection, CloudFront follows the principle of least privilege with S3 bucket owners configuring origin access control to only permit requests from an authorized CloudFront service account rather than wide open public access. Furthermore, CloudFront integrates with the **Web Application Firewall (WAF)**, which allows crafting custom threat detection rules to filter incoming requests for signs of SQL injection, cross-site scripting, or other malicious patterns before reaching the origin infrastructure.

You can now examine two common patterns for using CloudFront: with an ALB origin and an Amazon S3 origin.

Caching Content from an ALB

In the scenario in *Figure 6.7*, an ALB distributes traffic to Amazon EC2 instances running a web application. To integrate CloudFront, you first create a CloudFront web distribution and specify the load balancer as the origin. This means that the Route 53 DNS record pointing to your domain to the load balancer will need to be updated. Change the `Alias` record to route traffic to the CloudFront distribution domain name instead. This ensures all requests go through CloudFront first before reaching the origin (*Figure 6.8*).

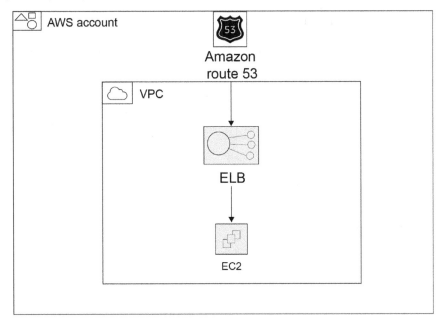

Figure 6.7: Simple architecture depicting a Route53 record pointing
to a load balancer fronting an EC2 instance

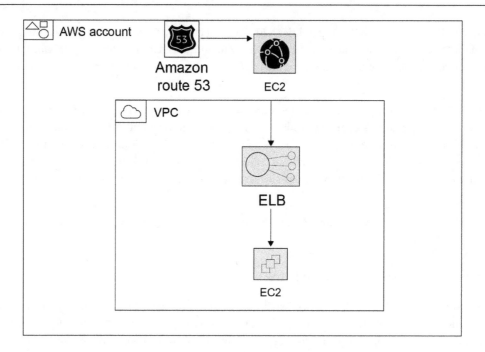

Figure 6.8: Simple architecture showing how Route53 now points
to CloudFront instead of the load balancer

To restrict direct access to the load balancer origin, two steps are required:

1. Configure CloudFront to add a custom HTTP header to all requests forwarded to the origin.

2. Update the load balancer listener rules to only forward requests containing the custom header and return 403 errors for requests without it.

This limits access to requests coming via CloudFront with the header. Use HTTPS between CloudFront and the load balancer to encrypt the custom header in transit. Rotate the custom header periodically for improved security.

Caching Content from an Amazon S3 Origin

Amazon S3 can be used to host static websites but lacks native HTTPS support, and sites are limited to the S3 bucket's regional location. CloudFront solves these problems. Create a CloudFront web distribution with the S3 bucket specified as the origin. Add an alternate domain name and SSL certificate to support HTTPS delivery. To restrict direct access to the S3 bucket, utilize CloudFront origin access identity and S3 bucket policies. First, create an origin access identity in CloudFront and associate it with the distribution. Then update the S3 bucket policy to only allow access to the files if requested through the identity. This removes public access to the S3 bucket and forces requests to go through CloudFront. With these patterns, CloudFront can cache content at the edge for lower latency, while also restricting direct origin access for increased security. You will read more about this use case in this chapter's lab.

Summary

In summary, DNS and load balancing are critical components for designing highly available and scalable cloud architectures. AWS provides robust services such as Route 53 and ELB to help manage DNS and distribute traffic across resources. Choosing the right routing policies and load balancer type according to the application requirements is key to building resilient and performant systems on AWS.

Exam Readiness Drill - Chapter Review Questions

Apart from mastering key concepts, strong test-taking skills under time pressure are essential for acing your certification exam. That's why developing these abilities early in your learning journey is critical.

Exam readiness drills, using the free online practice resources provided with this book, help you progressively improve your time management and test-taking skills while reinforcing the key concepts you've learned.

HOW TO GET STARTED

- Open the link or scan the QR code at the bottom of this page

- If you have unlocked the practice resources already, log in to your registered account. If you haven't, follow the instructions in *Chapter 16* and come back to this page.

- Once you log in, click the START button to start a quiz

- We recommend attempting a quiz multiple times till you're able to answer most of the questions correctly and well within the time limit.

- You can use the following practice template to help you plan your attempts:

Working On Accuracy		
Attempt	Target	Time Limit
Attempt 1	40% or more	Till the timer runs out
Attempt 2	60% or more	Till the timer runs out
Attempt 3	75% or more	Till the timer runs out
Working On Timing		
Attempt 4	75% or more	1 minute before time limit
Attempt 5	75% or more	2 minutes before time limit
Attempt 6	75% or more	3 minutes before time limit

The above drill is just an example. Design your drills based on your own goals and make the most out of the online quizzes accompanying this book.

First time accessing the online resources? 🔒

You'll need to unlock them through a one-time process. **Head to** *Chapter 16* **for instructions**.

Open Quiz	
`https://packt.link/SAAC03Ch06` OR scan this QR code →	

7
Data and Analytics

Over the last few decades, companies have been gathering huge amounts of data, and it has become increasingly challenging to get useful information from them. They need powerful tools to manage and analyze it effectively. AWS offers a wide range of solutions to help with these tasks. From AWS Glue for data integration and transformation, via Amazon Kinesis for real-time data streaming, to Amazon Aurora for storing transactional data, AWS offers tools or solutions to meet each use case. This chapter will explore the various AWS data and analytics services, teaching you how to evaluate the choices available.

Data and analytics on AWS cover a very wide range of services. At the time of writing, AWS offers 15 different databases and over 20 different analytics and data tools and pipelines. For the *SAA-C03 exam*, you will need to know the main differences between these tools and when to use each one, based on use cases. For some of the most commonly used services, you will also need to know how to carry out basic administrative and troubleshooting tasks.

In this chapter, you will explore the following main topics:

- Databases on AWS
- Analytics on AWS
- Machine learning and artificial intelligence tools
- Data ingestion and streaming

In the first section, you will learn about the different AWS databases available and how to choose the right one for any workload, as well as be able to differentiate their key functions and benefits.

Databases on AWS

As mentioned in the introduction, AWS currently offers 15 different databases for you to choose from. This is a huge number, and therefore, this topic is seen as one of the hardest by many solutions architects. For the *SAA-C03 exam*, you will need to know the basic use cases and benefits of each database type, and for the most used databases, you will also need to know how to perform basic admin and troubleshooting tasks. We will start by looking at relational databases.

Relational Databases

First, let's explain what relational databases are and why they exist. Back in the 1970s, when databases first became popular for data storage and retrieval, storage costs were extremely expensive. Any data that was duplicated or redundant was very costly. To prevent duplication, tables became a store for one type of object, and they were linked to other tables if you needed more details. For example, a table holding `Orders` would only hold `orderID`, `customerID`, and `productID`. To retrieve all the information about an order, you would need to search the `Customers` table for `customerID`, and the `Products` table for `productID`, returning the extra information held there. *Figure 7.1* demonstrates this relationship between data.

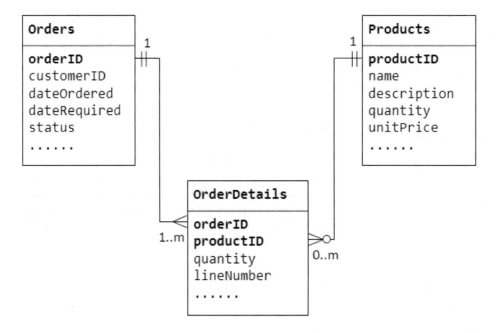

Figure 7.1: A relational database design

To date, relational databases are still the most popular type of database in the world, with an estimated 50 ZB (that is a zettabyte or 1 million petabytes!). While they are highly popular, they have many challenges, particularly when running on-premises. Databases need storage space and often grow, with new transactions and new data being loaded into them. They often have spiky usage patterns, whereby traffic during the day might be very high, but overnight, they are quiet; it can be very costly to have a high-performance system left idle overnight. They need regular patching, backups, and high-availability testing, all of which take time and skill. Let's take a look now at some AWS solutions designed to help manage these areas.

Amazon Relational Database Service (RDS)

As the name suggests, this is an AWS service designed to help manage relational databases. There is a choice of six different database engines or types to choose from, depending on the capabilities you need:

- Oracle
- SQL Server
- MySQL
- MariaDB
- PostgreSQL
- DB2

RDS was designed to help customers move their existing databases to AWS and allow them to offload the day-to-day management of those databases onto AWS. Let's take a deeper look at the specific tools offered by RDS.

Backups

RDS can be configured to take backups of your database on a schedule that meets your needs. The backups are stored and secured on S3 (S3 is covered in *Chapter 5, Storage*). The backups that are taken include transactional data, so you can recover a database to a specific point in time. By default, backups are enabled for seven days, unless you disable them, and the maximum retention period is 35 days.

You get backups up to the size of your database storage included in the price of RDS. This means that if you have allocated 100 GB of database storage, you get another 100 GB of backup storage too. Databases rarely use all their allocated storage, due to white space between data that can be ignored during backup, so the backup allocation can hold a full database as well as some of the transaction logs before you accrue any charges.

You can also make a manual backup at any time. These are called snapshots. The snapshots also count toward your free backup allocation, so if you had a database with 200 GB storage allocated and you create a 100 GB snapshot, you will have 100 GB left for automated backups before you are charged.

Snapshots can be shared with other accounts. This can be a useful method for creating a new testing database in a different account with genuine production data, or if you need to share data with a third party.

Patching and upgrading

Database **patching** (which is the process of updating software to fix bugs, improve security, or add new features) is hugely important, as older releases often have security or performance bugs that can be exploited by hackers. However, patching is often complex and results in downtime even for small changes. AWS allows you to automate patching or minor upgrades (for example, going from MySQL 5.7.38 to 5.7.44) without you having to do anything. You configure a maintenance window, typically during low-traffic periods, and AWS then applies the patch or upgrade during this window. AWS will run automated pre- and post-checks to ensure that everything has worked correctly. If you run a **Multi-Availability Zone** (**Multi-AZ**) deployment (which is covered later in this section), then AWS avoids downtime by patching the standby database first, switching over to the standby, and then applying the patches to the old primary. You can also invoke patching manually at a time to suit you. AWS does not enforce patching or upgrades unless the version you run on is fully deprecated, but you may encounter additional charges, called Extended Support, if you do not upgrade your version when it comes to the end of its standard supported life. AWS publishes these dates well ahead of time, allowing you to plan as needed. AWS will also never upgrade your database to a newer major version (for example, going from MySQL 5.7 to MySQL 8.0) automatically. These upgrades always need to be handled manually, either by using an in-place, one-click upgrade or by using other manual methods, such as Blue/Green Deployments (discussed next) or AWS Database Migration Service, which is discussed in *Chapter 8, Migrations and Data Transfer*.

A similar process occurs if the server the database runs on needs to be patched. As RDS is a fully managed service, you have less control over the server patch levels, as they are owned and controlled by AWS. You can manually initiate these patches for a time that suits you or let them complete during a maintenance window. If you delay the upgrades for too long and you go outside of the published upgrade schedule, AWS may enforce the upgrades upon you even if this is outside of your maintenance window. This may cause an unexpected outage to your database, so you should always plan for and complete required patches during the schedule.

Finally, you can look at **disaster recovery** (**DR**) and **high availability** (**HA**), which are other complex areas for database administrators.

Managing DR or HA

Many production databases need to handle failure gracefully and keep running with minimal downtime, even if they suffer an outage. These policies and procedures are known as DR and HA.

DR refers to being able to quickly get your systems back up and running should a major disaster strike. When running on-premises, this would include a data center being taken offline, a disk failure on your database, or a major networking failing. DR policies often include backups being stored in a different location to a database, and recovery operations are used to restore the database elsewhere. In AWS, DR is managed similarly by storing backups in a different Region to protect from a complete region failure (which has only happened twice in AWS history).

A manual snapshot can be sent to a different Region and saved there for recovery purposes, or you can use the **AWS Backup** service to send point-in-time backups to a different Region. The AWS Backup service supports more automation, making backups and restores easier. Many companies use AWS Backup instead of manual snapshots to reduce operational overheads and complexity.

HA is when you operate your database in a manner that allows it to continue working even when a part of it fails. In general, this is done via replication, which, when running on-premises, must be configured, monitored, and managed to ensure that it works correctly. You also must manage failovers when there is an outage to the primary server. When running on RDS, AWS offers you the option to run in Multi-AZ, which automatically replicates your database to a different AZ and automates switchovers and failovers to keep your database running, even if an entire AZ is unavailable. Multi-AZ deployment offers protection for an AZ outage. It also reduces downtime during any maintenance window. Multi-AZ deployments also offer an enhanced **service level agreement** (**SLA**) compared to a single-AZ deployment, which may be needed for your company's compliance rules (Multi-AZ having 99.95% uptime versus single-AZ having 99.5%).

Many companies use a combination of both HA and DR practices for their most critical databases.

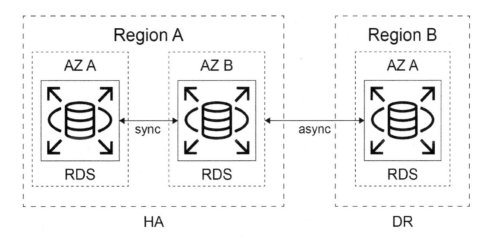

Figure 7.2: HA versus DR

The preceding diagram illustrates the difference between HA and DR, with HA located in the same region and DR cross-region. We will now discuss scaling an RDS instance to handle growth.

Scaling

Another area that can be a problem for database administrators is handling the scaling of both the resources for their database and the storage it has. On-premises, you would typically be running on a server with a fixed amount of CPU and memory. You might be running on a virtualized machine as part of a shared server, which may allow some flexibility in terms of adding additional CPU, but ultimately, you are still bound by the resources on the server itself. Adding additional CPU or memory would involve a procurement process to buy a new server or a full migration to a new server if you had one available. This would take a lot of time and cost and would incur significant downtime. Therefore, many on-premises databases are over-resourced and use a small percentage of the total resources or storage available, so they have room to grow without needing to buy a new server. As well as being wasteful in terms of the server, another impact of over-resourcing is many databases (such as SQL Server and Oracle) that have licensing terms to cover the number of CPUs you use. Over-resourcing in this way may cost more in license fees than is required.

Typically, storage on-premises can be extended, as most systems would use a **storage area network** (**SAN**) to share all the storage between systems. However, just like with the CPU on a shared server, the storage here would eventually be exhausted too.

When using RDS, you can choose from a wide choice of different servers to meet your needs. Some have a very high amount of memory while others are optimized for high processing power, offering more CPU cores to handle demanding workloads. The main benefit is that you can change between different instance sizes or types easily, and with minimal downtime when using a Multi-AZ deployment. This allows you to resource your database correctly without needing to worry about running out of CPU or memory capacity tomorrow, as you can simply upgrade. In addition, you can add extra capacity to your database by using read replicas, which are read-only copies of your database. Read replicas allow you to send read-only (select statements) queries away from the main instance, lowering the pressure and allowing it to focus on applying writes (`update`, `insert`, and `delete` statements). Read replicas are particularly useful when you make reports that run with complex queries, which can cause slowdowns on the database, and these queries can be offloaded to a different database, allowing your other traffic to operate unaffected.

Figure 7.3 shows how read replicas are provisioned and how they can run in a different AZ to the writer instance:

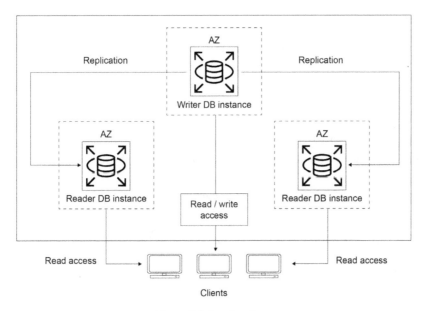

Figure 7.3: Read replicas

When it comes to storage, RDS allows you to increase allocated storage without any downtime. You can even set automatic storage increases to ensure that you never run out of space. However, you cannot reduce the allocated storage without migrating to a new instance, so make sure you only allocate the minimum storage you need. On RDS, the storage allocated also controls the amount of **input/output operations per second (IOPS)**. IOPS is the number of operations that your database can carry out against its storage disks – the higher the number, the greater the number of reads and writes that can be completed simultaneously. If you need higher IOPS than you are allocated, you will start to see disk queues rising, and your database performance will drop. There are three types of storage you can choose for RDS:

- **General Purpose 2 (gp2)**: Storage suitable for most use cases. You get 3 IOPS per GB of storage with a minimum of 100, up to a maximum that depends on the database engine.

- **General Purpose 3 (gp3)**: A newer version of gp2 that is now recommended for most databases. You now get 3,000 IOPS as a minimum, and this will increase with storage allocations, up to 12,000. You can additionally buy extra IOPS if needed.

- **Provisioned I/O (io1/2)**: The fastest and most reliable storage available. You control the IOPS you want. This is much more expensive than gp2 or gp3, so it is typically used for only the most critical and high-performance databases.

You can change between the different storage types typically without any downtime. In some cases, moving from gp2 to I/O storage can result in disks being locked for a few seconds when the process begins, but the database will remain open to connections.

Authentication

Creating and managing users on a database is both time-consuming and a security risk. It's all too common to have users using simple guess passwords or having far too many privileges for the role they need. RDS does not take away all the work of database administrators, but it offers tools to help remove the big problem of passwords being stored in text files.

Using AWS **Identity Administration and Management (IAM)** allows you to log into your database without needing to provide passwords. You create a role in IAM with the **connect permission** and assign that role to the users you want to grant access to. The role needs to map to a user created in the database itself, which still needs to be managed manually. IAM will not grant any permissions beyond the rights to connect to a database. If you want that user to be able to query anything or access system tables and views, you will need to grant those permissions at the database level. IAM authentication only works for MySQL, MariaDB, and PostgreSQL, so if you use SQL Server, DB2, or Oracle, you'll need a different option.

The alternative solution is to use Secrets Manager. Secrets Manager is simply a store of encrypted sensitive information that can be retrieved manually or programmatically. For RDS, you can store your password details for your applications, and then you change the application to ask the Secrets Manager for the password each time it connects, rather than storing the password in a config or text file on the application server, which represents a significant security risk. Used this way, Secrets Manager supports any database engine on RDS. If you use MySQL or PostgreSQL, you can also use Secrets Manager to rotate the security credentials within your RDS database on a schedule. This can help meet your compliance requirements for password rotation without having to do it manually.

Performance and Monitoring

AWS provides a range of tools to help monitor your RDS database, both at the database and server level. You can even enable query and wait level monitoring to allow your developers and database administrators to see poor performance in real time, as well as historical data, to quickly find problems.

CloudWatch provides detailed monitoring for Amazon RDS, offering metrics such as CPU utilization, database connections, read and write IOPS, disk space usage, and latency. These metrics help you understand the performance and operational health of your RDS instances. You can set up CloudWatch alarms to notify you when metrics cross predefined thresholds, allowing for proactive management and rapid response to potential issues. Additionally, CloudWatch logs can be used to store, access, and search your RDS logs, providing deeper insights into database operations and errors. You are charged for any data that is sent to CloudWatch, so make sure you housekeep it regularly and only keep what you need.

Performance Insights is a powerful tool integrated with Amazon RDS and CloudWatch that helps you analyze and optimize database performance. It provides a dashboard that visualizes database load and provides detailed information about SQL queries, wait events, and database load times. Performance Insights simplifies identifying and troubleshooting performance bottlenecks by offering granular, time-series data on database performance. By utilizing Performance Insights, database administrators can quickly identify inefficient queries, understand workload trends, and make informed decisions to enhance database performance. It also allows you to give access to database metrics without needing to grant permission to system tables, which can be a security risk. Performance Insights is included for free with a seven-day retention policy, but you need to pay if you want to keep the data for longer. *Figure 7.4* shows an example of the Performance Insights dashboard:

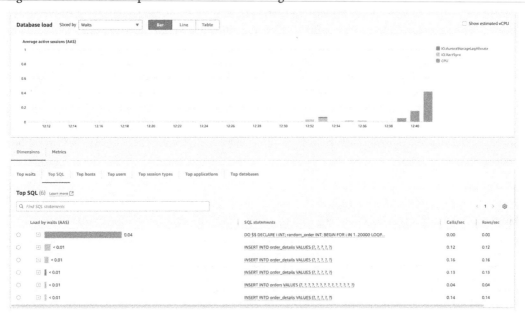

Figure 7.4: Performance Insights

Enhanced Monitoring for Amazon RDS provides a deeper level of visibility into the operating system metrics of your RDS instances. While standard CloudWatch metrics offer a high-level view, Enhanced Monitoring gives you real-time insights into over 50 CPU, memory, filesystem, and disk I/O metrics. This granular data is captured at a one-second resolution, providing a near real-time look at an instance's operating system. Enhanced Monitoring is particularly useful for diagnosing performance issues that standard metrics might not reveal, such as specific resource contention or system-level bottlenecks. The data collected through Enhanced Monitoring is accessible via the CloudWatch console, CLI, or API, enabling seamless integration into your monitoring and alerting workflows.

Parameters and Options

On-premises, a **database administrator (DBA)** might need to change certain database or operating systems parameters to improve the stability or performance of their database. However, RDS restricts direct access to the underlying hardware and operating system of database instances. **Parameter groups** are used instead to provide a way to customize database settings within the confines of AWS's managed environment.

Parameter groups allow you to manage the configuration settings of your RDS database instances. They serve as a container for engine configuration values that you can apply to one or more instances. Parameter groups can be applied to multiple databases simultaneously, allowing you to keep functionality consistent across databases with similar requirements; however, it is often considered best practice to create individual parameter groups for each system, allowing you to make modifications without impacting all other databases.

Parameter groups contain various settings specific to the database engine you use. These settings include configurations for memory allocation, cache sizes, connection limits, and query optimization. By modifying the parameters within a group, you can fine-tune the performance and behavior of your database instances according to your application's needs. For example, you might adjust the memory settings to improve query performance or change the connection limits to accommodate more concurrent users.

Option groups let you extend the functionality of your RDS instances by adding features and integrations not available by default. Like parameter groups, option groups are a way to manage settings and configurations in a controlled manner, given that RDS limits direct access to the server environment.

Option groups allow you to enable and configure additional features such as connecting to S3 or enhanced audit controls. When you create an option group, you can specify the options you need and configure their settings. Once an option group is associated with an RDS instance, the specified options are enabled, and their configurations are applied.

In summary, RDS acts as a management wrapper or layer around a database engine that works very similarly to an on-premises deployment. However, AWS also offers a database that it has built and designed to leverage the benefits of scale that the cloud offers. It is called Amazon Aurora.

Amazon Aurora

Aurora is a wire-compatible database engine that supports MySQL or PostgreSQL code. This means that, unlike RDS, Aurora is not simply a wrapper around a database; it is a different database that works with MySQL or PostgreSQL statements. This difference allows AWS to offer some groundbreaking features in Aurora, designed to support the largest and most demanding database workloads you may have.

The first thing to understand about Aurora is how different its architecture is compared to RDS. RDS follows a traditional database architecture. You have the database disks that store the data, a program installed on a server that accesses the disks and responds to queries, and a cache that holds frequently accessed data in memory on the database server. Conversely, Aurora decouples the storage layer from the database layer (an instance), allowing both to scale and operate independently of each other. This also allows some clever features, such as fast cloning, which you will learn about in this section. Aurora stores your data in six different locations by default across three different AZs, giving you true HA out of the box.

We will start by looking at backups on Aurora and how they differ from RDS.

Backups

Backups on Aurora are very similar to RDS, in that snapshots and continual backups are taken to allow recovery to a point in time; however, unlike in RDS, these backups cannot be switched off, and they are an integral part of the Aurora system. You can use AWS Backup to manage snapshots on Aurora and control restores.

Aurora additionally offers Backtrack for MySQL. Backtrack allows you to return a database to the state it was in at a certain time without restoring a backup. This makes it much faster to recover from a logical failure, such as someone accidentally deleting data. You can roll back and forwards with Backtrack to find the best restore point. For example, you can Backtrack by two hours and then slowly roll forward to find the exact timestamp where the mistake happened and restore just before. This minimizes any other data loss. Backtrack is almost instant, requiring only a short pause of the database to be implemented.

Patching and upgrading

Aurora automates the patching and upgrading of your database in a similar manner to RDS. Aurora uses its own numbering conventions to describe the version you run. For example, Aurora MySQL version 3 would run MySQL 8.0. Certain features on Aurora, such as Backtrack, are only available on the latest version of Aurora, which means upgrading the database engine. Upgrades may cause an outage when applied, but these are reduced if you run with reader instances such as running a Multi-AZ deployment in RDS.

Managing DR or HA

Aurora is HA by default. Aurora stores its data in six different locations across three different AZs, meaning you have extremely high fault tolerance in the storage layer. If an instance fails, Aurora will take action to restore a service almost immediately, either by using a reader instance (if you have one) or by creating a new primary instance. You can run up to 15 different reader instances in any AZ within the same region, but it's recommended to run in at least two AZs for increased fault tolerance. Your reader instances can be promoted to a primary instance during a failover. This occurs almost instantly, meaning there is very low downtime if there is any Aurora failure.

If you need cross-region replication, either for real-time performance benefits by having lower latency with your database and your global users, or for DR purposes, Aurora offers Global Database. Global Database allows you to run a copy of your database in multiple regions around the world. Aurora will keep these in sync, providing near real-time replication with a typical lag time of less than one second. This setup enables read-only operations to be offloaded to replicas in other regions, reducing latency for global users and distributing read traffic efficiently. In the event of a regional outage, you can promote a secondary region to be the new primary in less than a minute, ensuring minimal downtime and data loss.

Scaling

When discussing scaling in Aurora, there are four questions that you need to ask:

- Do you need more storage?
- Do you need more write resources for your database?
- Do you need more read resources for your database?
- Is your resource requirement going up and down a lot – that is, is it spiky?

Now, these can be answered in order.

Storage on Aurora scales automatically; you will never run out of space unless you hit account limits, and Aurora only charges you for the space you use, unlike on RDS, where you pay for allocated storage even if it isn't being used. There is no relationship between the storage size and the IOPS on Aurora either. However, on Aurora, you do pay for the IOPS that you use unless you pay an additional fee for I/O-Optimized.

When it comes to increasing the amount of resources available for your database (i.e., CPU and memory), you can either scale horizontally or vertically. Vertically means increasing the instance size to provide more resources in a single instance. This works well when the bulk of your traffic comes from write operations, as a database can only have one writer. If you have a higher number of reads on your system, then you can instead scale horizontally by deploying reader instances to handle the read-only traffic. This can have the additional benefit of increasing your HA options, as Aurora can fail over to the reader instances if the writer is unavailable. To help manage the connections to the readers, Aurora databases have two endpoints, one for read and write traffic and one for read-only traffic, and Aurora will route you to the best instance. You can also connect to a specific instance if you wish. This can be useful if you want to reduce cross-AZ traffic costs by preferring your application to communicate with a database instance in the same AZ. Aurora allows reader instances to auto-scale based on CPU usage.

Finally, let's assume that you have a spiky workload that goes up and down and only requires a high amount of CPU and memory for short periods of time. In this scenario, you might consider using Aurora Serverless instead of the standard Aurora Provisioned. Unlike traditional database instances, Aurora Serverless automatically adjusts its capacity based on an application's demands. This means that you do not have to manually provision or manage database instances. The database automatically scales up during peak times and scales down during periods of low activity, which helps to optimize costs. As a rule, Aurora Serverless is twice as expensive per unit (i.e., CPU and memory) as Aurora Provisioned, so it will only save costs if your workload is spiky and does not run at a constant level.

Authentication

Authentication on Aurora is very similar to RDS, with the option to use a username and password, IAM authentication, or AWS Secrets Manager. As Aurora only supports MySQL and PostgreSQL, any Aurora database can use password rotation via Secrets Manager too.

Performance and Monitoring

As well as the standard monitoring tools provided by RDS, Aurora offers several performance-enhancing features not available on RDS. Aurora can make use of its complex storage layer to speed up queries and allow for almost instant cloning of a database.

Aurora Parallel Query allows certain queries to be run directly against the storage layer, rather than going through the database itself. The main benefits of this are reducing strain on the database cache, allowing that to focus on standard queries, and reducing memory and CPU consumption on the database layer by offloading the work elsewhere. Parallel Query identifies ad hoc and batch-type queries and takes them outside of the database. This can result in higher I/O charges on Aurora, and Parallel Query is not used if you run in I/O-Optimized mode.

Aurora can create a copy of your database in minutes, regardless of the size. This is called **Fast Cloning**, and it uses the decoupled storage environment in Aurora. When the clone starts, only the database instance is created, and it is pointed to the existing data stored on the original database. As data is read by the clone, the blocks are copied into its own storage. Any changes written by the clone are also written to its storage, so in time, all the blocks are copied across. This is called lazy loading.

Parameters and Options

Parameter and option groups on Aurora behave like RDS, with the addition of a cluster parameter group. When you run multiple instances as part of the same database system, some of the parameters must be set at the cluster level, impacting all instances within the database system so Aurora has a cluster parameter group and individual instance parameter groups to support this. The Aurora parameter groups will contain some Aurora-specific parameters not found in RDS.

You now understand the key benefits and differences between RDS and Aurora. Now, we will learn about an additional service that AWS has released to help improve connection handling and failover times, as it applies to both Aurora and RDS.

RDS Proxy

Amazon **RDS Proxy** is a fully managed database proxy service for Amazon RDS and Amazon Aurora. A proxy sits between your application and a database, managing connections efficiently and improving performance and scalability. RDS Proxy is particularly useful for applications with unpredictable workloads or those that need to handle many simultaneous connections, as it pools and shares database connections to reduce the overhead on the database. RDS Proxy can also reduce downtime during failovers, as it is constantly aware of the status of the RDS system, so it can release sessions as soon as the system is available, even if the status in the console does not reflect that. RDS Proxy can also reduce application errors, as during a failover event, RDS Proxy holds or pauses connections rather than sending a failure. As such, an application does not need to manage these errors or resend the queries, as RDS Proxy will send them, in order, as soon as the failover is complete.

The benefits of using RDS Proxy include enhanced security, better availability, and improved application performance. By managing connections, RDS Proxy helps to protect your database from being overwhelmed by sudden spikes in traffic, which can lead to improved stability and responsiveness. Additionally, RDS Proxy integrates with AWS Secrets Manager for secure storage and automatic rotation of database credentials, enhancing the security of your applications.

EC2

So far in this chapter, you have learned about AWS's fully managed relational database options. But there is a third choice, self-hosted on EC2. When choosing between a self-hosted database on Amazon EC2 and Amazon RDS, it's important to consider flexibility, management, scalability, and cost.

Running a self-hosted database on EC2 gives you greater control over an environment, allowing for custom configurations and installations. However, this means you are responsible for all management tasks, such as backups, updates, and scaling. Scaling a self-hosted database on EC2 requires manual intervention, such as adding instances and managing replication. This provides flexibility but can be complex and time-consuming. Ensuring HA on EC2 involves setting up replication and failover mechanisms, which can be challenging to maintain.

Running a self-hosted database on EC2 can be cost-effective if you need maximum flexibility and control, but it comes with higher management overhead. Amazon RDS may have higher upfront costs for its managed services, but it often reduces the total cost of ownership by handling routine tasks and providing built-in features, such as backups and high availability.

You have now learned how relational databases run on AWS, and you should understand the main benefits, operations, and architecture of RDS, Aurora, and EC2 and when to use each. Now, let's turn your attention to NoSQL databases, starting with an overview of what NoSQL means and how these databases differ from relational databases.

NoSQL Databases

As you just learned in the previous section, relational databases use structured schemas and SQL to manage data, which is organized into tables with rows and columns. They excel in handling complex queries and transactions with strict data consistency. In contrast, AWS offers NoSQL databases such as Amazon DynamoDB, Amazon DocumentDB (with MongoDB compatibility), Amazon Neptune, and Amazon Keyspaces (for Apache Cassandra). DynamoDB is a key-value and document store designed for high performance and scalability, DocumentDB is optimized for JSON data, Neptune supports graph models for complex relationship data, and Keyspaces is built for wide-column storage. These NoSQL databases are ideal for applications requiring flexibility, high throughput, and the ability to store unstructured data at scale.

Now, we will learn about the different NoSQL databases offered on AWS that may feature in the *SAA-C03 exam*, starting with Amazon DynamoDB.

Amazon DynamoDB

DynamoDB is a fully managed, serverless, key-value pair database designed to support sub-millisecond query time at almost any scale, being able to handle over 20 million requests per second. Being fully managed means that AWS handles the hardware provisioning, setup, configuration, replication, software patching, and scaling. Serverless allows the database to scale elastically as required without provisioning specific-sized servers. This means you only pay for exactly what you use.

In a key-value pair database, data is stored in a simple structure where each piece of data is identified by a unique key. When you need to retrieve data, you provide the key, and the database returns the corresponding value. This makes lookups very fast and efficient but queries, where you need to search through the database, can be very costly and inefficient.

Let's take a more in-depth look at the specific features and benefits you will need to know for the SAA-C03 exam.

Capacity

DynamoDB can handle high request rates (over 20 million requests per second) and large amounts of data, with no hard limits on total storage capacity. It does this by using **partitioning** and **eventual consistency**. Partitioning is when your data is stored in different locations, based on the key value, to ensure that all similar keys are stored together. When your data is written to a partition, it is also stored in two other locations. The secondary writes may not occur immediately, so a subsequent read of the same data may not show the new data, depending on which location DynamoDB decides to read from. This is called eventual consistency. DynamoDB does support strongly consistent reads by only retrieving data from the location with the latest data, but this is more costly than standard reads. These two features are the trade-offs versus a relational database and are what makes DynamoDB able to handle much higher volumes of data and requests.

To handle different types of workloads, DynamoDB offers two capacity modes – **provisioned** and **on-demand**. Provisioned capacity is suitable for predictable workloads, while on-demand capacity automatically adjusts to your application's traffic.

To help you understand which type would be the best for a workload, you need to understand how billing is calculated in DynamoDB.

In **provisioned capacity mode**, you specify the amount of read and write capacity that your application needs. You pay for the specified capacity, regardless of whether you fully utilize it. The capacity is defined by capacity units for reads and writes. You pay for a specific number of **read capacity units (RCUs)** and **write capacity units (WCUs)**. One RCU represents two eventually consistent reads per second, or one strongly consistent read, for items up to 4 KB in size. One WCU represents one write per second for items up to 1 KB in size. If you use all your RCUs or WCUs, DynamoDB starts throttling requests, causing errors. To help prevent this, DynamoDB provides auto scaling to automatically adjust the provisioned capacity, based on usage patterns, helping you manage costs while ensuring availability. Auto scaling provisioned capacity is far slower than using on-demand capacity mode and typically results in throttling for periods of time before auto scaling kicks in. It's useful for steady workloads that might have occasional, unpredictable spikes rather than fully or mostly unpredictable workloads.

In on-demand capacity mode, you do not have to specify read and write capacity units. Instead, DynamoDB automatically adjusts to your workload, and you pay based on the actual read and write operations performed. You are billed for the actual read and write requests you make. This includes the number of **read request units (RRUs)** and **write request units (WRUs)** consumed. One RRU represents two eventually consistent read requests, or one strongly consistent read, for items up to 4 KB, and one WRU represents one write request for items up to 1 KB.

A Data Model

As previously explained, DynamoDB uses a key-value data model. It stores data in tables, which consist of items (rows) and attributes (columns). Each item is uniquely identified by a primary key, which can be a single attribute (partition key) or a combination of two attributes (partition key and sort key).

Every query in DynamoDB hits an index, and you can have multiple indexes on each table. You cannot query the data stored in a table directly, so this means that for each expected query you need to run, you must be able to answer how you will get the data you need from the indexes you have. For example, if you want to query based on a user ID, you need to have an index with a key defined on the `userID` column. For most applications, you would need multiple keys, and therefore, indexes, to be able to get the results you need.

To optimize query performance, DynamoDB supports two types of indexes – **global secondary indexes (GSIs)** and **local secondary indexes (LSIs)**. GSIs allow you to query on non-primary key attributes, and LSIs enable an additional sort key on the primary key. A sort key orders the results using the specified column. If you typically return the most recent results only, then using a sort key on a data column will ensure similar dated items get returned the fastest. You can define any sort key that fits your data model. GSIs are treated as if they are their own table, and they can be provisioned with their own RCUs/WCUs, which can be different from the main table. LSIs share the RCUs/WCUs with the main table.

> **Note**
>
> Make sure that you can do simple billing calculations for a DynamoDB table, as there are often exam questions on this. For example, you may be asked to calculate the number of RRUs used to retrieve a 5 KB item, using strongly consistent reads. The answer would be two RRUs, as one RRU can only retrieve a 4 KB item in strongly consistent mode, so you would need two for the entire item.

Performance

DynamoDB has two main optional features to enhance its performance, DynamoDB Streams and **DynamoDB Accelerator (DAX)**. DynamoDB Streams captures a time-ordered sequence of item-level modifications in a table. This feature allows for real-time data processing and integration with other AWS services, such as AWS Lambda. It can also be used for audit controls and logging to get real-time information on changes being made to your DynamoDB tables.

DAX is an in-memory cache that can greatly speed up your read queries by retrieving results from the cache, rather than needing to read from the DynamoDB table. In some situations, it can also reduce the number of RRUs/RCUs needed for your DynamoDB table, reducing your bill.

Monitoring and Management

DynamoDB integrates with Amazon CloudWatch to provide detailed metrics on key performance indicators, such as read and write throughput, latency, throttled requests, and error rates. You can set up CloudWatch alarms to notify you of any anomalies, such as exceeding provisioned throughput limits or increased latency, allowing you to take proactive measures. Using the usage statistics, you can get a better view of your workload and see whether switching between on-demand or provisioned mode would be cost-effective.

Backups

Amazon DynamoDB provides robust backup options to help protect your data. On-demand backup allows you to create full backups of your DynamoDB tables at any time, enabling you to safeguard data before major application changes or as part of a regular backup schedule. These backups are retained until you explicitly delete them and can be restored to a new table in minutes. **Point-in-time recovery (PITR)** offers continuous backups of your DynamoDB table data, allowing you to restore a table to any second within the past 35 days. This feature is particularly useful for protecting against accidental writes or deletes. Both backup options can be managed by AWS Backup. This integration allows for streamlined backup management and ensures compliance with organizational backup policies.

DynamoDB also offers export to S3, which lets you export table data to Amazon S3 for long-term storage, analytics, and archiving. This enables integration with other AWS services for further processing and analysis. Finally, while not directly a backup feature, global tables provide a multi-region, fully replicated database solution, ensuring HA and low-latency access to data across different geographic locations. This can be used as a DR strategy if an entire region was to fail.

Security

DynamoDB security features include encryption at rest, AWS **Identity and Access Management (IAM)** policies, and the use of VPC endpoints for private access. Fine-grained access control can be implemented using IAM policies to control access to individual items and attributes.

We will now take a look at Amazon ElastiCache.

Amazon ElastiCache

Amazon **ElastiCache** is a fully managed, in-memory caching service, designed to accelerate the performance of your applications by reducing the time required to access data stored in your primary database. ElastiCache supports two popular open source caching engines – **Redis** and **Memcached**. By caching frequently accessed data in memory, ElastiCache provides sub-millisecond latency, which significantly improves the responsiveness of your applications.

Common use cases for ElastiCache include caching, real-time analytics, gaming leaderboards, and speeding up machine learning workloads. By storing frequently accessed data in memory, you can reduce latency and improve application performance in scenarios such as session storage, user profiles, product catalogs, and database query results. Real-time analytics benefit from instant insights and decision-making capabilities. Gaming applications use ElastiCache to maintain high-score leaderboards and other rapidly changing data. Machine learning workloads are accelerated by caching model parameters and intermediate data.

ElastiCache supports Redis and Memcached. Redis is a powerful in-memory key-value store that supports complex data types, persistence, replication, and Lua scripting, making it suitable for use cases requiring HA, fault tolerance, and advanced data structures. Memcached is a simple, high-erformance, distributed memory object caching system, ideal for scenarios where you need to quickly retrieve data and do not require data persistence.

Capacity

Capacity is quite different on Elasticache to other database engines, as it does not have physical storage. Elasticache is an in-memory database, so you define its capacity in terms of how much memory it has to store records. If you try to exceed the maximum memory, then Elasticache will either start to evict or remove items, or it will throw an error. As a cache is often used to store the most commonly accessed data, you can set a **time to live** (TTL) policy that specifies which items should be removed first if the cluster is under memory pressure. To help Elasticache Redis decide which items should be evicted, you can set a cache eviction policy:

- **Volatile least recently used**: The items that have been accessed the least recently where they have an expiry or TTL set

- **All least recently used**: The items that have been accessed the least recently, whether they have an expiry or TTL set or not

- **Volatile least frequently used**: The items that have been accessed the least number of times where they have an expiry or TTL set

- **All least frequently used**: The items that have been accessed the least number of times whether they have an expiry or TTL set or not

- **Volatile TTL**: Removes the keys closest to their TTL date

- **Volatile random**: Randomly removes items where they have an expiry of TTL set

- **All random**: Randomly removes items whether they have an expiry or TTL set or not

- **No eviction**: No items will be removed, but errors will be sent back to the application instead

- For Memcached, the only options are "no eviction" or "least recently used." Memcached does not have a TTL option either, as it is a much simpler cache.

Deployment Modes

ElastiCache offers multiple deployment modes to meet different application requirements:

- **Standalone mode**: In this simplest form, a single node is used for caching, which is suitable for development and testing environments, or simple use cases where HA is not a concern.

- **Cluster mode disabled (Redis)**: This mode involves a primary node with read replicas to provide HA and failover support. It is suitable for applications that need HA and can benefit from read replicas to distribute the read load.

- **Cluster mode enabled (Redis)**: This mode allows you to partition your data across multiple shards, enabling horizontal scaling to handle larger datasets and higher request rates. It supports up to 250 shards and provides significant flexibility in scaling both reads and writes.

- **Memcached deployment**: Memcached can be deployed in a cluster with multiple nodes that share cache data without replication. This mode is useful for use cases requiring simple, high-performance caching without the need for data persistence or complex data structures.

Performance

Unlike a relational database, ElastiCache does not require tuning, or any schema design planning, like other NoSQL databases. The main consideration for performance relates to the size of the memory available and the cluster size. Memcached offers only a single node deployment, allowing you to scale vertically to get a larger cache. Redis offers clusters and sharding to spread data across multiple nodes for higher throughput and improved resilience.

Monitoring and Management

ElastiCache integrates with Amazon CloudWatch to provide comprehensive monitoring of your clusters. You can track key metrics such as CPU utilization, memory usage, cache hits and misses, and network throughput. CloudWatch also allows you to set up alarms to notify you of potential issues, enabling you to take proactive measures to maintain the performance and availability of your cache.

Backups

Additionally, ElastiCache offers automated backups and snapshots for Redis clusters, ensuring that your data is protected and can be restored if there is a failure. You can schedule backups to occur at regular intervals and retain them for a specified period. Memcached does not support any backups, as it is purely a memory store.

Security

ElastiCache provides multiple layers of security to protect your data. It supports encryption at rest and in transit, ensuring that your data is protected both when stored and during transmission. ElastiCache can be deployed within an Amazon **Virtual Private Cloud** (**VPC**), allowing you to isolate your clusters and control access using VPC security groups and network ACLs. AWS IAM policies can be used to control access to ElastiCache resources, defining fine-grained permissions to restrict access based on user roles and responsibilities.

Note

Be aware of the different engine types, Redis and Memcached. Both work very differently, so read the question carefully and make sure you know which engine is mentioned. In general, Memcached is a much simpler database and any answers that discuss clustering, multi-A, or backups are incorrect!

So, that is two NoSQL databases you have learned about – just four to go! From here on in, you do not need such deep insight, as any question in the exam will be based on when you would use one of these databases, rather than how to monitor or administer them.

Next, we will learn about briefly Amazon DocumentDB.

Amazon DocumentDB

Amazon DocumentDB is a fully managed, scalable, and HA document database service, designed to support **JavaScript Object Notation (JSON)** workloads. JSON is a method of storing data in a database that allows for a fluid and undefined schema. It is often used when different data needs to be stored together. DocumentDB is based on MongoDB (MongoDB is a document database that stores its data in a JSON-type format), and while they are not the same, many MongoDB commands and queries will run seamlessly on DocumentDB. DocumentDB's architecture separates storage and compute, allowing independent scaling of each to optimize performance and cost. In a similar manner to Aurora, it automatically replicates six copies of your data across three AWS AZs, providing robust fault tolerance and HA. It also offers managed failovers, backups, and patching.

DocumentDB also offers streams, like DynamoDB Streams, where all data changes are written to a stream that can be ingested by other systems for event processing.

You would use Amazon DocumentDB in scenarios where your application needs a flexible, schema-less data model that can handle a variety of data formats. For example, it is ideal for content management systems, catalogs, user profiles, and IoT applications where data structures can evolve over time without requiring complex migrations. It is also suitable for applications with high read and write throughput demands, given its ability to scale horizontally and support large volumes of concurrent operations.

> **Exam tip**
>
> DocumentDB is designed to be compatible with MongoDB commands, so if an exam question asks which database is best for storing JSON documents or migration from MongoDB, then the answer will be DocumentDB.

We will now look at a very different database type from what we have learned about so far – a graph database.

Amazon Neptune

Neptune is a graph database. A graph database is a NoSQL database that, instead of tables, columns, and keys, uses nodes, edges, and properties to represent and store data. This structure can be used to identify links between connection items on a graph and the strength of that connection. A typical use case for this type of data is a social media network, where the more friends you have in common with another person, the more likely you are to also want to be friends with them. Recommendation engines for online shopping websites also use graph data to recommend things, based on what others with a similar profile to you have also bought. The key components of a graph database are as follows:

- **Nodes**: These are the entities or objects in a graph. For example, in a social network graph, each person would be a node.

- **Edges**: These are the connections or relationships between nodes. In the social network example, an edge could represent a friendship between two people.

- **Properties**: Both nodes and edges can have properties, which are key-value pairs that provide additional information. For instance, a node representing a person might have properties such as name, age, and location, while an edge representing a friendship might have a property indicating when the friendship started.

Neptune supports both the property graph model and the **Resource Description Framework** (RDF) model, providing compatibility with popular graph query languages such as **Apache TinkerPop Gremlin** and W3C's **SPARQL**. With its highly optimized graph query processing engine, Neptune can handle complex queries involving deep traversals and intricate relationships among data points, making it ideal for applications that require sophisticated graph-based analysis.

You would use Amazon Neptune in scenarios where your application needs to navigate and analyze complex relationships within your data efficiently. For example, it is well-suited for use cases such as social networking applications, recommendation engines, and fraud detection systems. Neptune's managed service takes care of database maintenance tasks such as backups, patching, and scaling.

> **Note**
> Any exam question asking which database would work best that mentions connected data or recommendations almost always refers to Neptune.

We have now learned about Amazon Neptune and graph databases. Finally, we will explore the last two databases that AWS offers, Amazon Keyspaces and Amazon Quantum Ledger Database.

Amazon Keyspaces

Amazon Keyspaces is a fully managed database that supports **Apache Cassandra** workloads. Cassandra is a wide-column database that allows you to have different columns for each item in a row. This offers a lot of flexibility within a schema and allows for analytic-type queries to be run quickly and efficiently. In the exam, you would look for questions that ask about Cassandra's compatibility.

Amazon Quantum Ledger Database

Amazon Quantum Ledger Database (**QLDB**) is a fully managed ledger database that provides a transparent, immutable, and cryptographically verifiable transaction log. It is designed to track each application data change and maintain a complete and verifiable history of changes over time. QLDB uses a journal to record every data modification, ensuring that the history is immutable and cannot be altered or deleted. This makes it a good fit for systems that require a permanent and authoritative data record, such as financial systems, supply chain management, and regulatory compliance.

We have now learned about all the different databases that may come up in the *SAA-C03 exam* (except for Redshift, which AWS defines as analytics), so we can now move on to analytics.

Analytics on AWS

Analytics on AWS is an extremely wide range of tools and services to help organizations collect, store, process, and analyze data. AWS offers solutions for data lakes, data warehousing, real-time analytics, and machine learning. This helps businesses turn raw data into useful insights for better decision-making and innovation. With services such as Amazon Redshift, Amazon Athena, AWS Glue, and Amazon QuickSight, AWS makes it easy to work with different types of data, run complex queries, and create reports.

Amazon Redshift

Amazon Redshift is a fully managed, petabyte-scale data warehouse service designed for high-performance analysis of structured and semi-structured data. It enables organizations to run complex analytic queries against massive datasets, using familiar SQL-based tools and **business intelligence** (**BI**) applications. Common use cases include BI, predictive analytics, and big data processing, so it is used by many companies that need to analyze large volumes of data quickly.

Capacity

Managing capacity in Amazon Redshift is like Amazon RDS, where you define your instance size, but Redshift offers extra resize features to give more flexibility. For provisioned clusters, this involves selecting appropriate node types and numbers based on workload requirements. Elastic resize enables quick adjustment of compute capacity, while classic resize allows for more significant changes. **Concurrency scaling** automatically adds transient capacity for unpredictable query load spikes. Redshift Serverless automates capacity management, although you can set base capacity limits and maximum RPU to control costs.

Workload management (**WLM**) optimizes resource allocation by defining query queues and routing rules. It allows administrators to create multiple query queues, each with its own concurrency level, memory allocation, and timeout settings. WLM enables you to categorize and prioritize different types of queries based on various criteria, such as user groups, query groups, or specific SQL statements. By directing queries to the correct queues, WLM helps prevent resource-intensive queries from monopolizing cluster resources and ensures that critical workloads receive the necessary resources to execute efficiently. Redshift offers both automatic and manual WLM configurations. Automatic WLM uses machine learning to dynamically manage memory and concurrency, while manual WLM gives administrators more granular control over resource allocation.

Deployment Modes

Redshift offers two primary deployment options – provisioned clusters and Redshift Serverless. Provisioned clusters allow users to specify and manage the size and number of nodes, providing more control over performance and cost optimization. Conversely, Redshift Serverless automatically provisions and scales data warehouse capacity, making it ideal for applications with variable workloads or those that don't require constant use.

Performance

To deliver high performance, Redshift employs several techniques. It uses columnar storage, which allows for efficient compression and faster query performance. Its **massively parallel processing** (**MPP**) architecture distributes queries across all nodes in a cluster for parallel execution. Result caching speeds up frequently run queries, while automatic WLM prioritizes and allocates resources based on query importance and requirements.

Zero-ETL

The **zero-ETL** feature of Amazon Redshift allows direct, real-time access to operational data stored in other AWS services without traditional extract, transform, and load processes. This enables real-time analytics on the most up-to-date operational data, reduces complexity by eliminating the need for complex **ETL** pipelines, and improves cost efficiency by preventing data duplication.

Security

Security is a priority in Redshift, with support for encryption at rest and in transit, deployment within a VPC for network isolation, and fine-grained access control using AWS IAM. Column-level access control allows you to restrict access to sensitive data for specific users or roles.

Monitoring and Management

For monitoring and management, Redshift integrates with Amazon CloudWatch, providing comprehensive metrics on query performance, CPU utilization, and storage usage. CloudWatch alarms can be set up to alert on performance issues or capacity constraints. Redshift also automatically takes and retains snapshots of your cluster, with options for manual snapshots and cross-region snapshot copies for disaster recovery.

> **Note**
>
> For the exam, you need to understand the differences between provisioned Redshift clusters and Redshift Serverless and when each option is more appropriate, based on workload patterns and management preferences. You also need to understand WLM and whether it is automatic or manual.

Amazon EMR

Amazon Elastic Map Reduce (EMR) is designed to process very large amounts of data, using open source tools such as Apache Spark, Apache Hive, Apache Flink, and Presto. It provides a managed Hadoop framework that makes it easy, fast, and cost-effective to process and analyze massive amounts of data across dynamically scalable Amazon EC2 instances.

Deployment Options

EMR offers various cluster types to suit different processing needs. You can create long-running clusters for persistent workloads or transient clusters for short-term jobs. EMR supports both on-demand and spot instances for cost optimization. The service also provides EMR on EKS, allowing you to run EMR workloads on Amazon EKS for improved resource utilization and simplified operations.

You can use spot instances for lower-priority workloads, leverage instance fleets to automatically select the most cost-effective mix of instance types, and use EMR-managed scaling to automatically adjust cluster size based on workload.

EMR supports a wide range of open source tools and frameworks for big data processing. Apache Spark is commonly used for in-memory processing of large-scale data analytics. Hive provides SQL-like queries on large datasets, while Presto offers fast, distributed SQL query execution. For streaming data, you can use Apache Flink or Spark Streaming. EMR also supports machine learning frameworks, such as Apache MXNet and TensorFlow.

Performance

EMR automatically configures cluster compute resources and leverages instance fleets or instance groups for flexible scaling. You can easily add or remove instances during a cluster's lifetime to match your workload. EMR also supports the **EMR File System (EMRFS)**, an implementation of **Hadoop Distributed File System (HDFS)** that allows clusters to directly access data in Amazon S3, providing virtually unlimited storage scalability.

EMR Studio provides a web-based **integrated development environment** (IDE) for developing, visualizing, and debugging big data and analytics applications. It offers collaborative workspaces with Jupyter notebooks, making it easier for data scientists and analysts to work with EMR clusters.

Security

EMR integrates with AWS security services to provide a secure big data environment. You can run clusters in Amazon VPC for network isolation, use AWS IAM for fine-grained access control, and enable encryption for data at rest and in transit. EMR also supports Apache Ranger for centralized data governance and Lake Formation for simplified security management.

Monitoring and Management

EMR integrates with Amazon CloudWatch to monitor cluster performance and health. The EMR management console provides detailed information about cluster status, step execution, and instance groups. You can set up automatic scaling policies to adjust cluster size, based on utilization metrics, or schedule predictable capacity changes.

> **Note**
> Focus on understanding when to use EMR versus other AWS data processing services. Understand the benefits of EMR for big data workloads, its integration with other AWS services, and its cost optimization features. Be familiar with the concept of transient versus long-running clusters and how EMR can process data stored in S3, using EMRFS.

Amazon QuickSight

Amazon QuickSight is a cloud-native, serverless BI service that makes it easy to create and distribute interactive dashboards, reports, and visualizations. It is designed to provide insights to everyone in an organization, from business analysts to C-level executives, with minimal setup and maintenance. QuickSight offers an easy-to-use, drag-and-drop interface to create visually appealing dashboards and reports. It provides a rich set of visualization types, including bar charts, line graphs, heat maps, pivot tables, and geospatial charts. The service includes AI-powered features such as **AutoGraph**, which automatically suggests the best visualization type based on the selected data.

Data Sources

QuickSight can connect to a wide variety of data sources, both within AWS and external to it. It integrates seamlessly with AWS services such as Amazon RDS, Amazon Aurora, Amazon Redshift, Amazon Athena, and Amazon S3. It also supports connections to on-premises databases, third-party cloud databases, and **software as a service** (**SaaS**) applications. QuickSight's **Super-Fast, Parallel, In-Memory Calculation Engine** (**SPICE**) allows you to quickly import and analyze data.

Advanced Features

QuickSight's ML Insights feature leverages machine learning to provide automated narratives, anomaly detection, forecasting, and what-if analysis. These capabilities help users quickly identify trends, outliers, and potential future outcomes without requiring deep data science expertise.

With QuickSight's embedded analytics feature, you can embed interactive dashboards and visualizations into your own applications, portals, or websites. This allows you to provide data insights directly within your product or service, enhancing its value to end users.

Performance

QuickSight uses in-memory computing with its SPICE engine to deliver fast query performance. It also employs data caching and query result caching to further improve response times. For large datasets, QuickSight supports direct query mode, allowing it to push down complex calculations to the underlying data source.

QuickSight can automatically scale to support thousands of users without any capacity planning. It offers you a pay-per-session pricing model, making it cost-effective for organizations with many occasional users.

Security

QuickSight integrates with AWS IAM for fine-grained access control and supports row-level security. It provides encryption for data at rest and in transit, ensuring the security of your sensitive business information.

> **Note**
> Be familiar with QuickSight's serverless nature, its ability to connect to various data sources, and its embedded analytics capabilities. Know the differences between QuickSight and other AWS services, such as Amazon Redshift and Amazon Athena, and when to choose QuickSight for BI needs.

AWS Glue

AWS Glue is a fully managed ETL service that allows you to move data from one location to another and to make changes in-flight. This is very useful if you need to clean up data, as it supports near-real-time analytics. It automates much of the complex work involved in discovering, categorizing, cleaning, enriching, and moving data between various data stores and data streams.

Data Catalog and Discovery

At the core of AWS Glue is the Data Catalog, a central metadata repository. The Data Catalog provides a unified view of all your data across various data sources. Glue can automatically discover and catalog metadata from supported data sources, making it searchable, queryable, and available for ETL operations. This catalog integrates with other AWS services such as Amazon Athena, Amazon EMR, and Amazon Redshift Spectrum, enabling seamless data processing and analysis.

ETL Jobs

Glue allows you to create and run ETL jobs with minimal coding. It generates Python or Scala code for your ETL jobs, which you can further customize as needed. Glue provides a variety of built-in transformations to clean and transform your data, such as dropping fields, filtering rows, and joining datasets. For more complex transformations, you can write custom logic using PySpark. Glue also offers a visual ETL editor called Glue Studio, which allows you to create, run, and monitor ETL jobs through a graphical interface, making it accessible to users with varying levels of technical expertise.

Architecture

AWS Glue operates on a serverless architecture, automatically provisioning the resources needed to prepare and load your data. It can scale up or down based on the volume of data being processed, ensuring cost-effectiveness and eliminating the need for manual resource management. In addition to batch ETL jobs, Glue supports streaming ETL, allowing you to clean and transform streaming data in real time.

Data Quality

Glue DataBrew, a visual data preparation tool within the AWS Glue family, allows users to clean and normalize data without writing code. It includes over 250 pre-built transformations and can help identify data quality issues. AWS Glue also integrates with AWS Lake Formation, providing fine-grained access control and governance for your data lake.

Monitoring

For monitoring and error handling, Glue integrates with Amazon CloudWatch. You can track job runs, view logs, and set up alerts for job failures or performance issues. Glue also provides features for error handling and job tuning, helping you optimize your ETL processes over time.

> **Note**
> AWS Glue is serverless and can automate ETL processes while integrating with other AWS services. Be familiar with the concept of the Glue Data Catalog and how it serves as a central metadata repository. Know when to use Glue versus other data processing services, such as EMR or direct queries with Athena.

Amazon Athena

Amazon Athena lets you analyze data directly in Amazon S3 using standard SQL statements. It requires no infrastructure to manage, and you only pay for the queries you run. Athena is used for quick, ad hoc querying of data in S3. It is commonly used for log analysis, BI, and data exploration. Athena can be particularly useful when combined with visualization tools, such as Amazon QuickSight, to create dashboards and reports.

Data Sources and Integration

Athena works with a variety of data formats stored in S3, including CSV, JSON, ORC, Avro, and Parquet. It integrates seamlessly with the AWS Glue Data Catalog, allowing you to create a unified metadata repository across various AWS services. Athena can also query data from other sources through connectors, including on-premises data sources.

Performance

Athena uses Presto, a distributed SQL query engine, to execute queries. It automatically executes queries in parallel, providing fast performance even with large datasets. To optimize performance and reduce costs, Athena supports partitioning data, compressing files, and converting data into columnar formats such as Apache Parquet.

With Athena's serverless model, you're charged only for the queries you run. You can manage costs by compressing data, using efficient file formats, and leveraging partitioning. Athena also integrates with AWS Cost Explorer and provides usage reports to help monitor and optimize query costs.

Security and Access Control

Athena integrates with AWS IAM for access control. It encrypts results stored in S3 and supports querying encrypted data. When used with AWS Lake Formation, Athena provides fine-grained access control at the database, table, and column levels.

> **Note**
> For the exam, understand Athena's serverless nature and its ability to query data directly in S3. It integrates with Glue Data Catalog. Be aware of the best practices to optimize Athena's performance and cost, such as using columnar formats and partitioning data.

AWS Lake Formation

AWS Lake Formation simplifies setting up a secure data lake by using other AWS services, such as Athena, Redshift, and S3. It provides tools to ingest, catalog, clean, transform, and secure your data, allowing you to store data in its native format and run various types of analytics. Lake Formation's pricing is based on the amount of data processed and stored. You can optimize costs by leveraging data compression and partitioning, and using efficient file formats such as Parquet.

Data Sources

Lake Formation supports a wide range of data sources, including Amazon S3, Amazon RDS, Amazon Redshift, and on-premises databases. It integrates natively with the AWS Glue Data Catalog, enabling you to create a centralized repository of metadata for your data lake. Lake Formation uses the AWS Glue Data Catalog to automatically discover and catalog data from various sources. It provides a unified metadata repository that integrates with other AWS analytics services, such as Amazon Athena, Amazon Redshift Spectrum, and Amazon EMR. Crawlers and classifiers help to continuously update the metadata as new data is ingested into the data lake.

Lake Formation can ingest data from streaming sources such as Amazon Kinesis and Apache Kafka (which you will learn about later), as well as batch data from various AWS services and external databases.

Storage and Formats

Lake Formation leverages Amazon S3 as the primary storage layer for your data lake, supporting various data formats, including CSV, JSON, ORC, Avro, Parquet, and columnar formats. Additionally, it integrates with **Apache Hudi** and **Apache Iceberg** to manage large-scale datasets, providing transactional capabilities, efficient data updates, and support for complex data schema evolution. The following gives a comparison of the two different options:

- **Apache Hudi**: Hudi enables efficient data lake operations, such as **upserts (i.e., updates and inserts)** and deletions, with a focus on streaming data ingestion and incremental data processing. It provides snapshot isolation for data queries and supports time travel queries, allowing you to access historical data.

- **Apache Iceberg**: Iceberg is designed for handling large analytic tables with high efficiency. It supports schema evolution, partitioning, and optimized query execution. Iceberg's table format ensures reliable data consistency and performance across various compute engines. Once you have decided which data format to use, you need to make sure that only the people who should have access to it can do so. Security controls in Lake Formation are powerful when configured correctly.

Security

Lake Formation provides comprehensive data governance capabilities, including data classification, access control, and auditing. It integrates with AWS IAM to manage permissions and access policies. Lake Formation also supports fine-grained access control, enabling you to set permissions at the table, column, and row levels.

Data stored in Amazon S3 through Lake Formation can be encrypted at rest using AWS **Key Management Service** (**KMS**) keys. Lake Formation also supports querying encrypted data and ensures that all access is securely managed.

Performance

Lake Formation supports high-performance data querying and analytics by integrating with various AWS services. It leverages Amazon Athena for ad hoc SQL queries, Amazon Redshift Spectrum for complex analytic queries, and Amazon EMR for large-scale data processing. The use of data partitioning, indexing, and columnar storage formats enhances query performance and reduces costs.

> **Note**
>
> AWS Lake Formation simplifies creating and managing secure data lakes on Amazon S3. Focus on understanding how it integrates with AWS Glue for metadata cataloging and supports fine-grained access control with IAM. Be familiar with data ingestion, transformation, and governance features.

Machine Learning and Artificial Intelligence Tools

Machine learning is a part of **Artificial Intelligence** (**AI**) that allows systems to learn and improve from experience without being directly programmed to do so. ML systems analyze and interpret patterns in data, enabling applications to make predictions, automate decision-making, and enhance user experiences. On AWS, ML becomes accessible to developers and data scientists through a comprehensive suite of services and tools. AWS provides robust infrastructure, managed services, and scalable solutions that simplify the process of building, training, and deploying ML models, allowing organizations to harness the power of their data for actionable insights and advanced analytics. From Amazon SageMaker for end-to-end ML workflows to specialized AI services, such as Amazon Rekognition and Amazon Comprehend, AWS offers a diverse set of tools to accelerate and optimize ML initiatives.

We will start this section by looking at Amazon Sagemaker.

Amazon SageMaker

Amazon SageMaker enables developers and data scientists to build, train, and deploy ML models quickly and simply using standard tools. It simplifies the ML workflow, providing integrated tools for every step from data preparation to model deployment. It connects natively to a wide range of AWS data sources.

You use SageMaker when you want to create your own ML/AI models using your own custom data, rather than relying on pre-trained models that AWS offers.

Data Sources

SageMaker integrates with a variety of data sources, including Amazon S3, Amazon RDS, Amazon Redshift, and on-premises databases. It supports seamless data ingestion and transformation with built-in integration to AWS Glue for data cataloging and preprocessing. SageMaker also works with Amazon Athena, Amazon EMR, and AWS Data Pipeline, enabling you to prepare and process large datasets efficiently.

Models

SageMaker provides a wide range of tools for model building, including pre-built Jupyter notebooks, built-in algorithms, and support for popular ML frameworks such as TensorFlow, PyTorch, and scikit-learn. You can also use your own custom algorithms. For training, SageMaker offers a managed infrastructure that automatically scales to handle large datasets and complex models, with distributed training support to reduce training times.

It simplifies model creation with one-click deployment to managed endpoints, enabling real-time predictions with low latency. It supports A/B testing, multi-model endpoints, and auto-scaling to handle varying levels of inference traffic. For batch predictions, SageMaker provides a managed batch transform service that processes large datasets efficiently.

Cost Management

SageMaker's pricing model is pay-as-you-go, with charges based on the compute and storage resources used for training and inference. To optimize costs, use spot instances for training jobs and managed endpoints for scalable, cost-effective deployment. SageMaker also integrates with AWS Cost Explorer for detailed usage and cost tracking.

Security

SageMaker integrates with AWS IAM to provide fine-grained access control for users and resources. It supports the encryption of data at rest and in transit, using AWS KMS keys. SageMaker also complies with various security standards and certifications, ensuring robust security for your ML workflows.

> **Note**
> Sagemaker is used for customizable control of your models and when pre-built models do not offer enough control or customization.

Amazon Rekognition

Amazon Rekognition is a managed computer vision service that simplifies adding image and video analysis to your applications. It uses deep learning to detect objects, people, text, scenes, and activities in images and videos, and it can also perform facial analysis and recognition. Rekognition integrates seamlessly with AWS services such as Amazon S3, AWS Lambda, and AWS Step Functions, and it supports direct API integration to analyze visual data from any source.

Common use cases for Rekognition include enhancing security through facial recognition in surveillance footage, identifying inappropriate content to maintain platform safety, and gathering demographic information to measure customer engagement. Billing is based on the number of images and video minutes processed, with options to optimize costs through batch processing and by reducing image and video resolution when high precision is unnecessary. Rekognition integrates with AWS IAM for fine-grained access control and supports data encryption at rest and in transit, ensuring the security of your visual data.

Amazon Comprehend

Amazon Comprehend is a **natural language processing** (NLP) service that uses ML to extract insights from text. It can determine the sentiment, key phrases, entities, and language of text and classify documents by topic. Comprehend integrates easily with AWS services such as Amazon S3, AWS Lambda, and Amazon Redshift, and it can also be accessed directly through API calls for real-time text analysis.

Typical use cases for Comprehend include analyzing customer reviews and support tickets to understand sentiment and identify common issues, automatically classifying and organizing large volumes of text documents for easier retrieval, and extracting important entities from documents such as legal texts or medical records. Comprehend charges based on the amount of text processed, with cost optimization possible through text preprocessing and batch processing. It uses AWS IAM for access control and supports encryption for data at rest and in transit, ensuring the security and privacy of your textual data.

Data Ingestion and Streaming

When you need to move a large amount of data in near-real time to different locations, typically for further processing or analysis, this is known as **data streaming and ingestion**. For example, imagine you run a warehouse with sensors on every part of each machine to measure the throughput of items, temperature, the color of the things in the warehouse, and so on. This would generate a huge amount of data that would need to be processed quickly and efficiently to generate alarms if there was a fault, or to automatically recalibrate the machines if they were out of alignment. AWS offers several different tools to handle the data, depending on your needs.

We will start this section by learning about Amazon Kinesis and its different features.

Amazon Kinesis

Amazon Kinesis is a platform on AWS to collect, process, and analyze real-time, streaming data, enabling you to get timely insights and react quickly to new information. It provides a set of services to handle large streams of data records in real time.

Data Sources

Kinesis integrates seamlessly with a wide variety of data sources and services. You can stream data from sources such as web and mobile applications, sensors, logs, and many other systems. Kinesis Data Streams allows you to ingest and store streaming data, while Kinesis Data Firehose provides the capability to load the streaming data into destinations, such as Amazon S3, Amazon Redshift, Amazon OpenSearch Service, and even custom HTTP endpoints. Additionally, Kinesis integrates with AWS Lambda, enabling you to process streaming data in real time using Lambda functions.

Data Processing

Amazon Kinesis offers multiple services to process and analyze streaming data:

- **Kinesis Data Streams**: Captures GB of data per second from hundreds of thousands of sources. You can then write applications to process the data using the **Kinesis Client Library** (**KCL**) or stream processing frameworks, such as Apache Storm or Apache Spark.

- **Kinesis Data Firehose**: Automatically scales to match the throughput of your data and provides a simple way to load streaming data into data lakes, warehouses, and analytics services.

- **Kinesis Data Analytics**: Allows you to process and analyze streaming data using standard SQL. It provides the capability to query streaming data in real time and gain immediate insights.

- **Kinesis Video Streams**: Enables you to stream video data from connected devices to AWS for real-time and batch analytics, ML, and other processing. It supports secure video stream ingestion, and it integrates with services such as Amazon Rekognition for video analysis and Amazon SageMaker for building custom ML models.

Now you have learned about the different types of streams that Kinesis supports, let's move on to how to improve performance and scalability.

Performance and Scalability

Kinesis is designed to handle any amount of streaming data and process it with low latency. Kinesis Data Streams can scale from MB to TB per hour and automatically adjust throughput by adding or removing shards. Kinesis Data Firehose scales automatically to match the volume and throughput of your data streams, and Kinesis Data Analytics processes data in real time with HA and low latency. Kinesis Video Streams efficiently ingests, processes, and stores video streams and automatically scales to accommodate varying video input loads.

Security

Amazon Kinesis integrates with AWS IAM to manage access control, ensuring that only authorized users and applications can interact with your data streams. Data can be encrypted at rest and in transit, using AWS KMS for additional security. Kinesis also provides detailed monitoring and logging through Amazon CloudWatch, enabling you to track usage patterns, detect anomalies, and ensure compliance with your security policies.

Amazon Managed Streaming for Kafka

Amazon Managed Streaming for Apache Kafka (**Amazon MSK**) is a fully managed service that supports Apache Kafka to process streaming data. Apache Kafka is a distributed event streaming platform that can handle multiple simultaneous inputs and outputs. With Amazon MSK, you can have the benefit of having AWS manage the infrastructure for you while still maintaining compatibility with existing Kafka applications. Kafka is commonly used for the aggregation of data and log ingestion.

Data Sources

Amazon MSK integrates with a wide range of data sources and AWS services. You can ingest data from applications, websites, IoT devices, databases, and other sources. Amazon MSK integrates with Amazon Kinesis Data Analytics, AWS Lambda, and AWS Glue, among others, enabling you to build data processing and analytics pipelines. MSK also supports standard Kafka tools and frameworks, allowing you to use or migrate from your existing Kafka ecosystem.

Data Processing

MSK allows you to handle high volumes of streaming data with low latency, making it suitable for real-time analytics, monitoring, and event-driven architectures. You can integrate with popular stream processing frameworks such as Apache Flink, Apache Storm, and Apache Spark to process and analyze data in real time. MSK is also ideal for implementing event sourcing and **Command Query Responsibility Segregation** (**CQRS**) patterns, enabling scalable and resilient data architectures. CQRS is a design pattern that splits how a system handles reading and writing data. Commands are used to update or change data, while queries are used to fetch data without making changes. This separation can help make systems more scalable and efficient, especially in complex or high-traffic applications.

Performance and Scalability

Amazon MSK is designed for high performance and scalability. MSK automatically scales to accommodate varying loads, ensuring consistent performance as your data volumes grow. Kafka's partitioning mechanism allows you to distribute data across multiple brokers for parallel processing and fault tolerance. Running on optimized AWS infrastructure, MSK provides high throughput, low latency, and reliable performance.

Security

MSK supports encryption at rest using AWS KMS and encryption in transit using TLS, ensuring that data is protected both on disk and over a network. You can integrate with AWS IAM to control access to your MSK clusters, allowing you to enforce fine-grained permissions. MSK runs within your Amazon VPC, providing network isolation and security controls. MSK integrates with Amazon CloudWatch for monitoring and logging, enabling you to track usage patterns, detect anomalies, and ensure compliance with your security policies.

> **Note**
>
> For the exam, understand the main differences between Kinesis and Kafka, and know when to use each. If Kafka is mentioned in the question, then the answer likely involves Amazon MSK. If the question talks about IoT, devices, or video streaming, then it's likely Kinesis.

You have learned a lot of different topics, services, and use cases in the chapter. You can now practice building a data lake using Lake Formation, Glue, Athena, and QuickSight.

Hands-on Lab

In this lab, you will use a variety of different analytics tools to build a simple data lake with a QuickSight frontend for querying. You will end up with an architecture that looks like *Figure 7.5*:

Figure 7.5: A data lake architecture

QuickSight is a licensed product, and there is no free version. If you do not wish to pay for QuickSight for this lab, then you can use Athena to query the same data, but you won't be able to see some of the AI/ML features of QuickSight.

We will start by creating and setting up the data lake using Lake Formation.

Creating the Data Lake

Now you will create a data lake. Follow these steps to do this:

1. Open the AWS Management Console and navigate to S3.

2. To create an S3 bucket, click on `Create bucket`. Give it a name, such as `saa-c03-data-lake`. Remember that each S3 bucket name must be globally unique, so add some numbers to the bucket name. Leave everything else as default.

3. Navigate to `Lake Formation`. To create a data lake, on the Lake Formation console, click on `Get started`. Define an S3 bucket that will serve as your data lake (e.g., `saa-c03-data-lake`). Navigate to `Data lake locations` in Lake Formation. Click `Register location` and specify the `saa-c03-data-lake` S3 bucket.

4. Assign Lake Formation permissions to users or roles that will access the data. This typically includes granting database creation, table creation, and data location access permissions to specific IAM users or roles.

5. Now that you have a data store, you can collect the details of the data using Glue. To create a Glue crawler, navigate to `AWS Glue console`. Click on `Crawlers` from the left-hand menu. Then, click `Add crawler`.

6. You now need to configure the Crawler:

   - `Name`: Name your crawler (e.g., `saa-c03-crawler`).

   - `Data Store`: Choose S3 as the data store.

   - `Include Path`: Specify the path to your S3 bucket (e.g., `s3://saa-c03-data-lake/`).

   - `IAM Role`: Choose an existing IAM role, or create a new one with permissions to read from the S3 bucket and write to the Glue Data Catalog.

   - `Schedule`: Choose when to run the crawler. Select `on demand`.

   - `Output`: Create a new data catalog and give it a name (e.g., `saa-c03-data-catalog`).

7. Start the crawler to scan the data in the S3 bucket, and populate the Glue Data Catalog with table definitions. The crawler will create tables that match your data in the S3 bucket. It should create several tables, including `TopGoalScorer`, `PlayerGoalTotals`, `PlayerAppearanceDetails`, and so on.

8. We can now use Athena to run some queries on our data stored in S3. To set up Athena, navigate to `Amazon Athena console`. Ensure that Athena is set up to use the same S3 bucket for query results (which you can specify in the settings) – for example, `s3://saa-c03-data-lake`.

9. Use SQL to query the data cataloged by Glue – for example, select `* FROM saa-c03-data-lake.topgoalscored LIMIT 10`.

10. Finally, you can use QuickSight to create both simple and complex dashboards and leverage built-in ML/AI analytics. To set up QuickSight, navigate to `Amazon QuickSight console`. Sign up for QuickSight if you have not already.

11. Connect to Athena. In QuickSight, navigate to `Manage data`. Click `New dataset`. Choose `Athena` as the data source. Configure the connection by specifying the Glue Data Catalog database, `saa-c03-data-catalog`, and the tables you want to use, such as `TopGoalScorer`, `PlayerGoalTotals`, and `PlayerAppearanceDetails`. Use your credentials or an IAM role that has permission to query Athena.

12. Now, you need to create analyses and dashboards. Use the dataset to create visualizations. QuickSight provides a variety of chart types, tables, and other visualization tools. For example, create a dashboard showing player statistics, game results, and score distributions.

13. Finally, combine visualizations into dashboards for comprehensive views of your sports data. Apply filters, aggregations, and custom calculations as needed.

These steps outline the process of setting up a data lake specifically for your sample data using AWS Lake Formation, cataloging data with AWS Glue, querying it with Amazon Athena, and visualizing it with Amazon QuickSight.

Summary

In this chapter, you have learned about the extensive range of data and analytics services provided by AWS, crucial for the *SAA-C03 exam*. We covered 15 different AWS databases and over 20 analytics tools, highlighting the importance of knowing their distinctions and practical applications for various use cases. You explored key services such as AWS Glue for data integration, Amazon Kinesis for real-time data streaming, and Amazon Aurora for transactional data storage. This chapter also introduced essential topics such as the different types of databases available on AWS, analytics options, ML tools, and strategies for data ingestion and streaming. Additionally, you learned the technical steps necessary to access and manage these services, including how to set up an AWS account and configure the AWS CLI. This knowledge will enable you to handle basic administrative functions and troubleshooting tasks for the commonly used AWS services, providing a strong foundation for your SAA-C03 exam preparation.

Exam Readiness Drill - Chapter Review Questions

Apart from mastering key concepts, strong test-taking skills under time pressure are essential for acing your certification exam. That's why developing these abilities early in your learning journey is critical.

Exam readiness drills, using the free online practice resources provided with this book, help you progressively improve your time management and test-taking skills while reinforcing the key concepts you've learned.

HOW TO GET STARTED

- Open the link or scan the QR code at the bottom of this page

- If you have unlocked the practice resources already, log in to your registered account. If you haven't, follow the instructions in *Chapter 16* and come back to this page.

- Once you log in, click the START button to start a quiz

- We recommend attempting a quiz multiple times till you're able to answer most of the questions correctly and well within the time limit.

- You can use the following practice template to help you plan your attempts:

Working On Accuracy		
Attempt	Target	Time Limit
Attempt 1	40% or more	Till the timer runs out
Attempt 2	60% or more	Till the timer runs out
Attempt 3	75% or more	Till the timer runs out
Working On Timing		
Attempt 4	75% or more	1 minute before time limit
Attempt 5	75% or more	2 minutes before time limit
Attempt 6	75% or more	3 minutes before time limit

The above drill is just an example. Design your drills based on your own goals and make the most out of the online quizzes accompanying this book.

First time accessing the online resources? 🔒

You'll need to unlock them through a one-time process. **Head to** *Chapter 16* **for instructions**.

Open Quiz	
https://packt.link/SAAC03Ch07 OR scan this QR code →	

8

Migrations and Data Transfer

In this chapter, you will learn about the processes and tools for migrating and transferring data to AWS. Understanding these processes is needed to ensure an easy transition to the cloud, maintain data integrity, and minimize downtime. This chapter will guide you through the various services AWS offers to facilitate seamless migrations and data transfers. You will read about storage migration via AWS Transfer Family, application migration via AWS Application Migration Service, and database migration via AWS Database Migration Service. By the end of this chapter, you will know how to migrate and transfer your data and applications to AWS confidently. All exam domains are covered in this section as knowing how to correctly migrate to AWS requires you to build secure, resilient, high-performing, and cost-effective architectures.

In this chapter, you will cover these main topics:

- AWS Transfer Family for storage

- AWS Application Migration Service

- AWS Database Migration Service

- By the end of this chapter, you will be able to optimally migrate your storage from on-premises to AWS using AWS Transfer Family.

Storage Migration

Imagine that you have been running a small company for several years and have built up a large amount of data stored on your users' laptops and shared storage drives. You are starting to use AWS for your applications and databases and want the storage to also be available in AWS. As a result, you are looking into different options to move the data across. The main questions to consider are as follows:

- Do you simply want to move the files as a one-off transfer?

- Do you want to replicate the data to AWS and keep it in sync with on-premises?

- Do you want to back up the data on AWS but keep it on-premises?

- Do you also need to share data with external parties or suppliers?

For example, you might want to simply move all your files from on-premises to AWS as a one-off transfer and then access those files from AWS only. A company doing an "all-in" migration to AWS may no longer need access to the files in their local data center. Alternatively, a company might want to store their local files in AWS as a backup or **disaster recovery** (**DR**) strategy and keep them in sync with those on-premises. AWS offers tools and solutions to meet all these different needs.

AWS services for data transfer can all sound very similar if you are not proficient in storage access and transfer mechanisms. Therefore, in the following sections, you will learn which one to use and when, using AWS exam terminology and use cases. You will not need to know the differences between **Network File Server** (**NFS**) and **Server Message Block** (**SMB**) filesystems or **File Transfer Protocol** (**FTP**) versus **Secure File Transfer Protocol** (**SFTP**), for example, unless you want to. However, you must know the AWS storage types, such as S3 and **Elastic File System** (**EFS**). Please return to *Chapter 5, Storage*, for a refresher if you do not.

Assuming you decide to move all the files to AWS and need them to be moved as quickly, cheaply, and efficiently as possible, for this scenario, you would likely want to use AWS DataSync.

AWS DataSync

AWS DataSync supports moving high volumes of data between on-premises storage and AWS. You can also use it to move data between AWS storage solutions, for example, between two different AWS accounts or from EFS to S3. You can also use AWS DataSync to transfer files from AWS back to on-premises if you wish. The *SAA-C03* exam often poses questions about needing to process some files in an on-premises data center, and AWS DataSync is typically a good choice for doing that.

Figure 8.1 demonstrates how DataSync connects to multiple endpoints, including source on-premises NFS and SMB file servers, and target AWS services such as EFS, S3, and FSx.

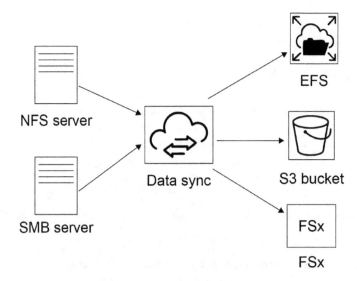

Figure 8.1: On-premises to AWS DataSync connections

> **Note**
> AWS DataSync does not support migration to EBS. DataSync supports moving files and not blocks; therefore, if the question asks how to move storage from on-premises to EBS, DataSync cannot be the correct answer.

You configure AWS DataSync via an agent package installed on an on-premises or EC2 server. This agent monitors the selection file locations for changes and uploads them following the rules configured. You can consider the agent as acting similarly to the Linux `rsync` command (this simple tool can monitor a directory on a server for any changes and then send the new files to a different location) or another file watcher tool. DataSync has many customizations to allow it to support differing needs of customers:

- **Scheduling**: You can use DataSync only to transfer data during specific time windows. Scheduling is helpful for companies who need to reserve their bandwidth for critical operations during the day but can allow DataSync to run overnight.

- **Incremental transfers**: DataSync can be set up to pull only incremental changes to save bandwidth and costs. The incremental selection is handled at the file level, so any modifications, no matter how small, to a file would result in the whole file being retransferred. Incremental transfers are the recommendation in all scenarios as all changes are still synced but without having to send all files again, even ones that haven't changed, which is more cost-efficient.

- **Bandwidth limits**: Bandwidth limits restrict how much data per second DataSync can transfer. While this can help protect operational activities from running out of bandwidth, this can cause DataSync to lag and, in some cases, end in failure if it cannot catch up. Companies that have limited bandwidth available will benefit from this technique as this allows them to protect critical production traffic by limiting the bandwidth available for DataSync.

- **Data verification**: DataSync offers an optional data verification process. The verification involves taking a checksum, an algorithmic calculation unique for each file, before the transfer and verifying that it matches after the transfer. This calculation guarantees data consistency, but this can cause an overhead and slow DataSync down. Using data verification is useful when the data consistency of the files being transferred is of more importance than the speed. This would typically be the case in any financial, legal, or customer-facing documentation.

DataSync is monitored through the console or API commands. You can see all the data throughput statistics to ensure you have sufficient bandwidth to transfer your files, and you can review the data verification checks if you have enabled them.

DataSync is very powerful but it has some limitations. DataSync requires the installation of an agent, and you cannot push or pull files from EBS. Your company may already use a specific file transfer protocol or tool to send data to other non-AWS locations. If you want to keep using those existing tools and workflows, you can use AWS Transfer Family.

AWS Transfer Family

AWS Transfer Family is a managed service that lets you use standard file transfer protocols such as SFTP to move files into and out of S3 and only S3. You use Transfer Family when a company already uses FTP in its workflows and wants to migrate to AWS without making any code changes. *Figure 8.2* shows how the AWS Transfer Family service sits between your on-premises server and an S3 bucket:

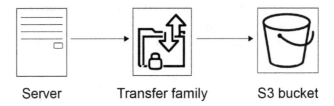

Server   Transfer family   S3 bucket

Figure 8.2: AWS Transfer Family

Transfer Family integrates directly with AWS IAM and supports fine-grained access controls to limit individual file-level access. You can also use an external identity management provider alongside IAM to simplify the security when moving files from on-premises. Transfer Family uses encryption in transit via **Secure Sockets Layer/Transport Layer Sockets (SSL/TLS)**, which supports encryption at rest through S3 server-side encryption. In addition, you can monitor all usage of Transfer Family through AWS CloudTrail and Amazon CloudWatch, down to the individual files that have been accessed.

You can configure workflows to manage post-upload processing. The workflow can be as simple as creating rules to move the files into different S3 storage classes based on their size or file types or as complex as creating an AWS Lambda function to run some custom processing of the files or even moving them into a different storage service. You can use a combination of Transfer Family and DataSync to quickly and securely migrate the files into EFS. First, use Transfer Family to migrate the files into S3. Then, you can use DataSync to move the files from S3 into EFS.

> **Note**
> AWS Transfer Family only supports migrations into and out of S3. If the question mentions another AWS storage service or does not specify S3, then Transfer Family is almost certainly the incorrect answer.

So, if you need to use SFTP to move your files to AWS and are happy with them being stored initially in an S3 bucket, then Transfer Family is the best choice.

You have learned which service to choose when transferring data into or out of AWS. Still, a company occasionally needs to extend its storage into AWS rather than moving its files or data directly across. If you need this, then AWS Storage Gateway is likely the best fit.

AWS Storage Gateway

Storage Gateway is very different from DataSync or Transfer Family as you do not always need to move any data to use it. It is designed to support hybrid cloud workloads running in both AWS and on-premises. You can use it when you need to seamlessly access your data in both locations and use AWS as a storage backup. You can also use Storage Gateway to store your tape backups in AWS without changing your backup system. For example, you have latency-sensitive applications running in a local data center but have moved the analytics service into AWS. Both systems need access to the same data and files using the same access protocols.

Storage Gateway consists of three different services for different requirements:

- **File Gateway**: Your on-premises data is stored in S3, and your on-premises applications or users can access them as if they are stored locally. File Gateway supports SMB/NFS. File Gateway caches the most accessed files, which lowers latency even further. This could be used when the majority of your workloads are running in AWS but you still have important services or applications running on-premises.

- **Volume Gateway**: There are two versions of Volume Gateway – cached and stored. Using stored, your on-premises data remains on-premises but it is asynchronously backed up to AWS to offer DR capabilities. This is used when a company wants to have backups of their data held in a different location to ensure that a physical issue with their data center would not result in any data loss. Using cached mode moves your data to S3 but the regularly accessed files are written to an on-premises cache, such as File Gateway. Volume Gateway cached mode supports **Internet Small Computer Systems Interface (iSCSI)**, not SMB/NFS, so it supports application volume storage, not file storage.

- **Tape Gateway**: This emulates a tape-based backup system and integrates with your on-premises backups, but stores them securely within AWS. You can archive and retrieve data using the same backup software you currently use. Companies use Tape Gateway to allow them to continue to use their existing tape backup service and protocols.

Figure 8.3 shows how each of the different AWS Storage Gateway options works.

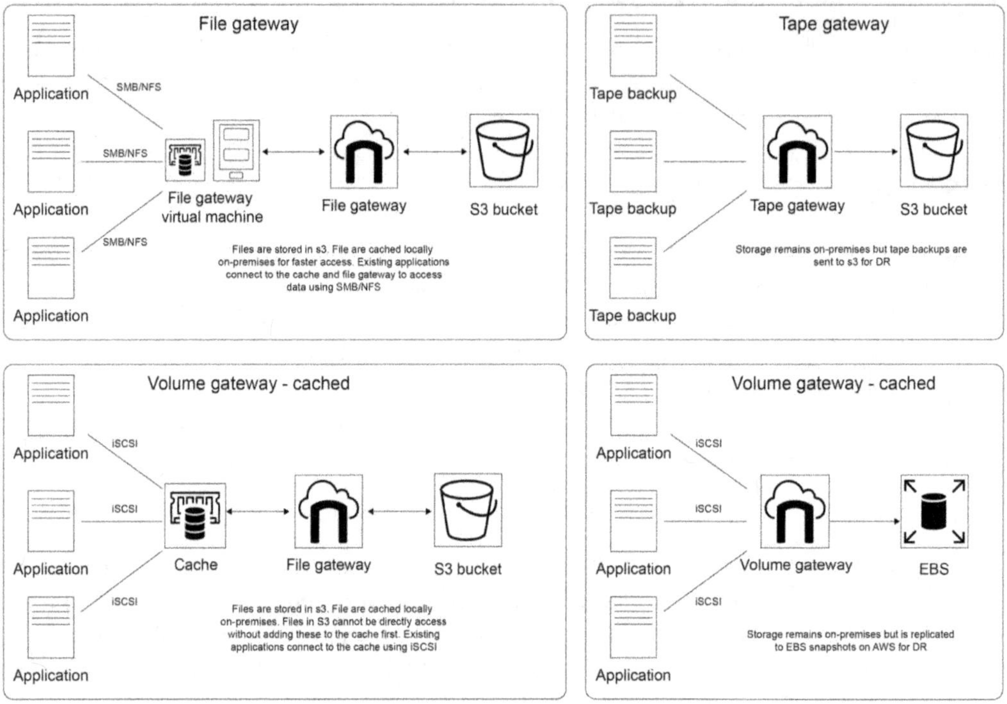

Figure 8.3: AWS Storage Gateway

The final storage transfer service is very different from the others. DataSync, Storage Gateway, and Transfer Family all rely on data being sent over the internet to migrate it, but what happens if the amount of data you have is too large to be sent over the internet in a timely manner or if the data is so sensitive that you cannot risk it being sent over the internet, even if it was encrypted? In these cases, the AWS Snow Family is your solution.

AWS Snow Family

In simple terms, AWS Snow Family devices are portable hard drives. You receive one in the post, plug it into your data center servers, download the data, and post it back to AWS. AWS then uploads the data into S3. Depending on your chosen device, it can run automated tasks, like in DataSync, to move your files from S3 into EFS or FSx. However, these devices are much more than just portable hard drives as they contain a small computer that can run data processing jobs directly on the device without waiting for the data to be uploaded to AWS.

There are two different types of Snow devices. Snowcone is a compact, portable device designed for smaller data transfers and edge computing in environments where space, power, and cooling are limited. It has 8 TB of storage and can operate in harsh conditions, making it ideal for collecting and processing data in remote locations such as oil rigs, military bases, or disaster zones.

The other device is the larger Snowball. It has two main variants: **Snowball Edge Storage Optimized** and **Snowball Edge Compute Optimized**. These devices are larger than Snowcone, with storage capacities ranging from 42 TB to 210 TB, depending on the model. Snowball devices are designed for bulk data migration and support edge computing workloads. The Compute Optimized variant includes more powerful processing capabilities, making it suitable for running applications at the edge, such as IoT processing, machine learning inference, and data analytics, all while disconnected from the internet.

Edge computing with the Snow Family is used when you need to process data near where it is generated. For example, in a factory setting, you could use a Snowball Edge device to run real-time analytics on production data, allowing you to make instant decisions without waiting for data to be uploaded to the cloud. Similarly, Snowball Edge can perform advanced computations in remote exploration sites and store data locally, which can then be securely transferred to AWS for long-term storage and further processing when network connectivity is available.

Table 8.1 provides a review of the different storage services AWS offers:

Service	Description	Use Cases	Primary Target
AWS DataSync	Automates and accelerates data transfers between on-premises storage and AWS services	Large-scale data migrations, ongoing data transfers, cross-region data transfers, and disaster recovery	Moving large volumes of data between on-premises and AWS
AWS Transfer Family	Securely transfers files using SFTP, FTPS, and FTP directly into and out of Amazon S3	Integrating legacy file transfer workflows with AWS, secure file exchanges, and partner/customer data transfers	Maintaining traditional file transfer protocols with AWS
File Gateway	Stores on-premises files as objects in Amazon S3, with access via NFS or SMB protocols	Extending on-premises file storage to the cloud, simplifying cloud backup and archiving	Organizations with file-based workloads needing S3

Service	Description	Use Cases	Primary Target
Tape Gateway	Virtual tape library that stores backup data in Amazon S3 and archives in Glacier	Modernizing tape backup infrastructure, providing long-term archival storage, and reducing physical tape management	Companies using traditional tape backups
Volume Gateway	Provides cloud-backed storage volumes for block storage with local caching and asynchronous backups	Disaster recovery, data protection, hybrid cloud storage solutions, and low-latency access to cloud data	Organizations needing block storage with cloud backup
AWS Snow Family	Physical devices for transferring large datasets to AWS when online transfer isn't feasible	Data center migrations, large data transfers from remote locations, and offline data transfer needs	Moving petabyte-scale data where network speeds are slow

Table 8.1: Comparison of AWS storage transfer services

At the end of this section, you can now answer the storage transfer questions in the *SAA-C03* exam. Most of the time, these questions will be use-case and scenario-based. In the next section, you will learn how to migrate an application from on-premises to AWS using AWS Application Migration Service.

Application Migration

A common problem for many companies looking to migrate to AWS is what to do with their applications. Typically, they have been written to run on-premises, and modifying them or recreating them on AWS would result in too much work to make the migration worthwhile or cost-efficient. Most companies would prefer a lift and shift method where they can simply copy an entire server across to AWS to minimize the configuration changes needed and speed up the migration. **AWS Application Migration Service** (**AWS MGN**) allows you to migrate and modernize applications quickly with minimal downtime. It automatically converts your source servers to run natively on AWS without requiring application changes. This service simplifies and expedites migration by automating much of the manual work involved.

AWS MGN can also be used as a DR solution by keeping your on-premises servers in sync with a copy stored in AWS. If your local data center fails, you can cut over to the AWS version.

AWS MGN runs via a replication agent installed on-premises on the individual server level or at the hypervisor level. The agent connects to AWS and the local servers you want to migrate and acts as the controller. Once the agent is installed, you can initiate replication tasks via the AWS Management Console or the API. Similar to DataSync, you can set bandwidth limits and scheduling to minimize any impact on your day-to-day operations. When you configure a task, AWS creates small EC2 instances to act as replication servers, and they will handle the data transfer to the new servers in AWS.

Once the data is replicated, you can launch test instances to ensure everything works correctly before cutting over. You can use this time to modify any setting to allow the application to work with AWS. For example, you might need to change the storage location from an NFS share to an S3 bucket. When testing is complete and signed off, you can cut over to the new servers and remove the old on-premises infrastructure. If you are using AWS MGN to create a DR set of servers, you can leave the configuration in place and use continuous replication to keep them in sync. You would typically run the smallest instance sizes you can to keep the costs low, and when you need to cut or fail over, you can increase the size to handle the traffic. AWS MGN allows you to reverse the process after the on-premises servers are available again. Using this technique lets you move back and forth as required.

You have learned how to move your storage and applications to AWS. Now, you need to learn how to move the most complicated service: the database.

Database Migration

Imagine that your organization has operated a traditional on-premises database infrastructure for several years. Over time, your databases have grown in size and complexity, containing critical data for your applications and analytics. With the move toward modernizing your infrastructure and taking advantage of cloud benefits, you are considering migrating your databases to AWS. As you explore this transition, you will need to make important decisions about the migration strategy and the tools to use. Key considerations in your migration planning include the following:

- Do you want to perform a one-time migration of the entire database to AWS, and are you prepared to accept downtime?

- Do you need to synchronize your on-premises and AWS databases during the migration process to minimize downtime?

- Are you considering changing your database engine – for example, moving from a proprietary system such as Oracle to an open source solution such as PostgreSQL?

For example, if your goal is to move all your data to AWS and decommission your on-premises databases, you might opt for a one-time migration. Alternatively, if you are looking to minimize downtime, AWS can help you replicate your data to AWS while keeping the source database active during the migration. Additionally, suppose you want to reduce costs and increase flexibility. In that case, you might consider switching from a proprietary database engine to an open source one, such as migrating from Oracle to PostgreSQL. AWS offers a service to handle all these scenarios: **Database Migration Service (DMS)**.

DMS is a fully managed AWS service designed to handle many different database migrations into and out of AWS. DMS offers four different migration types, which you can combine to make a custom migration. The types are as follows:

- **One-time migration**: AWS DMS can perform a one-time bulk migration of your database to AWS. This is suitable for scenarios where you plan to transition to AWS fully and do not need to maintain on-premises databases.

- **Continuous replication**: AWS DMS supports continuous data replication from on-premises databases to AWS databases. This feature helps reduce downtime during migration, as your applications can continue to write to the source database while AWS DMS replicates the data.

- **Data transformation**: AWS DMS offers data transformation capabilities if your migration involves switching database engines or schemas. This includes converting database schemas and applying custom mappings to ensure compatibility with the target AWS database. You may also utilize the **AWS Schema Conversion Tool (AWS SCT)** to help rewrite application code and stored procedures in the database to allow you to change the database engine.

- **Database conversion**: DMS supports changing the database engine. For example, AWS DMS allows migrating from a proprietary database such as Oracle to an open source database such as PostgreSQL, helping you reduce licensing costs and avoid vendor lock-in.

Consider a scenario where your company needs to migrate a mission-critical database from an on-premises data center to AWS. The database is large, and you cannot afford significant downtime. You might use AWS DMS to set up continuous replication in this case. This way, you can migrate your data in phases, reducing the risk of service disruption. During the migration, you may also transform your database schema to remove old data that is no longer needed. AWS DMS supports the migration of a subset of data, allowing you to reduce your storage footprint during the migration process, saving time and effort.

Furthermore, AWS DMS enables you to migrate from a proprietary database engine to a more cost-effective and flexible open source solution, such as moving from Oracle to PostgreSQL. In one migration task, you can not only move from on-premises to AWS with minimal downtime but also switch your database engine and remove old data that is no longer required. DMS's flexibility and power make it a highly regarded and heavily used tool by many AWS customers.

DMS has three main components:

- **Replication instances**: These are fully managed EC2 instances controlled by AWS with the DMS software installed. These instances have security groups attached to control what databases they can access, and they can be set to be either public or private. If you need to migrate from outside of AWS, these typically must be set to public. You also have the option to make the instance run as a Multi-AZ to allow for resilience and failover.

- **Endpoints**: These are the connections to either your source or your target databases. These are like a connection string containing the hostname or IP, connection port, and connection attributes. Connection attributes are used to control how DMS talks to the endpoints and how it retrieves and processes data. Before the endpoint can be used, its connectivity needs to be tested. This is done via the replication instance; hence, the instance needs to exist before you can create endpoints.

- **Replication tasks**: The tasks contain instructions for how DMS will retrieve, modify, and apply the data. In the task, you define the source and target endpoints, set up criteria for which schemas and tables will be included, and, optionally, add transformation rules to modify the data during the migration.

> **Note**
>
> DMS also offers a serverless option where you do not need to pre-create a replication instance, but this is not a feature in the *SAA-C03* exam.

Replication tasks are where you define how the migration will run. The first decision is whether you want to do a one-off migration (full load), a continuous one (with **change data capture** or **CDC**), or both. A full load is often the most straightforward and fastest migration method, but it requires you to stop any changes in the source database while it runs. CDC is used if you want to minimize downtime as you can sync the source and target databases and then switch over when you are ready. You can split the task as well. You can create a single task to handle the full load and then create a second task to handle the CDC. The benefits of doing this are that you have better control over the tasks and can run each part with different optimization settings. If you are doing this, you will need to start the CDC with the right timestamp to ensure all data changes are captured; otherwise, you risk data loss. If you want to combine the tasks into one for easier administration, you can set the task to pause after the full load is completed before the CDC starts. This allows you to make sure the full load has been completed properly before spending time waiting for the CDC part to run.

DMS integrates with CloudWatch for monitoring. When you run a task, you can control the amount of logging for each part. The logging can be set to minimally log using the ERROR level up to full and comprehensive logging using DETAILED_DEBUG. Any log settings above WARNING will generate a high volume of logs, which will be charged for at standard CloudWatch rates; therefore, you should only use DEBUG logging during testing or if you are hitting unexplained errors during the DMS task.

> **Note**
>
> For those preparing for AWS certification exams, it is essential to understand that AWS DMS is unsuitable for some data migrations. For example, if you need to migrate block storage (such as EBS volumes), AWS DMS would not be appropriate. Instead, you should investigate other AWS tools specifically designed for block storage migrations.

Summary

In this chapter, you have learned about AWS's key services for data and application migrations. AWS Transfer Family facilitates the migration of files to and from Amazon S3 and Amazon EFS. AWS Application Migration Service automates the process of moving and modernizing applications on AWS. AWS Database Migration Service ensures secure and efficient database migrations with minimal downtime. By choosing the most appropriate service, you can efficiently migrate your data and applications to answer the migration-based questions in the *SAA-C03* exam. In the next chapter, you will be learning about serverless and application integration, which covers services such as AWS Lambda, AWS Simple Queue Service, and Amazon EventBridge.

Exam Readiness Drill - Chapter Review Questions

Apart from mastering key concepts, strong test-taking skills under time pressure are essential for acing your certification exam. That's why developing these abilities early in your learning journey is critical.

Exam readiness drills, using the free online practice resources provided with this book, help you progressively improve your time management and test-taking skills while reinforcing the key concepts you've learned.

HOW TO GET STARTED

- Open the link or scan the QR code at the bottom of this page

- If you have unlocked the practice resources already, log in to your registered account. If you haven't, follow the instructions in *Chapter 16* and come back to this page.

- Once you log in, click the START button to start a quiz

- We recommend attempting a quiz multiple times till you're able to answer most of the questions correctly and well within the time limit.

- You can use the following practice template to help you plan your attempts:

Working On Accuracy		
Attempt	Target	Time Limit
Attempt 1	40% or more	Till the timer runs out
Attempt 2	60% or more	Till the timer runs out
Attempt 3	75% or more	Till the timer runs out
Working On Timing		
Attempt 4	75% or more	1 minute before time limit
Attempt 5	75% or more	2 minutes before time limit
Attempt 6	75% or more	3 minutes before time limit

The above drill is just an example. Design your drills based on your own goals and make the most out of the online quizzes accompanying this book.

> **First time accessing the online resources?** 🔒
> You'll need to unlock them through a one-time process. **Head to** *Chapter 16* **for instructions.**

Open Quiz	
https://packt.link/SAAC03Ch08 OR scan this QR code →	

9
Serverless and Application Integration

Serverless computing has transformed the landscape of cloud-based infrastructure, providing users with scalable and highly available methods of running code without the need for direct server management. This chapter explores the core principles and services that underpin the serverless paradigm, with a focus on equipping you with the knowledge and skills required to design and implement efficient, cost-effective, and resilient serverless applications.

You will begin with an overview of serverless computing, where you will explore its key advantages, such as automatic scaling, pay-per-use pricing, and reduced operational overhead. This contextual foundation sets the stage for a detailed examination of AWS Lambda. You will gain a comprehensive understanding of the Lambda function architecture, including the concepts of event-driven invocation, concurrency management, and execution environment reuse. Having established the fundamentals of standalone serverless functions, the chapter dives into the realm of application integration, exploring the role of services such as Amazon SQS, Amazon SNS, and Amazon EventBridge. These managed messaging and event bus solutions enable the decoupling of microservices and the creation of scalable, event-driven architectures. You will learn about message ordering, deduplication, and dead-letter queues, as well as the trade-offs between standard and FIFO queues.

The final section of the chapter introduces AWS Step Functions, a powerful workflow orchestration service that allows the design and execution of complex multi-step processes. You will become familiar with the various state types available and how to use them to build serverless applications that are highly maintainable and extensible. By the conclusion of this chapter, you will have a good understanding of the key serverless and application integration services provided by AWS.

You will learn about the following topics in this chapter:

- Overview of Serverless

- AWS Lambda

- Serverless Integration

This expertise will prove invaluable as you prepare for the *AWS Certified Solutions Architect - Associate (SAA-C03)* examination.

Overview of Serverless

The name "serverless" is somewhat misleading. It implies that no servers are involved when running your code. But, of course, you know that code must run on something. Serverless is a deployment model that allows you, the users, to run your code in the cloud without having to worry about building the infrastructure. The code still runs on servers, but the servers are managed by the cloud provider, in this case, AWS.

The serverless model has many advantages:

- **Flexible, automatic scaling**: AWS ensures that the serverless service can scale up and down seamlessly to meet the demands of your application. This makes serverless great for spiky workloads where traffic patterns cannot be predicted.

- **Only pay for what you use**: With serverless, you do not pay for idle capacity. You pay only for the execution time of the job and storage.

- **Resiliency**: Fault tolerance is built into AWS serverless services by default, with no additional input from you. This is achieved by spreading your underlying infrastructure across different Availability Zones and removing single points of failure.

- **No server management**: You do not need to remember to patch your servers or keep them updated. Simply manage your application code. You will have to make sure any libraries you import are patched appropriately, however. This results in reduced time to market.

So, what use cases are serverless technologies used for? Every use case you can imagine – serverless has been used to create web applications, process data, build ML data pipelines, and so much more. One of the more famous users of serverless is Netflix. Netflix heavily relies on serverless technologies to process media files for presentation on its website for users to stream.

With the basics of serverless covered, you can now explore some of the serverless technologies that AWS offers. You will learn about the following:

- AWS Lambda

- Amazon SQS and Amazon SNS

- Amazon EventBridge

- AWS Step Functions

AWS Lambda

Arguably one of the most well-known serverless technologies, AWS Lambda is an event-driven code service that allows you to run code in several programming languages without provisioning a single server.

What Does Event-Driven Mean?

Event-driven means that the service or application is triggered by events. An event could be something like a change of state in an item of infrastructure, or it could be the receipt of a request to an API gateway. Lambda will execute code based on an event that it receives. Most services in AWS will generate an event when something changes, and Lambda can be configured to run in response to these events. Event-driven architectures are an effective way to build out an application with fully decoupled microservice components. In any event-driven architecture, there are typically three components: an event producer, an event ingestor, and an event consumer. AWS Lambda is an event consumer.

Lambda Functions

Each instance in AWS Lambda is called a Lamba function. There are three components to a Lambda function: the input, the function, and the output.

The input is how your Lambda function will be invoked. There are several ways to invoke a Lambda function:

- **Direct invocation**: This may be via the console, **command-line interface** (**CLI**), or **software development kit** (**SDK**), and may be synchronous or asynchronous.

- **Event trigger**: Many AWS services can generate events that trigger your Lambda to be invoked. Combined with EventBridge, you can even trigger your Lambda functions on a schedule.

- **Lambda function URLs**: For Lambda functions that you want to trigger directly from the internet, you can provision an HTTP endpoint.

The function contains your code, imported libraries, and configuration features, such as how much memory your Lambda function needs to run and environment variables it might need. The more memory you allocate to your Lambda function, the more expensive it is to run, so allocate memory wisely. Lambda supports several language runtimes: Java, Go, PowerShell, Node.js, C#, Python, and Ruby. If you need to use a runtime that is not natively supported, you can use your own runtime, but note that, in this case, you will be responsible for any library or language support you may require.

> **Note**
>
> A Lambda function can run for a maximum of 15 minutes. This is an important limit to remember and will often determine architectural choices. If an exam question mentions long-running workloads, Lambda will not be the correct option.
>
> Another important limit to remember is Lambda's hard limit of 10 GB for memory.

The output is what happens once your function has completed its execution. This is optional and depends on your use case, but you may want to complete additional actions once your code has run, such as sending an email via SNS, invoking another Lambda function, or sending an event to EventBridge.

Concurrency

Several invocations of your Lambda function can run in parallel, and this is called **concurrency**. While AWS handles the scaling to allow concurrent function executions, you should be aware of some limits and features that relate to this. First, by default, you are limited to 1,000 concurrent Lambda executions across all functions in a region. This limit can be increased if necessary.

There are two types of concurrency that can be configured in AWS Lambda, but to understand them, you first need to understand at a high level how Lambda works under the hood.

Each Lambda function invocation is launched in its own secure execution environment. This means that the environment first must be initialized. This is what is referred to as a "cold start" (i.e., the time taken to initialize the execution environment prior to code execution). The time to initialize an execution environment can vary depending on the runtime being used and the code to be executed. For some runtimes (Java, for example), this initialization period can be substantial. Once the environment is initialized, the code is then executed. If the Lambda function is invoked again while the first invocation is in progress, a new execution environment will be created to handle the new request. This means two invocations are running concurrently. When the first invocation completes, the execution environment will persist for a short amount of time, and if the Lambda function is invoked once more during this time, that execution environment will be reused. This invocation will be slightly quicker than the first and second executions because it will not have to be initialized again. If the Lambda function is not invoked soon after the previous invocation, the execution environment will be shut down.

Now that you have a better understanding of concurrency, look at the two types of concurrency you can configure in AWS Lambda: reserved concurrency and provisioned concurrency.

Reserved Concurrency

Remember that concurrency limits are applied to all Lambda functions in a region. Say, for example, you had a concurrency limit of 10 and 3 Lambda functions. At a particular point in time, Function A has four invocations running and Function B has five invocations running. This means that Function C could only have one invocation running until Function A or B finishes its invocations. You might have a critical Lambda function that always needs to have a minimum number of concurrent executions. You can configure reserved concurrency for a Lambda function to ensure it always has X number of concurrent executions available. Because these will always be available to that one function, they cannot be used by any other Lambda function, even if they are not in use. This is important to remember because this reduces the number of concurrent executions the rest of the Lambda functions in the account can use. Reserved concurrency is free.

Provisioned Concurrency

Sometimes, applications are very sensitive to latency, and even the several-millisecond cold start initialization time of an execution environment can add too much time to an execution. When this occurs, you can provision concurrency. This will ensure that you have X number of execution environments pre-warmed at all times ready for your invocations. There is an additional charge for provisioned concurrency, so it should only be used when latency is more important than cost.

Logging and Monitoring

Logging and monitoring with AWS Lambda are straightforward because Lambda is integrated with CloudWatch by default.

Lambda provides several options for logging and monitoring functions:

- **CloudWatch Logs**: Lambda automatically logs function execution metadata and logs to CloudWatch Logs. This includes logs from the Lambda service as well as any logs produced within the function code. Logs are organized into log groups and streams. Functions can write logs to stdout/stderr, and they will also be sent to CloudWatch Logs. The log level can also be configured.

- **CloudWatch Metrics**: Key Lambda metrics such as invocation count, duration, and errors are published to CloudWatch Metrics. This provides performance monitoring over time. You will also find concurrency metrics here.

- **X-Ray tracing**: Lambda functions can be traced using AWS X-Ray to analyze requests as they travel through the application. This helps identify bottlenecks and errors.

Lambda is great for short workloads, but what if you have a workload that you know will take longer than 15 minutes to run? This is where you begin to consider containers, and specifically, Fargate. You can read more about Fargate in *Chapter 4, Compute*.

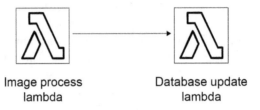

Image process
lambda

Database update
lambda

Figure 9.1: One Lambda function calling another Lambda function

Lambda functions are often small components that make up a larger application, and you might have Lambda functions call other Lambda functions (*Figure 9.1*). It is therefore important to ensure communication between these Lambda functions takes place seamlessly. Depending on the use case, there are several services that can orchestrate communication between Lambda functions and other AWS services. This topic is known as application integration.

Application Integration Services

Application integration is the process of connecting different applications or application components to allow them to share and exchange data. This helps you build applications that can reuse existing services and systems to do more with less coding. Take a walk through some use cases and use the right tool for each one.

In *Figure 9.1*, you have one Lambda function directly invoking another Lambda function. This can be problematic. If the second Lambda function has reached its scaling limit at the point it has been invoked, the request will simply be lost. Ideally, you need a buffer to hold requests until the Database Update Lambda function is ready to accept them. This is the purpose of message queues and, on AWS, that service is Amazon SQS. Take a look at *Figure 9.2*, which explains this:

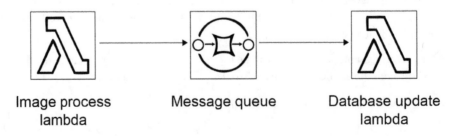

Image process
lambda

Message queue

Database update
lambda

Figure 9.2: A message queue acts as a middleman, storing messages for consumers

Amazon SQS

Imagine a busy restaurant kitchen, where chefs are constantly receiving orders from the wait staff. Without a proper system in place, the flow of orders could quickly become chaotic and overwhelming. The chefs might find themselves bombarded with orders, unable to keep up with the pace, leading to confusion, delays, and, potentially, even lost or incorrect orders.

This is similar to the challenge faced by many IT systems and applications, where different components need to communicate and exchange data. Without a mechanism to manage and buffer these communications, the system can become overloaded, leading to lost or dropped messages, and ultimately, a breakdown of the overall application.

This is where message queues come into play, much like a centralized order management system in the restaurant kitchen. The message queue acts as an intermediary, receiving and storing messages from producers (such as web applications or mobile apps) and then delivering them to consumers (such as backend services or databases) at a controlled, manageable pace. In AWS, this service is called Amazon SQS.

Amazon SQS is a fully managed message queuing service that can be used to decouple and scale microservices, distributed systems, and serverless applications. Producers can send messages to a queue and consumers, such as Lambda or EC2, can receive and process messages from the queue. In effect, the message queue acts as a middleman, storing messages until they can be processed by the consumers (*Figure 9.2*).

A typical flow with SQS is as follows:

1. An application creates a message and sends it to an SQS queue.
2. A consumer will either listen for messages entering the queue or poll the queue for new messages.
3. When the consumer selects a message, this message is locked, and a visibility timeout is activated. This prevents another consumer from picking up a message for processing.
4. When the consumer has completed processing the message, it should send a `DeleteMessage` API call to the message queue. This ensures that the message is not reprocessed.

Understanding how SQS works will help you choose the correct answer to questions about how Lambda picks up messages from queues.

It is the responsibility of the consumer application to remove the message from the SQS queue. This is not done automatically.

> **Note**
>
> Ensure that the visibility timeout is longer than the processing time of the message. For example, if it takes a Lambda function 15 seconds to process a message, ensure the visibility timeout is greater than 15 seconds. The default timeout is 30 seconds.

If a message cannot be processed, it will become available in the queue once more to be processed by the next available consumer. This is great for accommodating transient issues with consumers, but what if there is a problem with the message itself? This could result in an infinite loop of consumers trying to process the message. This is where a dead-letter queue is required.

Dead Letter Queues

Dead letter queues capture messages that cannot be processed and store them until you can investigate the problem. You define the maximum number of times a message can be received by a consumer, and when that number has been reached, the message is placed in the dead letter queue.

Polling Methods

SQS is a poll-based message queue. This means that consumers must check, or poll, the queue for available messages to process. There are two polling methods: short polling and long polling. By default, SQS uses short polling. In short polling, the `ReceiveMessage` API call will query a subset of SQS servers and return any messages it found or return empty if no messages were found. In long polling, the ReceiveMessage API call will query all servers for an SQS queue. It will return a response only when it finds a message or the poll request times out. There is a maximum of 20 seconds for the long polling timeout.

Queue Types

SQS has two different queue types: standard and **First In, First Out (FIFO)**.

Standard queues are the default queue type for SQS. They attempt to order messages in the order they entered the queue, but this is not guaranteed. It can support nearly unlimited transactions per second and guarantees at-least-once delivery of a message. As mentioned previously, if the visibility timeout is not set correctly, a message could be processed more than once.

FIFO queues maintain strict ordering of messages as they enter a queue, within the message group they are assigned. This means that only one message can be in flight at any one time, and this affects the throughput capacity to around 300 transactions per second. FIFO queues are more expensive than standard queues, so be mindful of questions that ask for the most cost-effective solution.

Message Ordering

Sometimes, you want to ensure that messages are processed in the exact same order that they entered the queue. To do this, SQS uses message groups, and this concept can be tough to understand. The following steps outline what happens when a message enters a FIFO queue:

1. Each message is assigned a unique message group ID and message deduplication ID when sent to the FIFO queue.

2. Only one message within a message group can be received from the queue at a time. Messages within the same group will be received in the order they were sent.

3. After a message is received, it is not available to be received again because of message deduplication, ensuring each message is processed only once (exactly-once processing).

4. Messages from different message groups can be processed concurrently, allowing parallel processing of ordered message streams within the same queue.

This is how messages are ordered correctly. But you will notice that message deduplication is mentioned in *Step 3*. What exactly is message deduplication?

Message Deduplication

Message deduplication is the process of removing duplicate messages from a queue. This might happen if a Lambda function accidentally picks up the same message twice because of an incorrectly set message timeout. The steps for this process are as follows:

1. When a message is sent to a FIFO queue, it is assigned a unique message deduplication ID.

2. If a message with the same deduplication ID is sent again within five minutes, it will not be delivered to the queue. SQS will ignore the duplicate message to prevent it from being processed more than once.

3. After five minutes, if the same deduplication ID is used, SQS will accept the message but will not deliver it until the original message with that ID is deleted from the queue. This ensures exactly-once processing.

4. The five-minute deduplication window allows time for the first message to be processed and deleted normally before a duplicate can be delivered, preventing duplicates, even if messages are processed out of order.

In addition to deduplication by ID, as described in the preceding steps, SQS FIFO also supports content deduplication. When enabled, SQS will create a SHA-256 hash using the body of the message and this becomes the message deduplication ID. If a message with the same body is received, the hash will be the same and it will not be processed.

Table 9.1 shows a comparison between standard and FIFO SQS queues:

	Standard	FIFO
Ordering	Best effort ordering	Order is maintained within message group
Throughput	Nearly unlimited transactions per second	300 transactions per second
Delivery	At least once delivery	Exactly once delivery

Table 9.1: Table comparing standard and FIFO SQS queues

After a Lambda function has finished processing, you may wish to notify several downstream services or people that the processing is complete in what is called a **fan-out pattern**. SQS is a one-to-one asynchronous service, which makes it unsuitable for this job. There are two services that can be used to address this need: Amazon SNS and Amazon EventBridge. Let's take a look at SNS first.

Amazon SNS

Amazon Simple Notification Service (SNS) is a fully managed pub/sub messaging service that uses a one-to-many model. Pub/sub means it uses a publish/subscribe model of operating. Publishers will publish messages to an SNS topic, and subscribers will subscribe to a topic to receive the messages that were published to it. SNS is a synchronous service; the messages are not held in the topic but, instead, are pushed out to subscribers as soon as they are received. Once a message is pushed out, there is no way to recall it. Each topic can have over 12 million subscribers, which means it has a huge fan-out distribution.

SNS can send messages in two ways, **application-to-application (A2A)** or **application-to-person (A2P)**. A2A messaging supports AWS Lambda, Amazon SQS as Amazon Kinesis Data Firehose endpoints as subscribers, as well as other HTTPS endpoints. A2P messaging lets you fan out messages via SMS, email, and mobile push notifications.

Like Amazon SQS, SNS also has standard and FIFO SNS topic types. The features are similar to SQS FIFO and have been outlined in *Table 9.2*:

	Standard	FIFO
Ordering	Best effort ordering	Order is maintained
Throughput	Nearly unlimited transactions per second	300 messages per second
Delivery	At least once delivery	Exactly once delivery
Subscription types	Amazon SQS, Amazon Kinesis Data Firehose, AWS Lambda, HTTPS, SMS, email, mobile push	SQS FIFO queues only

Table 9.2: Comparison of Standard and FIFO SNS topics

Dead letter queues can be configured for SNS to store messages that could not be sent to subscribers.

Finally, SNS supports encryption both at rest and in transit.

Now, let's take a look at Amazon EventBridge.

Amazon EventBridge

Amazon EventBridge is a relatively new service in AWS. It is very similar to SNS in that it allows messages to be fanned out at a huge scale, but it has some unique features that might make it the more appropriate choice for a use case.

Amazon EventBridge is a serverless event bus service that makes it easy to connect applications together using events. It supports ingesting events from various sources such as AWS services, applications, and third-party SaaS applications.

The EventBridge service uses new concepts that you may be unfamiliar with:

- **Message bus**: While this sounds complicated, a message bus is essentially just a container for a group of messages with logic for how to process those messages, much like an SNS topic.

- **Events**: A JSON structure that contains the payload and other metadata. This is essentially a "message."

- **Rules**: In EventBridge, you configure rules that define how a message should be routed to downstream consumers. For example, if the payload contains a particular keyword, route to Target X. A key restriction to note here is that each rule has a limit of five targets. You can also define a schedule rule that will run at a time scheduled in a `cron` expression you define.

- **Targets**: A target is simply a downstream consumer of the event.

One of the unique features of EventBridge is that it has built-in support for third-party integrations. This means you can ingest data from a whole range of third-party SaaS applications without needing to write any code. You can only use supported third-party integrations.

EventBridge has several features:

- **Pipes**: EventBridge Pipes is a no-code method of creating rules to connect producers to consumers. The pipe is the rule, and a number of sources can send messages to the pipe, such as SNS, SQS, and third-party SaaS providers. This can be useful for streaming data from DynamoDB to Kinesis.

- **Scheduler**: EventBridge Scheduler allows you to schedule the execution of tasks or workflows at user-defined intervals using cron expressions or schedule rates.

- **Schema registry**: The EventBridge schema registry is a way to define and manage the structure, or schema, of the events that flow through your EventBridge event bus. It acts like a central catalog of event schemas. This allows you to ensure that the data in your events is consistent and easy to understand so that both the source and consumer applications expect the same event. The default AWS schema registry contains all schemas for all events produced by AWS services. There is also a discovered schema registry, which collects the schemas of events from non-AWS components if schema discovery has been enabled on the event bus.

You should have a high-level understanding of each of the features of EventBridge so that you can understand which answer to select in the exam. Often, questions will ask for the easiest or simplest way to implement a solution, and EventBridge provides several out-of-the-box managed solutions that make development much simpler.

SNS or EventBridge?

With so many similarities between SNS and EventBridge, how do you decide which one to use?

Ultimately, it comes down to your use case. EventBridge is the ideal tool when you need to ingest data easily from supported SaaS providers, when you want to do complex filtering on incoming events, and when you want to schedule events that run at a time you define. When you require high throughput and need to reach a large number of subscribers simply, SNS is the better option.

SQS, SNS, and EventBridge are excellent for providing communication between serverless application components. But what if you had several Lambda functions or API calls that you needed to orchestrate in a particular order or based on conditions? You could include complex logic in your Lambda, but that wastes processing time that could be spent doing more useful tasks. This is where AWS Step Functions comes in handy.

AWS Step Functions

AWS Step Functions is a fully managed workflow orchestration service. With Workflow Studio, you can build your workflow in a drag-and-drop manner, or you can write your workflows programmatically using **Amazon States Language** (**ASL**). ASL can be written in either JSON or YAML.

A workflow in Step Functions is called a state machine, and each step in the workflow is a state. If you are unsure of what a state machine is, let's consider a vending machine. A vending machine will go through several states as the user provides input to the machine. This might look something like *Figure 9.3*:

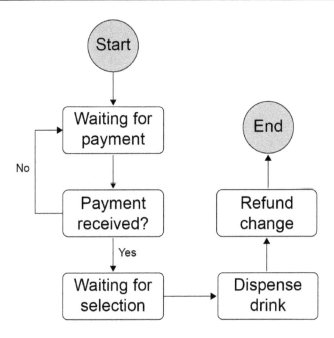

Figure 9.3: Simple diagram of a potential vending machine state machine

Data is passed from step to step so that each state can evaluate the data to make decisions. In this case, the payment amount will be transferred from step to step so that, in the end, the change can be calculated and returned.

There are several types of state that can be used in an AWS Step Functions function:

- **Pass**: A pass state simply takes the input and passes it to the output.
- **Task**: A task state is an action that will be performed, such as invoking a Lambda function or calling an AWS service API.
- **Choice**: A choice state provides conditional logic to determine the next action that should be taken.
- **Wait**: This state simply waits for a specified amount of time. It is useful when the previous step is asynchronous and takes time to complete.
- **Succeed**: This state stops an execution with a `Success` end state.
- **Fail**: This state stops an execution with a `Failed` end state.
- **Map**: The map state runs a defined set of actions for each item in a dataset in parallel. You define how many maps can be run in parallel.
- **Parallel**: The parallel state allows you to branch your workflow and run states in parallel.

- With this in mind, take a look at *Figure 9.4* that shows how the vending machine state machine might look as a step function:

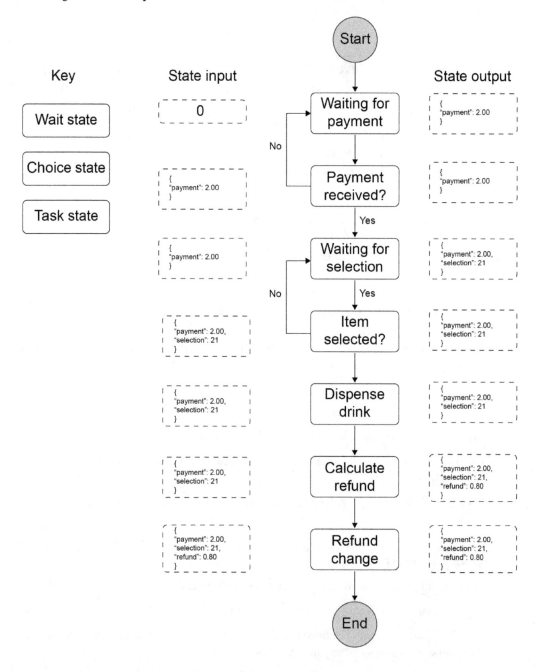

Figure 9.4: Step function workflow of a vending machine process

While this might not be an exact implementation of what a vending machine step function might look like, it gives a good overview. A step function uses JSON structures containing data that get passed from state to state. It is fully within your control what data is passed in and out of each state, which is useful because there is a hard limit of 1 MB for the request size. This also includes the request headers.

In *Figure 9.4*, you can see the type of state for each step. The blue task states in this example are small Lambda functions that only perform the task for that state. But in other use cases, these task states could be calls to SNS to send out emails or even API calls to an external HTTPS endpoint.

There are two types of step function: standard and express. Standard is the default state machine type and is the best option for most use cases, but if you are building a state machine that will have a high event rate with a short execution duration, you may want to consider express workflows.

The main differences between standard and express workflows are shown in *Table 9.3*:

	Standard	**Express**
Execution	Exactly-once execution	At-least-once execution
Duration	One year	Five minutes
Pricing	Per state transition	By execution length and memory consumption
Retries	Yes	No

Table 9.3: Comparison of standard and express workflows

Ultimately, express workflows are high-performance, lightweight state machines, and standard workflows fit most use cases.

Summary

In this chapter, you have gained a comprehensive understanding of the key serverless and application integration services provided by AWS. You have explored the benefits of serverless computing through AWS Lambda, including its event-driven model, concurrency management, and monitoring capabilities. Additionally, you have learned about the role of services such as Amazon SQS, SNS, and EventBridge in enabling asynchronous communication and fan-out distribution for your serverless applications. Finally, you have explored how AWS Step Functions can help you orchestrate complex workflows by coordinating the execution of various AWS services and Lambda functions. With this knowledge, you are now equipped to design and build robust, scalable, and event-driven serverless architectures on the AWS platform, which are highly relevant for the *AWS Certified Solutions Architect - Associate exam*. You will learn about the key AWS security services in the next chapter.

Exam Readiness Drill - Chapter Review Questions

Apart from mastering key concepts, strong test-taking skills under time pressure are essential for acing your certification exam. That's why developing these abilities early in your learning journey is critical.

Exam readiness drills, using the free online practice resources provided with this book, help you progressively improve your time management and test-taking skills while reinforcing the key concepts you've learned.

HOW TO GET STARTED

- Open the link or scan the QR code at the bottom of this page

- If you have unlocked the practice resources already, log in to your registered account. If you haven't, follow the instructions in *Chapter 16* and come back to this page.

- Once you log in, click the START button to start a quiz

- We recommend attempting a quiz multiple times till you're able to answer most of the questions correctly and well within the time limit.

- You can use the following practice template to help you plan your attempts:

Working On Accuracy		
Attempt	Target	Time Limit
Attempt 1	40% or more	Till the timer runs out
Attempt 2	60% or more	Till the timer runs out
Attempt 3	75% or more	Till the timer runs out
Working On Timing		
Attempt 4	75% or more	1 minute before time limit
Attempt 5	75% or more	2 minutes before time limit
Attempt 6	75% or more	3 minutes before time limit

The above drill is just an example. Design your drills based on your own goals and make the most out of the online quizzes accompanying this book.

First time accessing the online resources? 🔒

You'll need to unlock them through a one-time process. **Head to** *Chapter 16* **for instructions.**

Open Quiz

https://packt.link/SAAC03Ch09

OR scan this QR code →

10
Security

Security in the cloud is more important than ever before. As companies increasingly move sensitive data and critical applications into the public cloud, securing those assets needs to be a top priority. The shared responsibility model of the cloud means that while AWS handles the security of the underlying cloud infrastructure, you are responsible for securing the resources that you deploy into the cloud.

Neglecting cloud security can lead to disastrous outcomes, including data breaches, service disruptions, financial loss, and damaged reputations. No organization wants to become the next high-profile data breach headline in the news. AWS has a vast variety of services to help with security, and knowing where to start can be a challenge.

This chapter provides an overview of the key AWS security services. Security features included in services will be covered in their relevant chapter. In this chapter, you will focus on the services that specifically deliver security features, such as Amazon Macie and Amazon GuardDuty.

Controlling Access

Role-based access control (**RBAC**) is a major approach for managing permissions and access to resources in AWS.

With RBAC, access is determined by assigning users to roles that have been pre-defined with specific privileges associated with them. For example, a **developer** role might have permissions to create, delete, and modify resources in services such as EC2, S3, and DynamoDB. Meanwhile, a **security analyst** role has read-only access to some logging and monitoring services. As new employees join, they are assigned the appropriate role(s) for their job function. Roles simplify administration since privileges are tied to the role, not each individual user. Changing permissions means updating the role rather than many user accounts. Please see *Chapter 3, Identity and Access Management*, for more information about **identity and access management** (**IAM**) and RBAC.

In addition to IAM roles, RBAC can be applied across several other AWS services. S3 buckets can have bucket policies defined. The purpose of a bucket policy is to define who can or cannot access the contents of that bucket, as well as the actions that users can perform. You can restrict access to specific IP addresses, force encryption, or require multi-factor authentication, making it a versatile tool in the AWS security toolbox.

Policies can also be applied to KMS keys, but unlike bucket policies, it is mandatory for a KMS key to have a policy, and KMS keys can only have a single policy. You will read about KMS keys in more detail in the *Encryption and Secrets Management* section of this chapter, but essentially, KMS keys are encryption keys used to encrypt data on AWS.

Finally, **service control policies (SCPs)** are policies applied at the organization level that restrict what services can be used within accounts in your organization. They do not grant permission to users or roles in your organization but, instead, set limits on the actions that the users and roles can perform. You will learn more about organizations and SCPs in *Chapter 11, Management and Governance*.

Encryption and Secrets Management

In this section, you will explore encryption and secrets management and the relevant services for both of these concepts in AWS.

Encryption is a fundamental aspect of data security, transforming data into a secure format that is unreadable to unauthorized users. This process is crucial for protecting sensitive information from unauthorized access and ensuring data integrity. AWS offers several encryption solutions to safeguard data both at rest and in transit, utilizing advanced encryption algorithms and key management services. You will first learn about how to encrypt data while it is being stored.

Encryption at Rest

AWS provides various methods to encrypt data. At-rest encryption protects data stored on AWS services such as **Simple Storage Service (S3)**, **Relational Database Service (RDS)**, and **Elastic Block Store (EBS)**, ensuring that stored data remains secure. Some services will encrypt data at rest by default, such as S3, while others require you to configure encryption, such as EBS and RDS. It is recommended that encryption be enabled wherever possible.

Data can be encrypted before it reaches AWS (client-side encryption), or it can be encrypted once it is stored in AWS (server-side encryption). Client-side encryption provides you with the most control over encryption because you encrypt the data with a key that only you possess, which means that data is encrypted throughout the movement process.

S3 supports both **server-side encryption (SSE)** and client-side encryption. For server-side encryption, you have the choice of using an S3-managed key (which is the default option to secure your objects), a KMS-managed key, or a customer-provided encryption key. If no key is provided, then S3 will encrypt data at rest by default using an S3-managed key. Client-side encryption requires the data to be encrypted before uploading it to S3.

EBS, Redshift, and RDS all support encryption using an AWS KMS key. Unlike S3, this must be configured and, in the case of EBS, encryption at rest will encrypt not just the data at rest but also the snapshots. For RDS, encryption at rest will encrypt the backups, read replicas, and snapshots.

DynamoDB will automatically encrypt data using AWS-owned keys if a KMS key is not provided, and Lambda will encrypt environment variables in the same way. In addition, any files you upload to Lambda, such as deployment packages or layer archives, will be encrypted.

Encryption in Transit

In-transit encryption secures data as it moves between AWS services and endpoints, preventing unauthorized access during transmission. AWS ensures that communication between AWS data centers is encrypted at the physical layer, and communication within a VPC or between peered VPCs is encrypted at the network layer. It is the user's responsibility to ensure further encryption takes place, for example, enforcing HTTPS with S3.

Use HTTPS endpoints where possible to ensure data is secured with TLS. Use AWS PrivateLink to ensure private access to AWS services within your VPC to prevent traffic from going out to the public internet. Use AWS Direct Connect to establish secure connections with your on-premises environment, which can be encrypted using IPsec.

Consider using certificate-based encryption in transit for websites. When you connect to secured websites, you have probably noticed a small padlock next to the browser bar, depending on the web browser that you prefer to use. This padlock indicates that additional encryption is in use on that website using a certificate.

Two protocols are often used for securing websites: **Secure Sockets Layer (SSL)** and **Transport Layer Security (TLS)**. While these protocols work similarly, TLS is the more modern protocol and is used more. When you make a request to a website secured with SSL/TLS, the server will present the certificate to prove its authenticity. The client determines whether the certificate is legitimate for the website that you're trying to access and, if satisfied, continues the networking handshake process to establish the connection, ensuring that the traffic between the client and the server is encrypted. This is a simplified explanation but gives an overview of how certificates work.

In AWS, **AWS Certificate Manager** (**ACM**) simplifies the provisioning, managing, and deploying of SSL/TLS certificates, which secure network communications and verify the identity of websites and internal resources. ACM allows you to easily request both public and private certificates, with automatic renewal to ensure continuous security without manual intervention. These certificates can be deployed with AWS services such as CloudFront, Elastic Load Balancing, and API Gateway. ACM provides a centralized interface for managing all your certificates, making tracking and renewal straightforward. Public certificates from ACM are free, eliminating additional costs. Additionally, ACM offers AWS Private Certificate Authority (CA) for managing private certificates for internal applications, maintaining the same ease of use and automated features. This service significantly enhances security and reduces administrative overhead, allowing you to focus on your applications.

AWS Key Management Service (KMS)

You have seen KMS being mentioned several times so far – you can now explore what KMS is and how it can be leveraged in AWS environments.

AWS KMS allows you to create, manage, and control cryptographic keys across a wide range of AWS services. The key features include the following:

- **Centralized key management**: Manage keys for various AWS services from a single location
- **Key policies and IAM integration**: Define permissions and access controls for keys using IAM policies and KMS key policies
- **Automatic key rotation**: Enable automatic rotation of keys to enhance security
- **Auditing and logging**: Monitor key usage with AWS CloudTrail

KMS allows you to create and manage **customer master keys** (**CMKs**), which are used to control access to encrypted data. These keys can be either symmetric, where the same key is used for both encryption and decryption, or asymmetric, where a public and private key pair is used. Symmetric keys are commonly used for data encryption, while asymmetric keys are often used for digital signatures and other operations requiring a pair of keys. Keys can be single-region or multi-region, where multi-region keys let you decrypt data in a different Region from the one it was encrypted in.

When you create a key in KMS, you can define permissions using AWS IAM policies and KMS key policies, giving you granular control over who can use and manage the keys. KMS supports the creation of keys that are managed entirely by AWS, customer-managed keys that you control, and customer-provided keys that you import into KMS.

One of the key features of AWS KMS is automatic key rotation, which enhances security by periodically changing the key material without requiring manual intervention. This ensures that the encryption keys remain secure over time without disrupting access to the encrypted data. You can configure key rotation policies to suit your security requirements and compliance needs.

KMS also provides detailed logging and auditing capabilities through AWS CloudTrail. Every use of a KMS key is logged, allowing you to track how and when keys are accessed or used. This audit trail is crucial for security monitoring, forensic analysis, and compliance reporting, ensuring that you have visibility into all cryptographic operations performed with your keys.

AWS KMS is charged by each key created as well as the number and type of requests to the key. For AWS-managed keys, you will be charged for API requests to the key. As always, check the AWS website for the latest pricing information.

AWS Secrets Manager

Secrets management involves securely storing, accessing, and managing sensitive information such as passwords, API keys, and cryptographic keys. It ensures that these secrets are protected from unauthorized access and misuse while facilitating secure access by authorized users or applications.

AWS Secrets Manager is a fully managed service designed to simplify and enhance the security of managing sensitive information within your AWS environment. It provides a scalable solution for securely storing, retrieving, and automatically rotating secrets such as database credentials, API keys, and other sensitive data.

One of its key features is secure storage, where secrets are encrypted at rest using AWS KMS. This ensures that sensitive information remains protected from unauthorized access. Fine-grained IAM policies allow you to customize access controls, specifying who has permission to access and manage secrets within your AWS account. This granular control ensures that only authorized users and applications can retrieve or modify sensitive information.

AWS Secrets Manager automates the process of rotating secrets, such as database passwords and API keys, based on configurable schedules. Automated rotation helps improve security by regularly updating credentials without manual intervention, reducing the risk of unauthorized access due to compromised secrets. This can be done in one of two ways: managed rotation, where Secrets Manager configures and manages the rotation, or Lambda function rotation, where a Lambda function is used to update the secret and resulting database or service using that secret.

Managed rotation is supported by a limited number of services: Amazon Aurora, Amazon ECS, Amazon RDS, and Amazon Redshift. For Aurora, RDS, and Redshift, managed rotation can only rotate the master user or admin credentials. For any other user credential rotations, Lambda function rotation should be used.

Version control is maintained within Secrets Manager, keeping a history of previous versions of secrets. This feature enables you to audit changes over time and retrieve previous versions if necessary, ensuring traceability and compliance with security policies.

All interactions and API calls made to Secrets Manager are logged using AWS CloudTrail, providing detailed audit logs for monitoring and compliance purposes. This visibility helps track access to secrets and changes made to them, enhancing security monitoring.

AWS Secrets Manager supports integration with AWS CloudFormation, enabling you to define and manage secrets resources using infrastructure-as-code principles. This capability facilitates automation and consistency in deploying secrets across your AWS environment.

> **Note**
>
> There is a comparable service within Systems Manager known as Parameter Store. Parameter Store enables the storage of various plaintext values necessary for different automation tasks, including secrets that can be encrypted. However, a significant distinction between Secrets Manager and Parameter Store lies in secret rotation capabilities. Unlike Secrets Manager, Parameter Store does not support automatic secret rotation. Therefore, when faced with an exam question specifying a requirement for secret rotation and both Parameter Store and Secrets Manager are options, selecting Secrets Manager would be the appropriate choice.

Threat Detection

Threat detection in AWS involves the proactive identification and mitigation of potential security risks and malicious activities within your cloud environment. It includes a range of techniques and tools designed to monitor, analyze, and respond to suspicious behaviors or anomalies that could indicate security threats or breaches. Effective threat detection in AWS helps ensure the integrity, confidentiality, and availability of data and applications by swiftly identifying and mitigating security incidents before they escalate. The four services that we will cover in relation to threat detection are AWS Security Hub, Amazon Inspector, Amazon GuardDuty, and Amazon Macie.

You do not need to know these services in detail for the SAA-CO3 exam, but you should understand what they are at a high level and understand how each service differs from the others. This will help you determine the correct answer for exam questions.

Given how large an AWS estate can be, how can you identify vulnerabilities across all your AWS resources and accounts? Amazon Inspector is the perfect solution.

Amazon Inspector

Amazon Inspector is an automated security assessment service. It helps you identify vulnerabilities and deviations from security best practices in Amazon EC2 instances and container images.

One of the key features of Amazon Inspector is its ability to perform comprehensive security assessments using pre-defined rules packages. These rules packages are regularly updated to check for **common vulnerabilities and exposures (CVEs)**, unintended network accessibility, and non-compliance with security best practices. This helps you identify and address potential security issues before they can be exploited by malicious actors.

Amazon Inspector also offers the ability to create custom security assessment templates and rules packages, allowing you to tailor the service to your specific security requirements and regulatory compliance needs. This level of customization is particularly valuable when operating in highly regulated industries or industries with unique security challenges.

Another important feature of Amazon Inspector is its integration with other AWS security services, including AWS Security Hub and Amazon GuardDuty. This integration allows you to centralize and correlate security findings from multiple sources, providing a more holistic view of your security posture. This enables faster and more effective incident response and remediation.

Amazon Inspector is great for detecting vulnerabilities, but there are more threats to monitor than just vulnerabilities. Most businesses will leverage real-time threat-monitoring tools to protect their platforms. Take a look at Amazon GuardDuty.

Amazon GuardDuty

Amazon GuardDuty is a threat detection service that continuously monitors and analyzes specific AWS data sources and logs within your AWS environment. By leveraging threat intelligence feeds and machine learning models, GuardDuty identifies and alerts you to unexpected and potentially unauthorized activities. These activities include escalation of privileges, use of exposed credentials, and communication with malicious IP addresses and domains. GuardDuty also detects malware presence on Amazon EC2 instances and container workloads, as well as newly uploaded files in Amazon S3 buckets. Moreover, it scrutinizes login event patterns on databases for anomalies. For instance, GuardDuty can uncover compromised EC2 instances running malicious software or engaging in unauthorized activities such as cryptocurrency mining. It also monitors AWS account access for suspicious behavior, such as unusual infrastructure deployments in unfamiliar regions or atypical API calls suggesting security policy modifications.

Each finding in GuardDuty is categorized as high, medium, or low and provides recommendations for remediation. The foundational features of GuardDuty need to be enabled, and it monitors CloudTrail event logs and management events, VPC flow logs, and DNS logs. Additional insights can be gained for EKS, Lambda, RDS, and S3, plus additional malware detection for EC2 and runtime monitoring. Each of these is available as its own package and is available at an extra cost.

Finally, GuardDuty can be integrated with Security Hub, which allows you to see a snapshot of your security posture in one place.

Amazon Macie

Amazon Macie is a fully managed data security and data privacy service. It is designed to help you discover, monitor, and protect your sensitive data stored in Amazon S3 buckets.

Key features of Amazon Macie are as follows:

- **Sensitive data discovery**: Macie uses machine learning and pattern matching to automatically discover and classify sensitive data, such as **personally identifiable information** (**PII**), financial data, and intellectual property, stored in Amazon S3.

- **Continuous monitoring**: Macie continuously monitors data access and usage activity in S3 to detect and alert on potential data security and privacy issues, such as unauthorized access, data leaks, or unusual user behavior.

- **Anomaly detection**: Macie uses machine learning to establish a baseline of normal data access and usage patterns, and then alerts you to any anomalous activity that may indicate a potential security or privacy risk.

- **Compliance reporting**: Macie provides customizable reports and dashboards that help organizations track and demonstrate compliance with various data protection regulations, such as GDPR, HIPAA, and PCI-DSS.

- **Centralized visibility**: Macie integrates with other AWS security services, such as AWS Security Hub and Amazon GuardDuty, to provide a centralized view of your data security and compliance posture across your AWS environment.

Pricing for Amazon Macie is based on the amount of data stored in Amazon S3 that Macie analyzes and the number of sensitive data types that Macie detects. Customers are charged a per-gigabyte rate for data analyzed and a per-sensitive-data-type rate for each type of sensitive data detected. There is also a minimum monthly fee.

> **Note**
>
> If you have an exam question that has Macie as an answer, first establish in the question whether the data is stored in S3. If not, then you can exclude Macie as the correct answer.
>
> In addition to this, Macie specifically looks for PII. If the exam question is about PII, then look for an answer containing Macie and shortlist it.

AWS Security Hub

AWS Security Hub is a comprehensive security and compliance tool that provides a unified view of your security posture across your AWS environment. It is designed to help you centralize security data from multiple sources, analyze security trends, and prioritize and respond to potential security issues.

Key features of AWS Security Hub include the ability to aggregate security findings from various AWS services and third-party security tools, such as Amazon GuardDuty, Amazon Inspector, and AWS Config. It then analyzes these findings, identifies security trends, and provides prioritized recommendations to address identified security risks. Security Hub also supports compliance monitoring and reporting, allowing you to track your adherence to various security standards and regulations.

Another key feature of Security Hub is the ability to automate security responses. You can create custom security workflows to automatically take actions, such as triggering an investigation, notifying relevant teams, or remediating identified issues. This helps security teams respond more quickly and effectively to potential security threats.

Pricing for AWS Security Hub is based on the number of security findings processed and the number of Amazon S3 objects scanned for configuration compliance. Customers are charged a per-finding rate for the first million findings processed each month, and a reduced rate for any additional findings beyond that. There is also a per-object rate for scanning Amazon S3 objects for configuration compliance.

Detecting threats in your environment is good practice because if someone is determined to get into your platform, they will find a way, and you need to detect when that happens. But how can you make it harder for an attacker to infiltrate your AWS platform? Let's consider how to protect AWS applications.

Protecting Applications

Protecting applications from web-based threats is a critical concern for organizations operating in the cloud. AWS provides several security services to help safeguard web applications and APIs, including the AWS **Web Application Firewall** (**WAF**) and AWS Shield.

AWS WAF

AWS WAF is a web application firewall service that helps protect web applications and APIs from common web-based attacks. It is designed to provide a comprehensive security solution for anyone who hosts their web applications on the AWS cloud.

One of the key features of AWS WAF is its ability to protect against a wide range of web-based threats, including SQL injection, **cross-site scripting** (**XSS**), and other types of malicious activity. AWS WAF analyzes the incoming traffic to web applications and APIs and can be configured to block or allow specific traffic based on customizable rules. This helps you maintain the availability and integrity of your web-based assets, while also reducing the risk of data breaches and other security incidents.

Another important feature of AWS WAF is its seamless integration with other AWS services, such as Amazon CloudFront, Amazon API Gateway, and AWS Elastic Load Balancing. This integration allows you to easily deploy and manage your web application security within their existing AWS infrastructure, without the need for complex configuration or additional infrastructure.

AWS WAF also offers advanced features, such as the ability to create custom rules, set up rate-based rules to mitigate DDoS attacks, and integrate with AWS Lambda functions for custom threat detection and response. These features enable you to tailor the service to your specific security requirements and enhance your overall security posture.

AWS Shield

AWS Shield is a managed **distributed denial of service (DDoS)** protection service. It safeguards web applications and APIs from DDoS attacks, which are attempts to overwhelm and disrupt the availability of online resources by generating excessive malicious traffic.

A key feature of AWS Shield is its ability to provide always-on, automated DDoS attack detection and mitigation. The service continuously monitors traffic to web applications and APIs and quickly identifies and mitigates DDoS attacks before they can impact the availability of these resources. This proactive approach helps ensure that you can maintain the continuous operation of your mission-critical web-based services, even in the face of large-scale DDoS attacks.

In addition, AWS Shield integrates with other AWS services, such as Amazon CloudFront, Elastic Load Balancing, and Amazon Route 53. This tight integration allows AWS Shield to leverage the scalability and resilience of the underlying AWS infrastructure to handle even the most sophisticated DDoS attacks, without requiring organizations to manage complex DDoS mitigation solutions themselves.

AWS Shield offers two service tiers: AWS Shield Standard and AWS Shield Advanced. AWS Shield Standard is provided at no additional charge to all AWS customers and offers basic DDoS attack protection, while AWS Shield Advanced provides more comprehensive DDoS mitigation capabilities, including access to dedicated DDoS response teams and advanced analytics, for a monthly fee based on the protected resources.

> **Note**
>
> When deciding between Shield or WAF as the correct answer, look for whether the question is specifically asking for DDoS protection. If yes, Shield is probably the correct answer. If the question is more concerned about things such as SQL injection or XSS, then WAF is likely to be the correct answer. In reality, though, both should be used to provide a holistic security approach.

Hands-on Lab

Encryption is crucial to implement on AWS, and that is the topic of this chapter's lab. You will create an S3 bucket and encrypt the data within it with a KMS key that you create yourself. By working through this exercise, you will become familiar with using encryption and managing KMS keys:

1. Log in to the AWS Management Console – `http://console.aws.amazon.com/`.

2. Navigate to `Key Management Service`.

3. From the left-hand menu, select `Customer managed keys`.

4. Click `Create key`.

5. **Select** `Symmetric` **and** `Encrypt and Decrypt`.

6. **Click** `Next`.

7. **Give your key an alias, that is, a name it will be known by. Click** `Next`.

8. **Select which users and roles can administer this key. Make sure you select whichever user or role that you are logged in as.**

9. **Click** `Next`.

10. **Select which users or roles can use this key. Make sure you select whichever user or role that you are logged in as.**

11. **Click** `Next`.

12. **On the review page, you will see that the key policy has been created for you! Click** `Finish`.

13. **Congratulations! You have created a KMS key. Now you can use this key to encrypt objects.**

14. Navigate to S3.

15. Click `Create bucket`.

16. Give your bucket a name, remembering that it has to be globally unique.

17. Scroll down to `Default encryption` and select `Server-side encryption with AWS Key Management Service keys`.

18. Select `Choose from your AWS KMS keys` and, in the drop-down box, select the key you just created.

19. Click `Create bucket`.

20. Select `Upload`.

21. Click `Add files` and choose a file to upload to your S3 bucket. Click `Upload`.

22. Once the upload is complete, click X to return to your bucket.

23. You will now try to retrieve the file. To do this, you will need to open a terminal on your computer so that you can run AWS CLI commands. Make sure that you have authenticated to AWS before running any AWS CLI commands.

24. Run the following command, making sure to replace values where required:

25. `aws s3api get-object --bucket YOURBUCKETNAME --key YOURFILENAME outfile`

26. If this command runs successfully, your terminal will show you a summary of information from the object, where you will see that the object was encrypted and the key ID of the key it was encrypted with. After you exit the summary, check your directory, and you will see a new file called `outfile`. This is your downloaded file.

27. You will note that you did not have to provide the key to decrypt the object. S3 handles the decryption operation for you so, as long as you have permission to decrypt using a key on both your IAM policy and your KMS key policy, you will be allowed to download the object.

28. Try removing the permission to decrypt objects from your IAM role and see what happens when you try `get-object` again.

This concludes our KMS lab. In this lab, you created a KMS key and an S3 bucket that was configured to encrypt objects by default. You then learned that IAM permissions were important to the successful retrieval of the object. This can be important to remember for exam questions that might ask you to troubleshoot why a user is unable to perform an action.

Remember to clean up the resources you have created once you are finished.

Summary

AWS security services are essential for protecting sensitive data and critical applications in the cloud. The shared responsibility model means customers must secure their own resources, and AWS provides a range of services to help. RBAC with IAM roles, as well as bucket policies, key policies, and service control policies, allow granular control over permissions. Encryption is crucial, with options for protecting data at rest and in transit, along with the centralized AWS KMS. Secrets management with AWS Secrets Manager ensures secure storage and automated rotation of sensitive information. Threat detection services such as Security Hub, GuardDuty, Macie, and Inspector monitor for security issues, provide analysis, and generate alerts. Finally, the WAF and Shield services combine to safeguard web-based applications and APIs, blocking common attacks and mitigating DDoS threats. Understanding these key AWS security capabilities is vital for architecting secure cloud environments and passing the *AWS Certified Solutions Architect – Associate* exam. In *Chapter 11, Management and Governance*, you will learn about management and governance on AWS.

Exam Readiness Drill - Chapter Review Questions

Apart from mastering key concepts, strong test-taking skills under time pressure are essential for acing your certification exam. That's why developing these abilities early in your learning journey is critical.

Exam readiness drills, using the free online practice resources provided with this book, help you progressively improve your time management and test-taking skills while reinforcing the key concepts you've learned.

HOW TO GET STARTED

- Open the link or scan the QR code at the bottom of this page

- If you have unlocked the practice resources already, log in to your registered account. If you haven't, follow the instructions in *Chapter 16* and come back to this page.

- Once you log in, click the START button to start a quiz

- We recommend attempting a quiz multiple times till you're able to answer most of the questions correctly and well within the time limit.

- You can use the following practice template to help you plan your attempts:

Working On Accuracy		
Attempt	Target	Time Limit
Attempt 1	40% or more	Till the timer runs out
Attempt 2	60% or more	Till the timer runs out
Attempt 3	75% or more	Till the timer runs out
Working On Timing		
Attempt 4	75% or more	1 minute before time limit
Attempt 5	75% or more	2 minutes before time limit
Attempt 6	75% or more	3 minutes before time limit

The above drill is just an example. Design your drills based on your own goals and make the most out of the online quizzes accompanying this book.

First time accessing the online resources? 🔒

You'll need to unlock them through a one-time process. **Head to** *Chapter 16* **for instructions**.

Open Quiz	
https://packt.link/SAAC03Ch10 OR scan this QR code →	

11

Management and Governance

Imagine you are a cloud engineer at a business that is scaling rapidly. So far, you have been able to keep track of everything manually, but there are now more resources than you can monitor yourself and they're spread across different regions and accounts. You know you cannot continue to do this manually so you want to learn more about scaling on AWS.

AWS has many services that can help you with the management and governance of your cloud platform at scale. In this chapter, you will learn how to create compliance rules so that you can be alerted when rules are broken, how to auto-remediate broken rules, and how to enforce permissions across an entire cross-region, multi-account platform. You will also learn about logging and monitoring services. All these features and services will enable you to build according to AWS best practices.

The services that you will learn about are as follows:

- AWS Organizations and AWS Control Tower
- AWS CloudFormation and AWS Service Catalog
- AWS Config and AWS Systems Manager
- Amazon CloudWatch and AWS CloudTrail
- AWS Cost and Usage Reports and AWS Cost Explorer

Let's begin by looking at how you can use AWS Control Tower and AWS Organizations to create the foundation of your AWS platform with preventative guardrails.

Governance

Effective governance strategies on AWS are key to ensuring that your AWS platform is operating efficiently while mitigating risks and complying with relevant regulatory policies. This is particularly important for highly regulated industries such as banking or pharmaceutical manufacturing, but everyone can benefit from the governance features that AWS provides.

As you move away from a small AWS platform to a larger AWS platform, you will likely have several accounts to manage. Maybe you are centralizing your logs into one account, or maybe you have one account for all networking ingress and egress. As you gain more accounts to manage, enforcing controls across them becomes complex. As a platform administrator, you might want to restrict which services can be used in each account, ensuring that only approved services can be used. AWS Organizations was launched for this purpose.

AWS Organizations

AWS Organizations provides a way to create and manage multiple AWS accounts, set up organizational policies, and control access to AWS resources. To understand how AWS Organizations works, you will need to understand some new terms and phrases.

Accounts in AWS Organizations are structured in what are called **organizational units (OUs)**. These OUs allow you to group your accounts according to business functions, teams, or whatever logical structure makes sense for your platform. You can nest OUs within OUs up to five levels deep. This might be hard to visualize, so *Figure 11.1* shows an example:

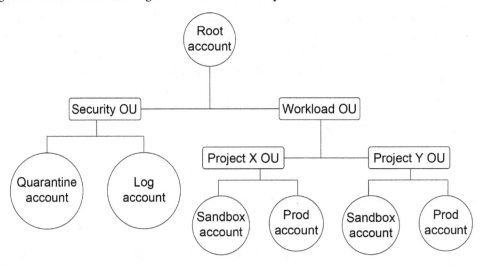

Figure 11.1: Example of an organizational structure in AWS Organizations

In any AWS organization, there must be a root account, as you can see in *Figure 11.1*. The root account is where the management of the organization takes place, as well as where billing is consolidated for all accounts in the organization. Under the root account, there are two OUs, the Security OU and the Workload OU, but these could be named anything according to your business needs. In the Security OU, there are just two AWS accounts, whereas in the Workload OU, you have additional OUs according to each project. The Project X OU is two OU levels deep, which means you could theoretically create another three levels of nested OUs within Project X. There is a limit to the total number of OUs you can have in an organization, however. The maximum number of OUs you can create is 1,000, while the default limit for the number of accounts that you can create or onboard into an organization is 10. This latter limit is a soft limit, however, and can be increased into the thousands.

The next term you need to understand for AWS Organizations is **service control policies (SCPs)**. SCPs are permissions policies that allow you to define the maximum permissions allowed for accounts in your organization. For example, the following policy will restrict users to only being able to provision the t3.small instance type:

```
{
  "Version": "2012-10-17",
  "Statement": [
    {
      "Sid": "RequireSmallInstanceType",
      "Effect": "Deny",
      "Action": "ec2:RunInstances",
      "Resource": [
        "arn:aws:ec2:*:*:instance/*"
      ],
      "Condition": {
        "StringNotEquals": {
          "ec2:InstanceType": "t2.micro"
        }
      }
    }
  ]
}
```

SCPs do not grant permissions; rather, they provide restrictions or guardrails on the actions that users can perform.

SCPs can be applied either to a specific account in an organization or they can be applied to an OU. If the SCP is applied to an OU, then all member accounts within that OU will inherit the permission restriction. Permission priorities remain the same as IAM, so if permission is denied at any level, it is blocked for that account, even if the local administrator grants broader access. This is a really powerful way to apply broad restrictions across your entire AWS platform.

You can also apply management policies in AWS Organizations. Management policies allow you to define tagging and backup policies across your entire AWS platform.

So, AWS Organizations makes it easy to manage large numbers of accounts. But if you want a way to create a new account that comes with pre-deployed networking configurations and enforces best practices, take a look at AWS Control Tower.

AWS Control Tower

At the core of AWS Control Tower is the concept of a "landing zone" – a pre-configured, baseline AWS environment that includes separate accounts for different workloads, teams, or business units, all with a set of pre-built guardrails to ensure adherence to security best practices and organizational policies. Think of Control Tower as an orchestrator using several AWS services, such as AWS Organizations to provision accounts, AWS Service Catalog to deploy networking infrastructure, and AWS IAM Identity Center to deploy IAM roles consistently across accounts.

When you create a Control Tower deployment, an AWS organization is created that contains two OUs: Security (required) and Sandbox (optional). In the Security OU, two AWS accounts are created: the Audit account and the Log Archive account. You can then create other OUs as you wish.

Guardrails

There are two types of guardrails that can be used with AWS Control Tower:

- **Preventative guardrails** are there to prevent actions from being performed if they don't conform to your policies. These are implemented with SCPs.

- **Detective guardrails** will monitor your resources and detect when a resource no longer conforms to your policies. For some detective guardrails, you can auto-remediate resolution, for example, by removing public access to an S3 bucket. These are implemented with AWS Config. We'll cover AWS Config in more detail later in this chapter.

A number of guardrails are mandatory and are deployed with every account that you create in your Control Tower environment, while others are either strongly recommended or elective, depending on your guardrail requirements.

Account Factory

When you want to automate the provisioning of a new account, making sure that it has all the right roles and networking infrastructure in place ready to be used by your end users, you can use Account Factory. You will define a blueprint that outlines what resources should be deployed to a new account and then use this blueprint during account creation to deploy the resources. This takes away much of the heavy lifting when creating and baselining new accounts.

Understanding, at a high level, the features that AWS Control Tower provides will be useful when answering questions on the *SAA-C03* exam. You won't need to know exactly which guardrails are mandatory and which are not, but understanding the difference between preventative and detective guardrails and the underlying services that provide those guardrails will be useful.

You've explored how to automate account setup and management in this section using AWS Organizations and AWS Control Tower. Now, take a look at how you might automate resource provisioning.

Provisioning and Orchestration

Clicking through the console to provision resources is great for learning, but when needing to create tens or even hundreds of resources, it soon becomes a very large manual task. Two key services help alleviate the burden here: AWS CloudFormation and AWS Service Catalog.

AWS CloudFormation

AWS CloudFormation is an **infrastructure-as-code (IaC)** service. You define the resources that you would like to deploy in either YAML or JSON, according to the CloudFormation syntax, and when this code is passed to AWS, it reads the code and deploys the configurations defined within. When you change the resource configurations in the code and pass it back to AWS, the resources will update to reflect the new changes.

Working with AWS CloudFormation is a really important skill to learn, not only because it will feature on the exam but also because IaC is becoming an integral part of any cloud-based job. In the scope of the exam, you may have to look at a snippet of CloudFormation and decide whether it is correct, as well as understand the features within CloudFormation, so it is highly recommended that you get used to working with it.

Anatomy of a CloudFormation Template

A code file containing CloudFormation YAML or JSON is called a CloudFormation template. It will always start with the version of the CloudFormation syntax being used in the template. Always use the most up-to-date version, which, at the time of writing, is **2010-09-09**. When the template has been deployed, this creates what is called a CloudFormation stack. A stack contains all the resources that you have deployed within that template. You can see a log of all events that took place in the deployment of those resources, as well as their current deployment state.

Take a look at a simple CloudFormation template in *Figure 11.2*:

```
AWSTemplateFormatVersion: "2010-09-09"

Description: 'AWS CloudFormation Sample Template EC2InstanceWithSecurityGroupSample

Metadata:
  License: Apache-2.0

Resources:
  EC2Instance:
    Type: AWS::EC2::Instance
    Properties:
      InstanceType: t3.micro
      SubnetId: subnet-123456
      SecurityGroups:
        - sg-123456
      KeyName: mykey
      ImageId: ami-1234567
```

Figure 11.2: A simple CloudFormation template to deploy an EC2 instance

This simple CloudFormation template is in YAML. At the very top, you can see `AWSTemplateFormatVersion`; there is then an optional description and metadata before you get to the meat of the template, the `Resources` block. In the `Resources` block, you define each of the resources you want to deploy. In this case, you are deploying one instance. Each resource must have a unique key that identifies it within the template. In this case, the key for your instance resource is `EC2Instance`. If you wanted to create another instance in the same template, you would have to ensure that the new instance had a unique key that differs from `EC2Instance`. You then set the values for the various instance configuration items, such as `InstanceType` and `SubnetID`.

If you keep the template like this, you will need a unique template for every instance because all those values have been hardcoded. Instead, you can use parameters and pseudo-parameters to automatically fill information for you at deployment. See what that looks like in *Figure 11.3*:

```yaml
AWSTemplateFormatVersion: "2010-09-09"

Description: 'AWS CloudFormation Sample Template EC2InstanceWithSecurityGroupSample'

Metadata:
  License: Apache-2.0

Parameters:
  LatestAmiId:
    Type: AWS::SSM::Parameter::Value<AWS::EC2::Image::Id>
    Default: /aws/service/ami-amazon-linux-latest/amzn2-ami-hvm-x86_64-gp2
  Subnets:
    Type: List<AWS::EC2::Subnet::Id>
  InstanceType:
    Type: String
    Default: t3.micro

Resources:
  EC2Instance:
    Type: AWS::EC2::Instance
    Properties:
      InstanceType: !Ref InstanceType
      SubnetId: !Select
        - 0
        - !Ref Subnets
      SecurityGroups:
        - !Ref InstanceSecurityGroup
      ImageId: !Ref LatestAmiId

  InstanceSecurityGroup:
    Type: AWS::EC2::SecurityGroup
    Metadata:
      guard:
        SuppressedRules:
          - INCOMING_SSH_DISABLED
    Properties:
      GroupDescription: Enable SSH access via port 22
      SecurityGroupIngress:
        - IpProtocol: tcp
          FromPort: 22
          ToPort: 22
          CidrIp: 0.0.0.0/0
```

Figure 11.3: Expanding on the first CloudFormation template to include parameters

In this new template, some new sections have been added. The first new section is the `Parameters` block. In the `Parameters` block, you can collect input values from the user at the point of deployment, so you do not need to know these in advance. You can even use Systems Manager Parameter Store to pull values from. For example, if you release your own AMIs, you can keep track of the latest version in Parameter Store, and then reference that parameter in your CloudFormation template. You see that here, in the case of `LatestAmiId`. This means that if a later version of the AMI is released, the template will always deploy with the latest AMI version. You can also present to the user a list of existing resources to choose from when selecting parameters. For example, `Subnets` has a value type of `List<AWS::EC2::Subnet::Id>`. This means that when the user goes to deploy this template, the `Subnets` parameter will present the user with a list of the existing subnets in the account being deployed to for the user to select from. From there, they can pick the subnet they would like to deploy to.

The other new block in this template is a new `Resources` block to define a security group. This is then referenced by its unique key in the instance block using the `!Ref` intrinsic function.

It is important to have a high-level understanding of intrinsic functions. There are several intrinsic functions that are used to get values at runtime. Some of the most used ones are as follows:

- `Ref` and `Fn::GetAtt`: Retrieve a specific value for a resource. `Ref` returns a default value while `GetAtt` allows you to select a specific attribute to return.

- `Fn::Join` and `Fn::Split`: These both do exactly what they say. You can join several strings or split a string with a delimiter.

You have now taken a look at some of the most used intrinsic functions.

Other Template Blocks

There are a few more optional template blocks that you should know of.

The `Mapping` template block allows you to create a map of keys to values. To reference a value within a map, you would use the `!FindInMap` intrinsic function. This is usually used to build a map of region names to AMI IDs so that, at runtime, you can pull the correct AMI for the region being deployed to.

The `Output` block allows you to output values that can be imported into other CloudFormation stacks. For example, you can output the instance ID of the instance deployed in the stack.

The `Conditions` block allows you to use conditional logic to determine whether a resource should or should not be deployed. For example, you could have an input parameter to capture the environment the user is deploying to (i.e., `dev`, `test`, or `prod`) and then have a condition that evaluates to `true` if `prod` is entered as the value. This can then be used to deploy a specific resource such as an instance.

CloudFormation Service Features

There are several CloudFormation features you should be aware of going into the exam. Take a look at some of them:

- **Nested stacks: Nested stacks** are a powerful feature that allows users to manage complex cloud infrastructures by breaking them into smaller, reusable templates. Instead of defining all resources in a single large stack, nested stacks enable you to split infrastructure into logical components, each defined in its own template. These individual templates are then referenced in a parent stack using the `AWS::CloudFormation::Stack` resource type. This modular approach simplifies management, promotes reusability, and makes the infrastructure more maintainable. Changes in one nested stack can be isolated from others, making updates safer and reducing the potential impact on other resources. Additionally, this technique enhances collaboration by allowing teams to work on different components independently while still combining them in a cohesive architecture.

- **Stack sets: Stack sets** allow users to deploy and manage CloudFormation stacks across multiple AWS accounts and Regions from a single template. This feature is particularly useful for organizations that operate in multi-account environments or need to ensure consistent infrastructure across regions. With StackSets, you can define a CloudFormation template once and then deploy it to multiple target accounts and Regions, ensuring that infrastructure remains uniform. StackSets also offer automated, large-scale operations, such as performing updates or deleting stacks across multiple accounts simultaneously. They support both self-managed and service-managed permissions, giving users flexibility in how they control deployment. This centralized approach simplifies cross-account management, reduces operational overhead, and helps enforce governance policies across an organization's AWS environment.

- **Change sets**: Change sets identify how your resources will change when you apply an update to a deployed stack, allowing you to see whether a resource will be replaced or updated. They will also detect drift in your deployments, where a change might have been made to your resources outside of the code.

- **Custom resources**: Custom resources allow you to create resources that CloudFormation doesn't natively support.

- `cfn-init`: This is a helper script that retrieves metadata from CloudFormation to perform tasks on an EC2 instance such as install packages, create files, or start services.

The best way to understand CloudFormation is to use it, and that will be the topic of this chapter's lab.

CloudFormation is excellent for deploying infrastructure and letting developers define their own configurations. Sometimes, you might have strict requirements, which means that you must enforce specific resource configurations – for example, an EC2 instance that must be deployed with specific security group rules. With CloudFormation, developers could potentially put any configuration down, and while you might be able to define guardrails to prevent unwanted deployments, this can become time-consuming and complex to manage and define. This is where AWS Service Catalog is useful.

AWS Service Catalog

AWS Service Catalog allows you to maintain a catalog of resources or products that can be accessed by users in a portal to deploy approved resources to your AWS environment. These products are IaC templates, either in CloudFormation or Terraform. Users do not get access to the template; they can only access the portal and modify the parameters of the product that you allow them to modify.

Administrators can version products so that if a change is made to a template, it does not break existing deployed provisioned products.

Service Catalog is how Control Tower deploys infrastructure across your landing zone.

You need not know much more about Service Catalog than this for the exam. So far, you have learned about provisioning new resources, but how do you look after resources once they've been deployed? Centralizing operations tasks reduces the burden on operations engineers. Take a look at how that can be done on AWS.

Centralized Operations

Centralized operations allow you to manage your IT infrastructure anywhere, on-premises, at the edge, or in the cloud. You can take advantage of built-in best practices and automations to streamline your operations. Now that you have your infrastructure in place, take a look at how you can perform operations at scale across the entire fleet with AWS Systems Manager.

AWS Systems Manager

AWS Systems Manager (SSM) provides a centralized platform for managing and configuring resources, automating routine tasks, and ensuring the security and compliance of your systems. By installing the SSM agent, it can gather data from not just EC2 instances but also on-premises servers and edge devices and then act upon that data. The service offers a wide range of capabilities, including patch management, remote command execution, parameter storage for securely storing and retrieving configuration data, inventory management, and more. For the *SAA-C03* exam, it is a good idea to have a high-level understanding of the key features of SSM.

Patch Manager

Patch Manager allows you to define and apply patch baselines that you can then schedule for deployment to your fleet. A wide variety of operating systems are supported, including Amazon Linux, Red Hat Enterprise Linux, SUSE Linux Enterprise Server, Ubuntu Server, and Windows Server. You can also observe patch compliance statistics across your fleet.

Run Command

Run Command is a powerful feature that allows you to remotely execute commands or scripts on your managed instances, whether they are Amazon EC2 instances, on-premises servers, or other resources. This capability lets you automate a wide range of administrative tasks, such as software installations, system configurations, and troubleshooting, without the need to individually access or log in to each target system. It can be run on multiple targets simultaneously.

This feature leverages an SSM Command document, which is a YAML or JSON document that defines which commands should be executed.

Parameter Store

Parameter Store allows you to store either plain text or encrypted parameters that can be used by other AWS services and SSM features. Remember, in *Chapter 10, Security*, you learned the difference between Secrets Manager and Parameter Store. Parameter Store does not support native secret rotation and isn't intended to be a secret store. Parameter Store also supports versioning, parameter policies, and parameter locking, ensuring that your critical configuration data is properly secured and audited.

Inventory

Inventory is a feature that provides a comprehensive view of your computing resources, both on-premises and in the cloud, by collecting detailed metadata about your managed instances, software, and other assets. This centralized inventory helps you better understand and manage your IT environment. The service automatically discovers and adds new resources to the inventory, and you can schedule regular data collection to ensure the information remains up to date. Inventory also provides powerful search and filtering capabilities, allowing you to quickly find and analyze the specific resources you need.

Automation

Automation is similar to Run Command. It allows you to remotely execute commands on managed nodes, using SSM automation documents. Typically, automation documents are more complex, multi-step workflows or procedures that can involve not just command execution but also conditional logic and even other AWS services. The structure of the documents is largely similar, however, using either YAML or JSON as their language.

SSM has many, many more features than the ones listed here, and one could probably write a standalone book just on it. But these are the features that are most likely to appear in the exam. SSM is not the whole story, however. It is a good idea to ensure that there are detections in place to identify when your resources no longer conform to the rules that you have in place. Take a look at AWS Config.

AWS Config

AWS Config is a fully managed service that provides a detailed view of the configuration of AWS resources in an organization's environment. It continuously monitors and records changes to these configurations, enabling organizations to assess, audit, and evaluate the configurations of their AWS resources.

With AWS Config, users can create customizable rules to detect and record non-compliant resource configurations, helping to ensure that their infrastructure adheres to internal best practices and external regulations. The service also provides a comprehensive timeline of configuration changes, allowing users to quickly identify when and how a resource's configuration has been modified. This historical data can be invaluable for troubleshooting, auditing, and compliance purposes.

It's key to note that AWS Config does not prevent changes from happening; it simply detects that a change has taken place. However, you can configure auto-remediation using either a predefined action or by creating a custom SSM document.

Logging and Monitoring

Arguably, logging and monitoring is one of the most important things to have properly configured in your AWS environment. It's the first thing you will look at when something does not behave as expected or when a change has taken place that you were not expecting. AWS has two logging and monitoring solutions – AWS CloudTrail for API logging and Amazon CloudWatch for application-level logging.

AWS CloudTrail

AWS CloudTrail enables the continuous monitoring and logging of your AWS infrastructure. It records all actions taken within your AWS account, including API calls made by users, roles, or services, and stores this data in durable and highly available storage. This information can be used to track changes, investigate security incidents, and ensure compliance with regulatory requirements. CloudTrail provides a comprehensive audit trail, allowing you to understand who accessed which resources, when, and from where.

CloudTrail is enabled by default and stores the last 90 days of events for free in the event history. If you want a custom view of AWS activities, you can create a trail. When you configure a trail, you specify which events you would like to log, where the log files will be stored (which S3 bucket), which regions the trail should track, and whether you want to be notified of new log files being created. You can configure multiple trails, each with its own settings.

When creating trails, it is important to understand the two types of events that a trail can log:

- **Management events**: API calls made to your AWS account that create, modify, or delete your AWS resources, or that change the configuration of your AWS resources. Management events are free to track and store.

- **Data events**: API activity that captures the resource operations performed on the actual content or data within your AWS resources, such as accessing an S3 bucket or invoking a Lambda function. These are not free to record and store.

By understanding this distinction, you should be able to handle any cost-related questions on CloudTrail. The final key point to remember about CloudTrail is that it is not a real-time service. It can take around 15 minutes for an activity to appear in CloudTrail. This is a key point to understand for the exam.

Amazon CloudWatch

Amazon CloudWatch enables you to collect, analyze, and act on various metrics and logs generated by your AWS resources, as well as resources outside of AWS. CloudWatch can monitor metrics such as CPU utilization, network traffic, storage usage, and custom application-specific metrics, allowing you to gain visibility into the health and performance of your infrastructure and applications. There are several key features within CloudWatch.

CloudWatch Metrics

CloudWatch Metrics allows you to collect and track metrics from AWS services, applications, and custom sources. This provides real-time monitoring of metrics such as CPU utilization, HTTP errors, and IOPs, among many others. You can create alarms to trigger based on metric thresholds. There are a lot of metrics that have been pre-created for you and these are free to use; however, you can also configure your own custom metrics and these incur an additional cost.

CloudWatch Logs

CloudWatch Logs collects log data with excellent integration with other AWS services, in particular Lambda, and provides an interface to filter and search these logs. This will be the first place to go to debug a Lambda function that isn't working as expected. Pricing of CloudWatch Logs is based on the amount of data ingested and stored. It is best practice to only store the logs you need because prices can increase quickly if you don't apply a relevant lifecycle.

CloudWatch Alarms

As mentioned previously, you can set alarms based on metric thresholds or when an anomaly is detected. Notifications (which can be email, SMS, or Amazon SNS) are sent when an alarm is triggered. Alarms can also trigger actions, for example, you could trigger an autoscaling action when an alarm has triggered. You are charged based on the number of active alarms you have configured.

You may also see references to **CloudWatch Events** when reading material online. CloudWatch Events was rebranded to Amazon EventBridge, which was covered in *Chapter 10, Security*. If you read material that references CloudWatch Events, it is likely out of date. Make sure you understand the difference between CloudTrail and CloudWatch as that will be key to selecting the right answer in the exam. Remember, CloudTrail tracks AWS API actions, while CloudWatch is more application-level logging and metric tracking.

Cost Management

An important component of managing any IT system is managing cost. With the pay-as-you-go nature of the cloud, costs can spiral quite quickly if they are not being monitored. In this section, you will learn about three services that can help you understand and keep on top of your AWS costs: AWS Budgets, AWS Cost Explorer, and AWS Cost and Usage Reports. We will not go into huge detail, but it's important you understand the differences between them for the exam.

AWS Budgets

AWS Budgets enables users to monitor and manage their AWS spending. One of the key features of AWS Budgets is the ability to create budgets for specific services, cost categories, or the overall AWS account. These budgets can be set based on actual spend, forecasted spend, or a combination of both.

If a budget is exceeded, you can configure an automated action to run, such as applying an IAM policy or SCP, or targeting an EC2 or RDS instance to be stopped.

AWS Cost Explorer

One of the key features of AWS Cost Explorer is the ability to view and analyze cost and usage data for AWS services, including detailed reports on the specific services, usage types, and other cost dimensions that contribute to the overall AWS expenditure. You can filter reports based on service, timeframe, and tags, and it is capable of forecasting future AWS spending based on past historical data.

AWS Cost and Usage Reports

While Cost Explorer provides a nice user interface to explore AWS costs, AWS **Cost and Usage Reports** (**CUR**) provides a CSV or Parquet file that can be used with the user's analytical tool of choice but provides the same functionality of being able to filter and include or exclude data as the user decides.

This gives you a high-level overview of the cost management services at AWS. You may not get asked about these services, but they may feature in the questions, so it is a good idea to understand each of these.

Hands-on Lab

In this lab, you are going to build and deploy a CloudFormation template that deploys a single S3 bucket. You will learn how to use parameters and pseudo-parameters, as well as how to use conditions. Let's dive in.

You will use the following YAML template as a starting point: AWSTemplateFormatVersion: '2010-09-09'

```
Description: 'A simple CloudFormation template to deploy an S3 bucket'

Resources:
  S3Bucket:
    Type: AWS::S3::Bucket
    Properties:
      BucketName: what-is-a-name
```

You can now follow the given instructions:

1. Open your text editor of choice. It is best to use an IDE such as Visual Studio Code when working with code as it comes with lots of tools to ensure your syntax and whitespace usage are correct. This helps you avoid issues during deployment.

2. Either copy the preceding code or write it out into a new document, taking special care to use the correct quotes and tabs. For example, there is a one-tab indent at the start of the line containing S3Bucket and two tabs indenting the line containing Type.

3. Now that you have the base code written out, let's add a parameter. All bucket names have to be globally unique, so you are going to create a parameter that will be a prefix to your bucket name. Create a new line between Description and Resources. Then, enter the following:

```
Parameters:
  Prefix:
    Type: String
    Default: saaco3
```

This will create a parameter that can be referenced by its logical ID, `Prefix`, of the `String` type. If no value is provided, it will use the `saaco3` value. Your code should now look like *Figure 11.4*:

```
1    AWSTemplateFormatVersion: '2010-09-09'
2
3    Description: 'A simple CloudFormation template to deploy an S3 bucket'
4
5    Parameters:
6      Prefix:
7        Type: String
8        Default: saaco3
9
10   Resources:
11     S3Bucket:
12       Type: AWS::S3::Bucket
13       Properties:
14         BucketName: what-is-a-name
15
```

Figure 11.4: CloudFormation snippet containing a simple S3 bucket definition

4. Now, you need to modify the bucket name to use this prefix. Update the value of `BucketName`, making sure to keep the same indentation:

```
BucketName: !Sub "${Prefix}-bucket"
```

You have now created and used your first parameter!

5. Next, you will add a pseudo-parameter to the bucket name to place the region name in the bucket. Update the `BucketName` value:

```
BucketName: !Sub "${Prefix}-${AWS::Region}-bucket"
```

You did not add a parameter to capture this new pseudo-parameter. It will pull the information from the AWS control plane at runtime. This is useful for making templates that can be deployed across many regions.

6. Finally, you are going to add a condition that will determine whether the bucket will be deployed with versioning or not. First, add a new parameter. This will be a `String` parameter that takes just two options – `true` or `false`:

```
Versioning:
    Default: false
    Type: String
    AllowedValues: [true, false]
```

7. Now, add a new `Conditions` block between the `Parameters` block and the Resources `block`:

```
Conditions:
  CreateVersioning: !Equals
    - !Ref Versioning
    - true
```

In this `Conditions` block, you have created a condition that will evaluate to `true` if the `Encryption` parameter has a value of `true`.

8. You will now modify the resource to accommodate this condition. Add a new property underneath `BucketName`:

```
VersioningConfiguration:
        !If
        - CreateVersioning
        -
          Status: Enabled
        - !Ref "AWS::NoValue"
```

This logic says that if the `CreateVersioning` condition is `true`, then add the `Status: Enabled` configuration parameter to `VersioningConfiguration`; otherwise, place no value.

9. Your completed template will now look like *Figure 11.5*:

```
1    AWSTemplateFormatVersion: '2010-09-09'
2
3    Description: 'A simple CloudFormation template to deploy an S3 bucket'
4
5    Parameters:
6      Prefix:
7        Type: String
8        Default: saaco3
9      Versioning:
10       Default: false
11       Type: String
12       AllowedValues: [true, false]
13
14   Conditions:
15     CreateVersioning: !Equals
16       - !Ref Versioning
17       - true
18
19   Resources:
20     S3Bucket:
21       Type: AWS::S3::Bucket
22       Properties:
23         BucketName: !Sub "${Prefix}-${AWS::Region}-bucket"
24         VersioningConfiguration:
25           !If
26           - CreateVersioning
27           -
28             Status: Enabled
29           - !Ref "AWS::NoValue"
30
```

Figure 11.5: Final CloudFormation snippet containing conditions and variables

Save this file.

10. Now, you are going to deploy this bucket. Log in to the AWS Management Console and then navigate to CloudFormation.

11. In the CloudFormation console, click Create Stack.

12. On the page that appears, ensure that Choose an existing template is selected, then select Upload a template file. Select the file you have just created and then click Next.

13. Enter a stack name. This is just so that you can identify the stack in the list of CloudFormation stacks.

14. Below the stack name, you will see the parameters that you configured in your template, showing the default values that you configured. Change the value for `Prefix` to something unique to you, ensuring that it is all lowercase. If you leave the default value, you will likely encounter an error that someone else has used that bucket name.

15. For now, leave `Versioning` as the default, `false`. You can change this later. Click `Next`.

16. On this page, you can configure how CloudFormation should roll back in case of failure, among many other configurations. For the sake of this lab, leave the defaults and click `Next`.

17. You will now see a summary of the stack you are going to create. Click `Submit`.

18. Now, your stack is being created. You will see the `Events` tab of the stack, which shows you all the information about the steps CloudFormation is taking to deploy your resources, as well as whether it was successful or not. Wait until the stack finishes deploying. This might take a minute.

19. Once the resources have successfully deployed, you will see a `CREATE_COMPLETE` status on both the stack and the stack events. Click the `Resources` tab.

20. In the `Resources` tab, you can see a list of resources that were created in this deployment. You only deployed a single S3 bucket so that will be the only resource listed. Click the hyperlink to the bucket name in the `Physical ID` column. This will open a new window taking you to the S3 bucket in the S3 console.

21. Click on the `Properties` tab. You'll see that `Bucket Versioning` is currently disabled. Let's enable versioning.

22. Return to the browser tab containing the CloudFormation console.

23. Ensure that the stack you just created is selected, then click `Update` on the right-hand side of the window.

    Select `Use Existing Template`. This will continue to use the file you first uploaded. Click `Next`.

24. In the `Versioning` drop-down box, select `true`. Click `Next`.

25. On the `Review` page, scroll to the bottom and you will see the `Change set preview`. This gives you an overview of the changes that will be made with this update. Click `Submit`.

26. Once again, wait for the stack to finish making its changes.

27. Once the stack status shows `UPDATE_COMPLETE`, click into the `Resources` tab, then click on the S3 bucket physical ID to open S3.

28. Click on the `Properties` tab. You should now see that bucket versioning has been enabled on the bucket!

29. Congratulations! You have created your first CloudFormation template and explored parameters and conditions as well as how to deploy and update a template.

30. To clean up, select the stack you have just deployed, then click `Delete`. This will remove the S3 bucket that you just deployed.

During this lab, you built out a CloudFormation template that deploys an S3 bucket and performed an update to the bucket by changing a parameter value in the template. This is a common workflow with CloudFormation and formed a good first step to understanding how CloudFormation works. Continue to work with CloudFormation and test out some of the features that we didn't include in the lab.

Summary

In this chapter, you learned about the various AWS services and features that can help a cloud engineer manage and govern a rapidly scaling cloud platform. You gained an understanding of AWS Organizations and AWS Control Tower, which provides a way to create and manage multiple AWS accounts, set up organizational policies, and enforce compliance through preventative and detective guardrails.

The chapter also covered infrastructure provisioning and orchestration using AWS CloudFormation and AWS Service Catalog, which enables the definition and deployment of resources through IaC and the creation of a centralized catalog of approved resources. To centralize operations tasks, you learned about AWS Systems Manager and AWS Config, which offer capabilities such as patch management, remote command execution, resource inventory, and compliance monitoring. The importance of logging and monitoring was emphasized, with AWS CloudTrail and Amazon CloudWatch being the key services discussed.

Finally, you were introduced to the cost management services of AWS, including AWS Budgets, AWS Cost Explorer, and AWS Cost and Usage Reports, which allow organizations to monitor, analyze, and control their AWS expenditure. In the next chapter, you will begin to learn how the information over the chapters learned so far fits into the exam. You will begin with the first exam domain, *Design Secure Architectures*.

Exam Readiness Drill - Chapter Review Questions

Apart from mastering key concepts, strong test-taking skills under time pressure are essential for acing your certification exam. That's why developing these abilities early in your learning journey is critical.

Exam readiness drills, using the free online practice resources provided with this book, help you progressively improve your time management and test-taking skills while reinforcing the key concepts you've learned.

HOW TO GET STARTED

- Open the link or scan the QR code at the bottom of this page

- If you have unlocked the practice resources already, log in to your registered account. If you haven't, follow the instructions in *Chapter 16* and come back to this page.

- Once you log in, click the START button to start a quiz

- We recommend attempting a quiz multiple times till you're able to answer most of the questions correctly and well within the time limit.

- You can use the following practice template to help you plan your attempts:

Working On Accuracy		
Attempt	Target	Time Limit
Attempt 1	40% or more	Till the timer runs out
Attempt 2	60% or more	Till the timer runs out
Attempt 3	75% or more	Till the timer runs out
Working On Timing		
Attempt 4	75% or more	1 minute before time limit
Attempt 5	75% or more	2 minutes before time limit
Attempt 6	75% or more	3 minutes before time limit

The above drill is just an example. Design your drills based on your own goals and make the most out of the online quizzes accompanying this book.

First time accessing the online resources? 🔒
You'll need to unlock them through a one-time process. **Head to** *Chapter 16* **for instructions.**

Open Quiz	
https://packt.link/SAAC03Ch11 OR scan this QR code →	

12

Design Secure Architectures

In the previous chapters, you learned about the relevant AWS services for the AWS *SAA-C03* exam. Now, it's time to understand how those services fit into the exam's domains. This chapter will focus on the *Design Secure Architectures* domain. While the content may not be entirely new, it will be presented in the context of the exam requirements. If you complete a test exam on the internet, you may get a breakdown per domain of how many questions you got right and wrong. You can use this and the following chapters to give you an overview of the topics you need to know to improve on each domain.

The *Design Secure Architectures* domain has three key task statements:

- Design secure access to AWS resources
- Design secure workloads and applications
- Determine appropriate data security controls

Each of these statements will be explored in more detail throughout this chapter. You will first learn about the *Design secure access to AWS resources* task statement.

Design Secure Access to AWS Resources

In this task statement, you are expected to have knowledge of access controls and management across multiple AWS accounts, AWS federated access and identity services such as IAM and AWS IAM Identity Center, the AWS Global Infrastructure, and AWS security best practices such as the principle of least privilege and the shared responsibility model. In terms of skills, you should be able to apply AWS security best practices to IAM users and root users, including using **multi-factor authentication** (**MFA**). You should be able to design a flexible authorization model using IAM users, groups, roles, and policies, as well as a **role-based access control** (**RBAC**) strategy leveraging services such as AWS **Security Token Service** (**STS**), role switching, and cross-account access. You must also be able to design a security strategy for multiple AWS accounts, utilizing features such as AWS Control Tower and **Service Control Policies** (**SCPs**).

Finally, you should be able to determine the appropriate use of resource policies for AWS services and when to federate a directory service with IAM roles. Overall, the emphasis is on demonstrating the knowledge and skills to design secure access to AWS resources across multiple accounts and identity management services.

As you learned in *Chapter 3, Identity and Access Management*, least privilege is one of the key principles to securing the AWS cloud environment. This principle ensures that principals are only allowed to perform the actions they need to perform and nothing more. This means having a robust IAM strategy that follows best practices.

Best Practices for Securing IAM Users

A common question topic that features on the AWS *SAA-C03* exam is around the root user for the AWS account. Remember, every account has a root user that has the ultimate access to your account. This root user should not be used for everyday tasks, and only used in the case of an emergency. This is to ensure that you minimize the risk of the root user being compromised. Make sure that the credentials for the root user are protected from unauthorized use. This might even mean writing down the password and storing it in a physical safe. But for the purpose of the exam, the key thing to remember is that the root user should never be used as a normal IAM user.

In addition to securing access to the root user, ensure that the root user is protected by MFA. This ensures the safety of your account, even in the scenario that the root user's password has been compromised. This should also be implemented for any other IAM users you have configured.

You also learned in *Chapter 3, Identity and Access Management*, that while you can use IAM users, it is best practice to configure federation and IAM roles to grant temporary credentials to your AWS accounts.

IAM Roles and RBAC

There are four main components used in IAM – users, groups, roles, and policies. Policies can be applied to users, groups, and roles and outline what permissions those entities are allowed to perform. When you have a platform that utilizes IAM users, by placing users in a group and applying a policy to that same group, you can implement restrictions to hundreds of users in one action, saving you vast amounts of operational overhead and removing the need to apply permissions to each individual user.

The best practice is to use federated identities and IAM roles, however, granting individuals temporary credentials. This can be done in a number of ways, using supported identity providers such as Google and Facebook, or using an existing identity directory such as Amazon Cognito or Azure AD/Entra ID. Once you have configured your identity store, you will use AWS STS to authenticate and temporarily assume a role with a set of permissions. This solves the problem of securing access to roles. But how do you decide what permissions a role should have?

When creating a robust RBAC strategy, it is important to define clear responsibilities for your roles. The worst thing that you could do is give admin permissions to everyone. Instead, identify the various job functions, responsibilities, and access requirements within your organization. For example, you might have a DevOps engineer who needs write access to CodeBuild and S3, but they may not need access to EKS or SageMaker. Likewise, you might have a data scientist who only needs access to SageMaker. You would create two roles: one for DevOps engineers that only has permissions for S3 and CodeBuild and one for data scientists that only has access to SageMaker.

> **Note**
>
> An important concept to understand for the exam is the policy evaluation logic, which determines whether an action is allowed or denied in an IAM policy. Remember, if an action is explicitly denied in one policy and explicitly allowed in another, and both policies are attached to an IAM principal, the deny policy will always take precedence.

Sometimes, an individual might have access to several roles. For example, an organization might move all IAM actions out into a role on its own to ensure that individuals cannot grant themselves extra permissions. To use this other role, the individual can leverage role switching to assume another role.

Finally, you might have an application that needs to access resources in another account; for example, you might have a central logging account. In this case, it is best practice to configure cross-account access, restricting the actions and permissions the application can perform and in which accounts.

IAM Permissions at Scale

As your AWS platform grows and begins to have more and more accounts, remember to leverage tools to simplify the management of IAM across your platform. Make use of SCPs to implement guardrails across your AWS organization and use Control Tower to ensure IAM roles and policies are standardized across your accounts.

Design Secure Workloads and Applications

So far, you have explored how to secure access to AWS, but you will now look at each of the ways that you can secure applications and workloads. The very first point to consider is how the application itself is accessed. Ensure that not only do your users have to authenticate to use your application but that you also have some authentication mechanism to manage your application, ensuring that you are storing any application secrets in AWS Secrets Manager.

There can be a number of threats that you need to be aware of when designing your applications.

Threat Vectors: Detections and Mitigations

The two common attacks that might feature on the *SAA-C03* exam are **distributed denial-of-service (DDoS)** and SQL injection attacks, which were taught in *Chapter 10, Security*.

DDoS is a type of attack whereby an application is flooded with so many bogus requests that legitimate requests cannot make it through to the application. There are several ways in which this attack can be protected against. Here, you can take a look at some such ways:

- **Scalable architectures**: The primary reason that DDoS is successful is that the application freezes up as its resources are fully utilized. If your application is scalable, then as your architecture is attacked, it can scale to meet the unexpected demand. The caveat to this solution is that it can be incredibly costly. Make sure there are guardrails in place to limit just how far your infrastructure can scale out to avoid unexpected costs. Use Route 53 to failover to healthy endpoints in the event of an attack and use CloudFront to distribute your incoming traffic to lessen the burden on your origin servers.

- **AWS Shield Standard**: This is a managed DDoS protection service that is automatically enabled for all AWS customers at no additional charge. This will mitigate basic, common DDoS attacks by scrubbing malicious packets and performing scaling activities. AWS Shield Advanced provides additional capabilities for an extra fee. For the exam, make sure to remember this pricing distinction.

- **Block malicious traffic**: Several services that have been covered in this book can help to block malicious traffic, such as AWS Network Firewall and AWS **Web Application Firewall (WAF)**.

Any of these topics could hold the answer for dealing with DDoS on AWS. Make sure you understand the difference between each of the security services. Learn which ones can actually perform mitigations and which ones are more about detection.

The second attack is SQL injection. This works by submitting a malicious SQL query to your backend database via the web frontend. At worst, this can result in the loss of your database, and it often results in the unauthorized retrieval of data.

The first thing that you can do to protect against SQL injection is not specific to AWS – it is to sanitize and sanity-check user inputs before passing them to the database. Check for query length, special characters such as wildcards, and anything that might be unusual for the query being performed. This is unlikely to appear in the exam but is good practice all the same.

The main AWS service to prevent SQL injection is AWS WAF. WAF allows you to create match conditions (a set of criteria or rules that the WAF uses to inspect and evaluate incoming web traffic) to identify malicious SQL code. This will likely be the correct answer for any question asking about the right way to prevent SQL injection in the exam.

Application Network Security

The other main way to protect and secure an application is by securing the network around an application. Throughout this book, you have learned about different ways in which a network can be designed to be secure. You can review them now.

Some resources in AWS, such as RDS databases and EC2 instances, are required to be deployed into a VPC, or virtual network. VPCs have a number of features that should be configured for security, such as security groups, network access control lists (NACLs), route tables, and NAT gateways. A common question that can appear on the *SAA-C03* exam is one that asks you to select the correct security group rule to accomplish a particular goal, so make sure you are familiar with the most common port numbers, which are given here:

- 22 – SSH

- 80 – HTTP

- 443 – HTTPS

- 3389 – RDP

> **Note**
>
> The CIDR notation 0.0.0.0/0 means everywhere. If you see this in an exam question or an answer, be careful to read what the question is asking for. If the question states that they want the most secure rule, it is unlikely to be an answer containing 0.0.0.0/0.

Remember that VPCs have subnets and that they can have public and private subnets. The rule of thumb is that anything public-facing, such as a web frontend, should be placed in a public subnet, while anything containing data should be placed in a private subnet. This may appear in the exam, so make sure you are comfortable with it. Also, make sure you understand the difference between an internet gateway and a NAT gateway.

Often, customers have on-premises environments that need to be connected to the cloud, and they can do this in a few ways, such as with VPNs and Direct Connect. Remember that Direct Connect is not encrypted by default, but you can use MACsec encryption or create a VPN tunnel encrypted with IPsec. When Direct Connect features in a set of answers as a solution to a question, read the question carefully and look for a requirement for speed. Direct Connect can take several months to implement, so if there is a requirement for the fastest possible solution, Direct Connect will not be the correct answer.

Your application may have a requirement to connect to AWS services that are not in your VPC, for example, S3. In this case, it is best practice to use VPC endpoints to connect to AWS services without your traffic leaving the AWS network to the public internet. This helps protect your network traffic. Remember that there are interface endpoints and gateway endpoints. Make sure you know the difference between the two as there is often a question that has both as options in the list of answers. If trying to connect to S3 or DynamoDB, it will be a gateway endpoint. If it is not one of those services, it will be an interface endpoint.

Now that you have learned how to protect applications, you will go a level deeper and look at how to protect data.

Determine Appropriate Data Security Controls

Data is one of the most important commodities in any business and it is crucial that it is protected. The key things you are expected to know for the exam in this regard can be broadly placed in two categories: controlling data and encrypting data.

Controlling Data

Controlling data is key to ensuring your data is protected. This means controlling who can access your data, how you can recover data in the event of a disaster, how you classify and retain data, and how you back up data.

Given how important data is, you want to ensure that access to the data is limited to only those people who need to access it. By now, you are well versed in how IAM works and you can leverage IAM to ensure that you restrict which principals can access AWS managed database services. However, databases can be hosted on EC2 instances as well as managed services, and that means you have to configure access restrictions yourself. Ensure that there is an authentication method on any self-hosted databases and, if using a username and password approach, that the password is stored in AWS Secrets Manager.

Companies will often think deeply about how to mitigate malicious threats to their data, but the biggest problem facing their data is human error. A simple mistake can wipe out an entire database in seconds, so it is important to have a good data backup strategy. This is often framed around the concept of the **recovery point objective** (**RPO**), that is, how much data the business is willing to lose in the event of an outage or problem. If this is set to an hour, then you will want to back up databases every hour. Pay attention to the exam question to work out whether an RPO has been defined and work backward from that.

Related to the RPO is the **recovery time objective** (**RTO**), that is, how fast your application can get back online after an outage. Your data recovery strategy can impact this greatly. For example, if you store all of your data in cold storage, it can take several hours to restore your data. Therefore, read the question carefully to understand whether an RTO has been stated to help you select the correct answer.

Data is rarely needed forever, but you may have compliance requirements that require you to keep data for a certain number of years, or conversely, you may be required to ensure you delete data after a certain number of years. Therefore, you may see exam questions about data retention strategies. Make sure you are familiar with data lifecycle policies in S3, as well as Intelligent-Tiering, and make sure you understand how to automate the deletion of data after a period of time.

You must also know how to protect data from accidental deletion, using S3 Versioning, S3 Object Lock, MFA delete, and RDS database delete protection.

Encrypting Data

To keep data secure, it should be encrypted throughout its life cycle. It should be encrypted at rest using AWS KMS and it should be encrypted in transit using TLS and a certificate stored in **AWS Certificate Manager (ACM)**. Some AWS services support encryption of data both at rest and in transit by default, so make sure you understand which services provide that capability.

While AWS can manage encryption keys for you, you can also manage your own keys in KMS. When managing your own keys in KMS, remember to ensure that you are locking down the key so that it can only be used and managed by the principals and applications that need access to it. You may be presented with an exam question that shows you a key policy and asks you to pick the correct answer about who can use or access the key, so make sure you are familiar with how key policies work in KMS.

It is also important to ensure that encryption keys are rotated regularly. This can be automated in KMS, so make sure you are familiar with that concept. Likewise, if encrypting data in transit, certificates are only valid for a set period of time and need to be renewed, so you should also know the process for renewing certificates in ACM. This is not a common exam topic but it can come up.

Summary

In this chapter, you have learned the key concepts and skills required to understand the *Design Secure Architectures* domain of the *SAA-C03* exam. You started by exploring how to design secure access to AWS resources. This includes understanding the importance of applying AWS security best practices, such as the principle of least privilege and the shared responsibility model, when configuring IAM users, groups, roles, and policies. You have learned how to implement a flexible authorization model by leveraging AWS STS for RBAC and cross-account access. Additionally, you discovered how to utilize AWS Control Tower and SCPs to centrally manage security across multiple AWS accounts.

Next, you delved into the design of secure workloads and applications. This involved learning how to implement authentication and authorization mechanisms for application access, as well as protect against common threats such as DDoS and SQL injection attacks. You explored the use of services such as AWS Shield, AWS WAF, and secure application architecture patterns to mitigate these threats. Finally, you focused on determining appropriate data security controls. This included understanding how to control data access using IAM and database authentication, implementing data backup and recovery strategies based on RPO and RTO requirements, and managing data retention and deletion using S3 life cycle policies and RDS delete protection. Additionally, you learned the importance of encrypting data at rest using AWS KMS and in transit using TLS and ACM, as well as the management of encryption keys, including key policies, rotation, and certificate renewal.

By understanding these concepts, you are now better equipped to design secure architectures that meet the requirements of the *Design Secure Architectures* domain. In the next chapter, you will cover the *Design Resilient Architectures* exam domain.

Exam Readiness Drill - Chapter Review Questions

Apart from mastering key concepts, strong test-taking skills under time pressure are essential for acing your certification exam. That's why developing these abilities early in your learning journey is critical.

Exam readiness drills, using the free online practice resources provided with this book, help you progressively improve your time management and test-taking skills while reinforcing the key concepts you've learned.

HOW TO GET STARTED

- Open the link or scan the QR code at the bottom of this page

- If you have unlocked the practice resources already, log in to your registered account. If you haven't, follow the instructions in *Chapter 16* and come back to this page.

- Once you log in, click the START button to start a quiz

- We recommend attempting a quiz multiple times till you're able to answer most of the questions correctly and well within the time limit.

- You can use the following practice template to help you plan your attempts:

Working On Accuracy		
Attempt	Target	Time Limit
Attempt 1	40% or more	Till the timer runs out
Attempt 2	60% or more	Till the timer runs out
Attempt 3	75% or more	Till the timer runs out
Working On Timing		
Attempt 4	75% or more	1 minute before time limit
Attempt 5	75% or more	2 minutes before time limit
Attempt 6	75% or more	3 minutes before time limit

The above drill is just an example. Design your drills based on your own goals and make the most out of the online quizzes accompanying this book.

> **First time accessing the online resources?** 🔒
> You'll need to unlock them through a one-time process. **Head to** *Chapter 16* **for instructions.**

Open Quiz https://packt.link/SAAC03ch12 OR scan this QR code →	

13

Design Resilient Architectures

In this chapter, you will cover the Design Resilient Architectures exam domain. Resiliency in any IT system is crucial to business operations and it is a key area to understand for the exam. This exam domain has two task statements:

- Designing scalable and loosely coupled architectures
- Designing highly available and/or fault-tolerant architectures

These are very broad task statements and cover an awful lot of detail because resiliency is important to consider across the entire AWS platform. You will begin with designing highly available and/or fault-tolerant architectures. By the end of this chapter, you will have an overview of the topics you need to know about to improve in the *Design Resilient Architectures* domain.

Designing Highly Available and/or Fault-Tolerant Architectures

Architectures that are highly available mean that in the event of an **Availability Zone (AZ)** going down, your applications can remain operational. Werner Vogels is famous for the phrase, "Everything fails, all the time," and they are good words to live by, especially when operating mission-critical applications and infrastructure. To explore the concepts in this chapter, you are going to see how you might transform a standard three-tier architecture to be highly available.

First, let us recap the AWS global infrastructure. Remember that there are Regions, which are geographically distinct locations around the world within which you can deploy resources. Within Regions, you have AZs. AZs may be made up of several data centers, and each zone is separated so that they are on different flood plains and using different energy suppliers. This means that a localized issue should never take out all of the AZs in a Region. This is how AWS ensures that it is highly available. However, you do need to be prepared for, at the very least, an AZ-level failure.

Figure 13.1 shows a typical three-tier web application with a web frontend, an application tier, and a database tier.

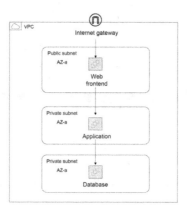

Figure 13.1: Typical three-tier application architecture in one AZ

The application tier and the database tier have been placed in private subnets for security and the web frontend is in a public subnet to receive web traffic from the internet gateway. However, this architecture is prone to a few issues. Take a minute and think about what the problems could be here.

You will notice that all the infrastructure is in a single AZ. This means that if the AZ was to go down, your application would stop working. To be more resilient, the architecture should make use of two different AZs, as shown in *Figure 13.2*:

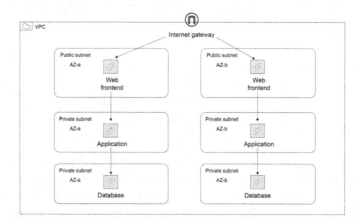

Figure 13.2: A three-tier web application spread across two AZs

As shown in *Figure 13.2*, if an AZ breaks, the application can continue to work in the remaining AZ. A common question that you may see in the exam will be about how many servers need to be deployed across how many AZs in order to meet a performance **service-level agreement (SLA)**. Make sure that the answer you select will always have at least one server up in any potential failure scenario.

This new architecture still presents issues. Now that there is infrastructure in two different zones, how does traffic know where to go? This architecture needs a load balancer. The load balancer will help to distribute traffic evenly across the infrastructure, making sure it does not send traffic to unhealthy instances. This means you do not have to worry if an AZ goes down; the load balancer will automatically send all traffic to the other healthy AZ for you (*Figure 13.3*).

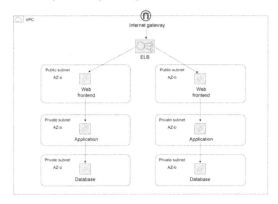

Figure 13.3: Three-tier web application with a load balancer

You will read about scaling in the next section, but there's still another improvement that can be made to this architecture. As it stands right now, the database is hosted on an EC2 instance. By replacing this database with a managed service, such as Amazon **Relational Database Service (RDS)**, it becomes easy to configure high availability with a secondary database. In the event of an AZ failure where the primary DB is located, RDS will fail over to the secondary DB to maintain your application uptime. Now, the architecture looks like *Figure 13.4*.

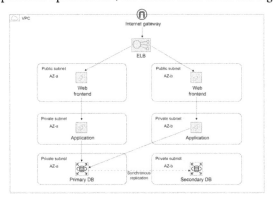

Figure 13.4: Three-tier web application across two AZs using RDS with a primary and secondary DB

One of the key issues with databases is that they can only sustain a certain number of connections. High-performing applications may need to open many more connections than the database can handle and this can result in the database refusing connections and potentially breaking an application. To get around this, you can use Amazon RDS Proxy to pool connections, lowering the burden on the database servers, while also offloading authentication to the proxy. It does come at an additional cost, however, so be mindful of any phrases in the exam question referring to the "most cost-effective solution."

Each of the preceding improvements has been made in the context of a failure occurring and small changes have been made to make the architecture more resilient to failures in an AZ. **Disaster recovery (DR)** is a very important topic to understand for the SAA-C03 exam because there will certainly be questions about it. There are two main concepts in the area of DR that you may see on the exam: **recovery point objective (RPO)** and **recovery time objective (RTO)**.

RPO refers to the maximum acceptable amount of data loss measured in time. It defines the point in time to which data must be restored after a disaster to resume operations. If the RPO is set to four hours, the backup strategy must ensure that the organization can recover data up to the last four hours before the disruption occurs. This means that data generated more than four hours before the outage is safe, but anything within that four-hour window may be lost.

RTO is the maximum acceptable amount of time that a system, application, or process can be down after a disaster before normal operations must be restored. If the RTO is set to two hours, the DR plan must ensure that all critical systems and processes can be back online and operational within two hours of the outage.

These two terms will almost certainly appear on the SAA-C03 exam, requiring you to understand DR strategies as well as data storage recovery options. For example, if the question states that RTO should be one hour, and one of the answers states that data should be restored from Glacier, you know this answer can be dismissed as wrong because Glacier takes several hours to restore data without additional fees.

Disaster Recovery Strategies

You may see DR strategies appear in the exam as part of a question. For example, a question may say something like: "A solutions architect has deployed an application in a pilot light configuration…". It is important for you to therefore understand the key DR strategies: backup and restore, pilot light, warm standby, and active-active failover.

Backup and restore is the simplest and most cost-effective DR strategy. It involves regularly backing up data and configurations to AWS and restoring them when needed. The recovery process can take hours or even days, depending on the amount of data and the complexity of the environment, and is therefore more suitable for non-critical workloads where downtime is acceptable and where higher RTO is acceptable.

The pilot light strategy, shown in *Figure 13.5*, involves keeping critical systems (such as databases) running in a minimal state in AWS. Other less critical components are turned off and only spun up during a disaster. This strategy is suitable for moderate RTO and RPO requirements as it is quicker than restoring all data. However, recovery involves scaling up the minimal environment to full production, which can still take some time.

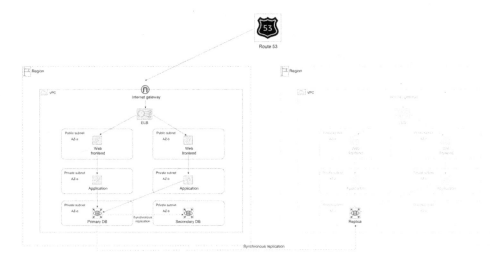

Figure 13.5: Pilot light DR strategy architecture

Warm standby (*Figure 13.6*) is similar to pilot light but it keeps all components running in a scaled-down manner. In the event of a disaster, this environment can be scaled up to handle production traffic. This has lower RTO and RPO than pilot light because you have more components already running.

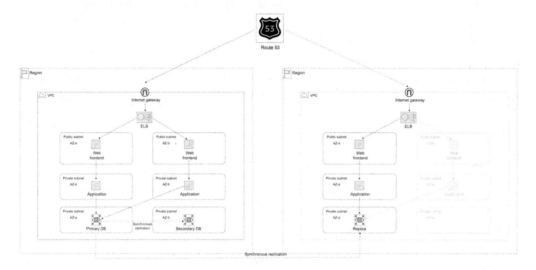

Figure 13.6: A warm standby DR recovery architecture – only half of
the infrastructure is running in the second Region

Active-active, shown in *Figure 13.7*, is the final DR strategy. This involves running a complete copy of your infrastructure in a second Region. This is the most expensive DR strategy, so pay attention to any signals in the question about cost-efficient options. However, this strategy does result in a near-zero RTO and RPO due to nothing needing to scale and no need to restore data.

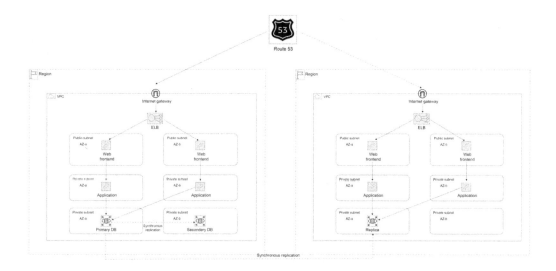

Figure 13.7: Active-Active DR strategy architecture – all infrastructure
components are fully scaled in two regions

Now that you know each of the different DR strategies, you will be equipped to answer questions about them. Most of the time, the DR strategy is used to set up the context of the question, but sometimes, the strategies form the answer, and you have to select the best option. You will next explore the *Designing Scalable and Loosely Coupled Architectures* section.

Designing Scalable and Loosely Coupled Architectures

By now, you should understand what is meant by loosely coupled. Let us recap anyway. **Loosely coupled** is a design principle where components of a system have minimal or no direct dependencies on each other. This means that if one component of the application were to break, the application may still continue to operate.

Begin with the single-region three-tier architecture that is shown in *Figure 13.4*. You have this architecture split into three tiers because it helps the application to be more scalable and resilient. If you had just one tier for the web frontend and application tiers, then if the server went down, it would take down the whole application. However, right now, this architecture is not particularly scalable and everything is very tightly coupled. If the application tier were to go down, the whole application would stop working. It might go down for a number of reasons, but one reason might be that there is too much traffic for the server to handle.

For this reason, it is crucial that the various components in this architecture can scale. The first thing that can be done is to scale out the instances using Auto Scaling. This is what is called **horizontal scaling**, and is shown in *Figure 13.8*:

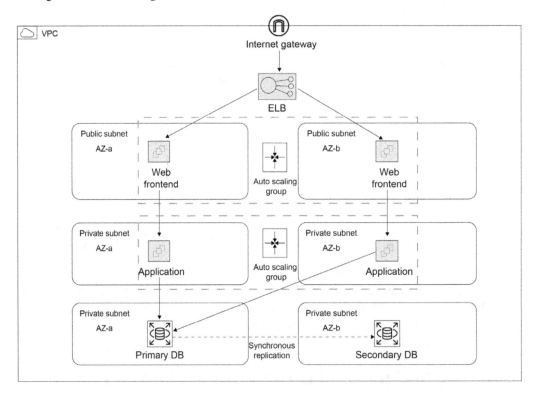

Figure 13.8: A three-tier web application with Auto Scaling groups for the web and app tiers

With auto-scaling in place, the instances can increase or decrease in number to accommodate real-time traffic fluctuations, ensuring that the application continues to work even with the toughest demands. Remember to set an upper bound for the scaling action, however. This will minimize unexpected costs.

The next component to scale is the RDS database. This can be scaled horizontally by adding read replicas. **Read replicas** offload read operations to the replicas so that the primary database can be focused entirely on write operations. Typically, there are more read operations than write operations in a database, so this can help to improve the resiliency of the database. However, if you have an increase in write operations, read replicas will do nothing to help. This is where it may become necessary to vertically scale your database, that is, to increase the size of the instance to a large instance type in order to assign more CPU and RAM.

For databases that perform the same query repeatedly – for example, an online shop fetching item prices, you can cache content using ElastiCache to reduce the burden on your database, as shown in *Figure 13.9*:

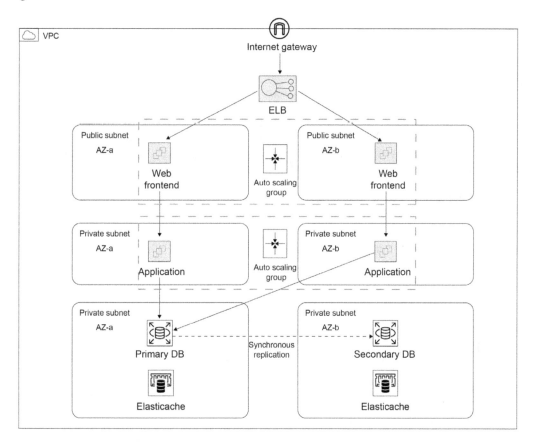

Figure 13.9: Add a caching layer to the three-tier architecture to
improve speed and reduce the burden on your database

By adding a caching layer to your database, you can not only improve your database performance (sometimes making read operations up to 80x faster), but it will also reduce costs by reducing the number of queries being made to your database.

Caching can also be done on static content that you serve on your web frontend. By using CloudFront, you can store your static content, such as web images, in S3, then use CloudFront to cache that content in edge locations all around the world, minimizing the need to pull content from a central bucket. This is a common topic for the SAA-C03 exam, so remember this.

So far, the strategies that you have learned about have been mainly in the context of EC2 instances, and a lot of them are also applicable to container workloads. But you also need to think about scaling and coupling in the context of serverless workloads.

Serverless Scalability

It is easy to forget that you need to design serverless workloads for scalability because the services themselves are fully managed and capable of scaling without you needing to lift a finger. But bottlenecks can occur between serverless services, as you learned in *Chapter 9, Serverless and Application Integration*.

Remember, when designing microservices, an important aspect is decentralization. Microservices are intended to be independently deployable and managed, often by different teams. This autonomy encourages decentralized data management, allowing each service to operate independently without being tightly coupled to other services or a central database.

A key decision to make when designing microservices is whether or not state is important. Stateless microservices do not retain any internal state between requests. Each request is processed independently, with no reliance on previous interactions. This design simplifies scaling and makes the service more resilient since any instance of the service can handle any request. It also allows for easier load balancing and failure recovery, as there is no need to manage session state or data persistence within the service itself. Stateless services are generally preferred in microservice architectures because they align well with the principles of independence and scalability.

In a microservices architecture, the goal is often to minimize statefulness as much as possible. However, when stateful services are necessary, careful design is required to ensure that they do not become bottlenecks or single points of failure.

When it comes to questions about loosely coupling architectures in the SAA-C03 exam, remember the **Simple Queue Service (SQS)**, **Simple Notification Service (SNS)**, and EventBridge service. These are the key services to decouple microservices and the correct answer will depend on the question being asked. Remember, SQS is one-to-one communication, SNS is one-to-many communication, and EventBridge is many-to-many communication. Remembering that distinction will often lead you to the correct answer.

When you have several Lambda functions that you need to coordinate, consider using Step Functions rather than decoupling using SQS. This gives you more control over the Lambda chaining process but also gives you logic to change what happens next without the need for a Lambda function to act as an intermediary. Typically, in questions that have several Lambda functions, Step Functions is often the correct answer, but make sure you read the question carefully in case there's some nuance that would impact the type of workflow you might choose.

In the last section, caching was used to reduce the burden on a database, but this can also be done at the application layer, by using API Gateway, as shown in *Figure 13.10*:

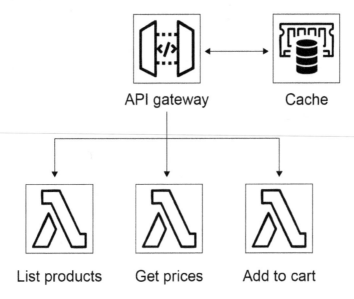

API gateway   Cache

List products   Get prices   Add to cart

Figure 13.10: Using a cache on API Gateway enables caching for stateless serverless workloads

In the same way as caching database requests, API caching will cache the API responses so that if the same request comes in again, the answer can be pulled from the cache running the task again.

Summary

In conclusion, designing resilient architectures is essential for ensuring the reliability and availability of IT systems, especially in mission-critical environments, and this is an important domain for the exam. This chapter emphasized the need to build scalable and loosely coupled architectures that can withstand failures and continue operating under adverse conditions. By transforming a standard three-tier architecture into a more robust system using multiple AZs, load balancers, and managed services, such as RDS, you can significantly enhance fault tolerance. Additionally, understanding and implementing appropriate DR strategies, such as backup and restore, pilot light, warm standby, and active-active configurations, is crucial for minimizing downtime and data loss. By applying these principles, organizations can achieve high levels of resilience, ensuring that their systems remain operational even in the face of unexpected challenges. In the next chapter, you will read about the principles and best practices for designing high-performing architectures on AWS.

Exam Readiness Drill - Chapter Review Questions

Apart from mastering key concepts, strong test-taking skills under time pressure are essential for acing your certification exam. That's why developing these abilities early in your learning journey is critical.

Exam readiness drills, using the free online practice resources provided with this book, help you progressively improve your time management and test-taking skills while reinforcing the key concepts you've learned.

HOW TO GET STARTED

- Open the link or scan the QR code at the bottom of this page

- If you have unlocked the practice resources already, log in to your registered account. If you haven't, follow the instructions in *Chapter 16* and come back to this page.

- Once you log in, click the START button to start a quiz

- We recommend attempting a quiz multiple times till you're able to answer most of the questions correctly and well within the time limit.

- You can use the following practice template to help you plan your attempts:

Working On Accuracy		
Attempt	Target	Time Limit
Attempt 1	40% or more	Till the timer runs out
Attempt 2	60% or more	Till the timer runs out
Attempt 3	75% or more	Till the timer runs out
Working On Timing		
Attempt 4	75% or more	1 minute before time limit
Attempt 5	75% or more	2 minutes before time limit
Attempt 6	75% or more	3 minutes before time limit

The above drill is just an example. Design your drills based on your own goals and make the most out of the online quizzes accompanying this book.

First time accessing the online resources? 🔒

You'll need to unlock them through a one-time process. **Head to** *Chapter 16* **for instructions**.

Open Quiz	
`https://packt.link/SAAC03Ch13`	
OR scan this QR code →	

14

Design High-Performing Architectures

Designing high-performing architectures is a critical responsibility for solutions architects, as these architectures must meet the rigorous demands of modern applications. Whether dealing with large-scale data processing, high-traffic web applications, or complex enterprise systems, the need for scalable, responsive, and efficient solutions is ever-present.

This chapter focuses on the *Design High-Performing Architectures* exam domain. It explores the key considerations across various components—storage, compute, databases, networking, and data ingestion—that collectively contribute to building solutions that not only perform well under current loads but are also scalable to accommodate future growth.

The following topics will be taught in this chapter:

- High-performing and scalable storage solutions
- High-performing and elastic compute solutions
- High-performing database solutions
- High-performing and scalable network architectures
- High-performing data ingestion and transformation solutions

By leveraging AWS services and following the AWS Well-Architected Framework, architects can design solutions that ensure optimal performance, resilience, and elasticity. This chapter provides an in-depth look at how to determine and implement high-performing solutions tailored to specific business needs, ensuring that your architecture can handle the most demanding workloads with ease and efficiency.

High-Performing and Scalable Storage Solutions

Determining high-performing and scalable storage solutions is essential for ensuring that applications can handle varying data loads efficiently and reliably. In this task, solutions architects must evaluate and select the appropriate AWS storage service—such as Amazon S3, EFS, or EBS—based on performance requirements such as latency, throughput, and IOPS. By understanding the unique characteristics of different storage types (object, file, and block storage) and their use cases, architects can design storage architectures that not only meet current demands but also scale seamlessly to support future growth and evolving business needs.

Types of AWS Storage Services

In *Chapter 5, Storage*, you learned about the key AWS storage services: Amazon S3, Amazon EFS, and Amazon EBS.

Briefly, Amazon S3 is an object store, making it ideal for a wide range of use cases, including data backups, content distribution, big data analytics, and archival storage. S3 provides features such as versioning, lifecycle policies, and fine-grained access controls, allowing you to manage data effectively throughout its lifecycle. It also offers various storage classes, such as S3 Standard, S3 Intelligent-Tiering, and S3 Glacier, enabling cost optimization by storing data based on access frequency and retrieval needs.

Amazon EFS provides simple, elastic file storage for use with AWS cloud services and on-premises resources. EFS is designed to be highly available and durable, automatically scaling to accommodate growing data needs without requiring upfront provisioning or capacity management. It supports the **Network File System** (**NFS**) protocol, making it easy to integrate with existing applications and share file data across multiple Amazon EC2 instances. EFS is ideal for workloads that require a shared filesystem, such as web serving, content management, data analytics, and media processing, offering seamless scalability and consistent low-latency performance. With features such as lifecycle management and multiple storage classes, EFS also enables cost optimization by automatically moving infrequently accessed data to lower-cost storage tiers.

Finally, Amazon EBS is a block storage service designed for use with Amazon EC2 instances. EBS provides persistent, low-latency storage that can be customized to meet the performance requirements of various workloads, including databases, enterprise applications, and transactional systems. With EBS, you can choose between different volume types optimized for throughput, IOPS, or cost, such as **General Purpose SSD (gp3)**, **Provisioned IOPS SSD (io2)**, and **Throughput Optimized HDD (st1)**. EBS volumes are automatically replicated within an AWS Availability Zone to ensure high availability and durability, and they can be easily resized and backed up using snapshots. EBS is ideal for applications requiring reliable, high-performance storage that can be tightly integrated with compute resources.

Selecting Storage Services Based on Performance Demands

Selecting the right storage service involves evaluating the specific performance needs of your application, such as required latency, throughput, and IOPS, and matching these with the capabilities of AWS storage services. It is therefore crucial to read the exam question carefully to determine any specific requirements for the storage. Does the question require the lowest cost solution? Or does it require high performance and low latency?

Amazon EBS is the go-to solution for applications requiring low-latency, high-performance block storage, such as databases and transactional systems. If the question requires low-latency storage, then EBS is likely to be the correct answer.

Amazon EFS is ideal for applications that require shared access to a file system across multiple instances, such as content management systems, web servers, and development environments. For the exam, look for requirements for NFS or multiple instances needing access to a shared file system.

Amazon S3 is optimal for scenarios requiring massive scalability and durability, such as content distribution, data lakes, and backup solutions. When examining the question for clues, look for requirements for low-cost, durable storage.

Designing Scalable Storage Solutions

Designing scalable storage solutions is vital for ensuring that your architecture can accommodate growing data volumes and evolving application demands without compromising performance or efficiency. In AWS, scalability is achieved by leveraging services that can automatically adjust to increased loads and by structuring your storage architecture to handle future expansion seamlessly.

Amazon S3 inherently provides massive scalability, allowing you to store unlimited amounts of data with ease. By utilizing S3's features such as lifecycle policies, you can automatically transition data between storage classes (e.g., from S3 Standard to S3 Glacier) based on access patterns, optimizing both cost and performance. S3's support for multi-Region replication further enhances scalability by distributing data across AWS Regions, ensuring both availability and performance on a global scale.

Amazon EFS offers elastic file storage that automatically scales up or down as you add or remove files, making it ideal for applications with unpredictable or rapidly growing storage needs. EFS's ability to scale without manual intervention simplifies the management of file systems in dynamic environments. For even greater scalability and cost efficiency, EFS allows you to choose between Standard and Infrequent Access storage classes, enabling you to optimize for workloads with varying access patterns.

Amazon EBS, while providing block storage tied to a specific EC2 instance, also supports scalability through volume resizing and performance adjustments. EBS volumes can be dynamically resized to increase capacity or IOPS, ensuring that your storage can grow alongside your application's demands. For applications requiring high availability and scalability across multiple instances, you can use EBS with Amazon EC2 Auto Scaling to automatically adjust compute resources and associated storage based on traffic or usage metrics.

When designing scalable storage solutions, it is crucial to consider both current and future needs, ensuring that your architecture can adapt as your business grows. By leveraging the inherent scalability of AWS storage services, combined with strategic use of features such as auto-scaling, data lifecycle management, and cross-region replication, you can create a robust, flexible storage infrastructure that meets performance demands today and in the future. Now that we have recapped storage, let's look at high-performance compute.

High-Performing and Elastic Compute Solutions

The ability to rapidly scale compute resources is critical for maintaining performance and handling varying workloads. This is where cloud services such as Amazon EC2, AWS Lambda, and AWS Fargate play a pivotal role. Each service offers unique capabilities that can be leveraged to optimize application performance and ensure elasticity. By understanding the strengths and appropriate use cases for these services, you can design solutions that are both responsive and cost-effective.

AWS Compute Services Overview

In *Chapter 4, Compute,* you learned about the different storage services that you can run your workloads on in AWS. Let's recap them quickly.

Amazon **Elastic Compute Cloud (EC2)** is a fundamental service that provides resizable compute capacity in the cloud. It allows users to run virtual servers, known as instances, which can be tailored to meet various performance and configuration needs. EC2 offers a diverse array of instance types optimized for different workloads, including general-purpose, compute-optimized, memory-optimized, storage-optimized, and GPU instances. This flexibility enables users to select instances based on their specific requirements.

EC2 instances can be easily scaled up or down to accommodate varying levels of demand. The service supports Auto Scaling, which automatically adjusts the number of instances in response to traffic fluctuations and workload changes. Additionally, EC2 offers both On-Demand and Reserved Instances. On-Demand Instances are billed based on actual usage, while Reserved Instances provide cost savings for long-term commitments.

AWS Fargate is a serverless compute engine for containers that integrates seamlessly with both Amazon **Elastic Container Service (ECS)** and Amazon **Elastic Kubernetes Service (EKS)**. Being a fully managed service, Fargate removes the operational overhead of managing underlying server infrastructure. Instead, users specify the CPU and memory requirements for their containers, and Fargate handles the provisioning and management of the compute resources.

Amazon ECS is a highly scalable container orchestration service that simplifies the deployment and management of containerized applications. It integrates with Fargate to allow users to run containers without managing the servers. ECS manages the scheduling and orchestration of containers, and with Fargate, users can focus on designing and building their applications rather than handling infrastructure concerns.

Similarly, Amazon EKS is a managed Kubernetes service that simplifies running Kubernetes clusters on AWS. Fargate integrates with EKS to enable serverless compute for Kubernetes workloads, providing the benefits of managed container orchestration along with the flexibility of serverless compute.

Fargate's automatic scaling feature adjusts the compute capacity for containerized applications based on demand, simplifying the scaling and management of these workloads. Its cost model, which is based on the resources used by containers, offers a cost-effective option for running containerized applications.

Finally, AWS Lambda is a serverless compute service designed to run code in response to events without the need for provisioning or managing servers. Lambda functions are executed in response to various triggers, such as data changes, HTTP requests, or messages from other AWS services. This event-driven approach allows for automated and responsive processing.

Lambda's automatic scaling capability ensures that functions can handle variable workloads without manual intervention. The service adjusts execution based on the number of incoming requests.

Lambda functions are inherently stateless, meaning they do not maintain state between executions. Any necessary state management must be handled externally, typically using services such as Amazon S3 or DynamoDB. AWS Lambda is particularly effective for event-driven applications, such as real-time data processing, API backends, and automation tasks.

Now that you remember the key compute services, let's consider some important concepts for high-performing architectures in the *SAA-C03* exam.

Decoupling Workloads for Independent Scaling

In modern cloud architectures, decoupling workloads is a key strategy for enabling independent scaling and optimizing application performance. This approach involves decomposing monolithic applications into smaller, more manageable components, each of which can be scaled independently based on its specific requirements. For instance, in a containerized web application, the web frontend can be scaled separately from the containers handling the application logic. This allows for increased scalability of the frontend during periods of high traffic, even if the application layer remains unaffected, such as when users visit the site without making API requests. Two key concepts central to this strategy are microservices and event-driven architectures, both of which play a significant role in enhancing the scalability and flexibility of compute solutions.

Microservices architecture is an approach to building applications as a collection of loosely coupled, independently deployable services. Each microservice is responsible for a specific business function and communicates with other services through well-defined APIs. Event-driven architecture complements the microservices approach by enabling services to communicate asynchronously through events. In this model, components produce and consume events to trigger actions and process data.

> **Note**
>
> Asynchronous communication means that applications can communicate without waiting for a response from the receiver. Think of it like sending a letter. You write your letter and put it in the mailbox for the mail carrier to collect, but you do not stand waiting by the postbox until you have seen the mail carrier has emptied the mailbox. You continue with your day instead, confident that the mail process will handle your letter for you. This is asynchronous communication.

For the exam, these concepts are crucial to understand in order to pick the right exam question. For example, you might be given a question that states you have decided to build a microservices architecture and then asks you to select the most appropriate answer. You would need to know what a microservices architecture is in order to select the correct answer.

Managing Compute Elasticity with Auto Scaling

Auto Scaling is a fundamental feature for managing compute elasticity in cloud environments. It automatically adjusts the number of compute resources in response to varying workload demands, ensuring that applications have the right amount of capacity at any given time. Auto Scaling is available for both Amazon EC2 instances and containerized applications running on services such as ECS and EKS.

With Amazon EC2, Auto Scaling policies can be configured to automatically add or remove instances based on criteria such as CPU utilization, network traffic, or custom metrics. This capability helps maintain performance during peak loads and reduces costs during periods of low demand. Read the exam question carefully to understand what metric should be used for auto-scaling activities.

For containerized applications managed by Amazon ECS or EKS, Auto Scaling adjusts the number of tasks or Pods based on demand. ECS integrates with Fargate to automatically scale containerized workloads without manual intervention, while EKS can leverage Kubernetes' Horizontal Pod Autoscaler to achieve similar results.

Selecting Compute Resources Based on Business Requirements

Selecting the right compute resources is crucial for designing efficient and scalable cloud architectures. This involves understanding the different types of compute resources available on AWS and choosing the appropriate ones based on specific business requirements. This means reading the question carefully!

Identifying Appropriate Instance Types and Sizes

Amazon EC2 provides a broad range of instance types, each tailored for different workloads. When selecting EC2 instances, start by evaluating the characteristics of your workload, including requirements for CPU, memory, storage, and network performance. For instance, if your application demands high processing power, compute-optimized instances such as the C6i series are ideal. These are designed for tasks such as batch processing and high-performance computing. Conversely, if your application requires substantial memory, memory-optimized instances such as the R6g series are better suited, making them appropriate for in-memory databases and real-time analytics. There are also instance types specifically for AI/ML workloads, such as the Tranium and Inferentia instance types.

Remember that AWS offers its own processor type, Graviton. Some instance types come with Graviton processors, and these can offer better performance than their Intel counterparts. It's unlikely this will appear on the exam, except perhaps in the question framing.

Storage needs also influence instance selection. Storage-optimized instances such as the I3 series are designed to handle high disk throughput, making them suitable for data warehousing and distributed file systems. Performance requirements such as throughput, **input/output operations per second (IOPS)**, and latency should guide your choice of instance type to ensure that it meets the necessary performance metrics for your application.

You may be expected to know what each of the instance family types are optimized for, so try to have a high-level understanding of each of the families.

Serverless Computing Options and When to Use Them

AWS offers serverless computing options such as AWS Lambda and AWS Fargate, which abstract away infrastructure management and automatically scale based on demand. AWS Lambda is particularly well-suited for event-driven applications where code is executed in response to events such as data changes or HTTP requests. Lambda automatically handles scaling, making it ideal for workloads with unpredictable or variable traffic patterns.

AWS Fargate complements serverless computing for containerized applications. It integrates with Amazon ECS and Amazon EKS, allowing you to run containers without managing the underlying server infrastructure. Fargate is well-suited to microservices architectures and applications requiring container orchestration with minimal infrastructure management. Serverless options often offer cost efficiency, as you only pay for the resources used during the execution of your code or containers, leading to potential savings compared to traditional compute resources.

Managing Distributed Computing Workloads

For applications involving distributed computing, such as large-scale data processing or high-performance computing, designing your system to distribute workloads across multiple compute resources is crucial. Using Amazon EC2 Auto Scaling, you can dynamically adjust the number of instances based on demand, ensuring that your application can handle varying workloads efficiently. For containerized applications, Amazon ECS or EKS with Auto Scaling helps manage the distribution of tasks or Pods, enhancing scalability and resilience.

AWS Batch can also be used to manage distributed computing workloads. AWS Batch simplifies the execution of batch computing workloads by dynamically provisioning the optimal quantity and type of compute resources based on the volume and resource requirements of the jobs submitted. It will automatically manage the execution of these jobs, including the provisioning of compute resources such as Amazon EC2 instances or AWS Fargate containers. This service is particularly useful for workloads that require significant computational resources but have sporadic or unpredictable usage patterns.

Incorporating load balancing is also important to ensure that incoming traffic is evenly distributed across multiple instances or containers. Amazon **Elastic Load Balancing** (**ELB**) offers different types of load balancers, such as **Application Load Balancer** (**ALB**) and **Network Load Balancer** (**NLB**), which cater to various traffic and routing needs.

Data distribution is another critical consideration. AWS services such as Amazon S3 provide scalable storage, while Amazon RDS and DynamoDB offer distributed database solutions. It is essential to design your architecture to support data partitioning and replication, maintaining performance and availability in a distributed environment.

Mastering these concepts is crucial for the *AWS Certified Solutions Architect – Associate (SAA-C03)* exam and for designing effective cloud solutions. By understanding how to choose and manage compute resources efficiently, you can create architectures that meet your organization's needs while achieving optimal performance and cost-effectiveness. This knowledge not only helps in passing the exam but also equips you with the skills necessary to build robust and scalable cloud environments.

High-Performing Database Solutions

Databases are central to most applications, storing and managing the data that drives business processes and user interactions. Choosing the right database solution and optimizing its performance are essential for ensuring that your applications can handle large volumes of data, provide fast access, and scale with demand.

Overview of Database Services

In *Chapter 7, Data and Analytics*, you learned about the different database services that AWS offers. Let's recap the main three: Amazon RDS, Amazon DynamoDB, and Amazon Aurora.

Amazon RDS is a managed service that simplifies the management of relational databases. It supports several popular database engines, including MySQL, PostgreSQL, MariaDB, Oracle, and SQL Server. With Amazon RDS, users benefit from automated backups, automated patch management, and easy replication. The service includes features such as Multi-AZ deployments, which enhance availability and failover support by replicating data to a standby instance in a different Availability Zone. Additionally, Amazon RDS provides the ability to create read replicas, which can distribute read traffic and improve performance. This service also supports both vertical and horizontal scaling, allowing users to adjust instance sizes or add read replicas in response to workload changes.

Amazon DynamoDB is a fully managed NoSQL database designed for applications requiring high performance with low-latency data access. It supports a key-value and document data model, making it well-suited for various applications such as gaming, IoT, and mobile apps. DynamoDB is known for its single-digit millisecond response times and automatic scaling capabilities, which adjust throughput capacity based on traffic patterns to ensure consistent performance. For applications that need multi-Region replication, DynamoDB offers global tables, providing low-latency access to data across multiple AWS Regions. Additionally, **DynamoDB Accelerator** (**DAX**) enhances performance further by reducing latency through in-memory caching.

Amazon Aurora combines the performance and availability of high-end commercial databases with the simplicity and cost-effectiveness of open source databases. Compatible with MySQL and PostgreSQL, Aurora delivers impressive performance, offering up to five times the performance of standard MySQL and three times the performance of standard PostgreSQL databases. Aurora automatically scales storage capacity up to 128 TiB as needed, and its high availability is ensured through data replication across multiple Availability Zones and continuous backups to Amazon S3. Aurora Serverless is a variant that automatically adjusts database capacity based on application demand, providing cost savings and flexibility. For globally distributed applications, Aurora global databases offer low-latency reads and fast cross-region replication.

An important topic for the *SAA-C03* exam is performance optimization in databases.

Performance Optimization in Databases

Optimizing database performance is crucial for ensuring that applications run efficiently and can handle varying workloads effectively. This section explores several strategies for enhancing the performance of databases within AWS, focusing on capacity planning, caching strategies, and replication.

Let's look at each of these strategies in the context of building a new database. When first creating a database, you need to determine how much traffic your database is likely to have.

Capacity Planning

Effective capacity planning involves provisioning adequate resources to meet current and future demands. Is the database going to have lots of write traffic, but very little read? Is it going to be balanced? These are questions that you need to ask yourself when provisioning a database.

For relational databases managed by Amazon RDS and Amazon Aurora Standard, you need to select the appropriate instance type and size to match your workload's requirements. Amazon RDS and Amazon Aurora Standard provide various instance types optimized for different tasks, such as compute-optimized, memory-optimized, or storage-optimized instances. Don't forget that you can scale vertically by changing instance types or sizes as your needs grow.

In addition to instance types, it is important to configure database storage settings to handle expected workloads. Amazon RDS allows you to provision IOPS for your storage, which can significantly impact the performance of database queries and transactions. By selecting the right IOPS settings and storage type (e.g., General Purpose SSD or Provisioned IOPS SSD), you can ensure that your database performs efficiently under high-load conditions.

Amazon DynamoDB and Amazon Aurora Serverless are fully managed, serverless services, so you do not need to determine your exact CPU requirements; however, you should still have a high-level understanding of your capacity requirements because you will need to assign capacity units when you provision your infrastructure. This can be changed if your needs change, so it isn't locked in place, but if you don't have enough capacity units provisioned, you may find that your database throttles or drops connections.

Caching Strategies

Caching is a vital technique for reducing database load and improving application performance by storing frequently accessed data in memory. Maybe you run an online shop and a couple of your products are much more popular than the others. You might want to cache the hits for these products to improve the loading speed for users.

For Amazon RDS, integrating with caching solutions such as Amazon ElastiCache can provide significant performance benefits. ElastiCache supports both Redis and Memcached, which can be used to cache query results, session data, or other frequently accessed data.

Caching reduces the need for repeated database queries, thus decreasing latency and increasing throughput. By strategically caching data that is read frequently but updated infrequently, you can offload read operations from your primary database and enhance the overall performance.

Replication and Read Replicas

Replication is another key strategy for optimizing database performance. Imagine you have a database that has loads of read traffic but very little write traffic, such as a webshop. Read replicas can help with this.

Amazon RDS supports replication through read replicas, which can be used to distribute read-heavy workloads and improve query performance. Read replicas allow you to offload read operations from the primary database instance, reducing its load and enhancing its ability to handle write operations.

Read replicas are beneficial for scenarios where applications require high availability and performance, such as reporting and analytics. They can also be used for data warehousing and business intelligence applications that demand extensive read operations. Amazon RDS makes it straightforward to create and manage read replicas, and you can configure them to be asynchronous or synchronous based on your consistency requirements. Read replicas are a common exam question topic, so make sure you understand what they can and can't be used for.

Monitoring and Tuning

Regular monitoring and tuning are essential for maintaining optimal database performance. Amazon RDS provides monitoring tools such as Amazon CloudWatch, which allows you to track key performance metrics, including CPU utilization, memory usage, and disk I/O. Analyzing these metrics helps you identify performance bottlenecks and make informed decisions about scaling or adjusting configurations.

Additionally, database parameter tuning can help optimize query performance and resource utilization. Amazon RDS offers parameter groups that allow you to adjust database engine settings to better suit your workload. For example, you might adjust parameters related to query caching, connection limits, or memory usage to achieve better performance.

By implementing these performance optimization strategies—capacity planning, caching, replication, and monitoring—you can ensure that your database systems remain responsive, reliable, and capable of handling your application's demands efficiently. Proper optimization helps in maintaining high performance and scalability, ultimately leading to a better overall user experience and more effective use of cloud resources.

Selecting Database Engines and Configurations

Choosing the right database engine and configuration is essential for designing a high-performing and scalable architecture that meets your application's specific needs. This is also important to understand for the exam as you may be presented with different database options in an exam question.

Comparing Relational and Non-Relational Databases

When selecting a database engine, one of the primary decisions is choosing between relational and non-relational (NoSQL) databases. Relational databases, such as those supported by Amazon RDS (MySQL, PostgreSQL, Oracle, and SQL Server), are ideal for applications requiring complex queries, transactional consistency, and structured data relationships. They use **Structured Query Language (SQL)** for managing and querying data, which is beneficial for applications that need strong data integrity and advanced querying capabilities.

Non-relational databases, such as Amazon DynamoDB, are designed for applications that require high scalability, flexibility, and performance with large volumes of unstructured or semi-structured data. They support various data models, including key-value and document formats, and are well-suited for scenarios where scalability and low latency access are critical. NoSQL databases excel in handling distributed data and accommodating varying data structures without requiring a fixed schema.

The key difference to note here is structured versus unstructured data. If the question states which type of data is being used, this will help you to eliminate incorrect answers.

Database Connections and Proxies

Effective management of database connections is important for optimizing performance and ensuring efficient use of resources. For relational databases on Amazon RDS, using connection pooling can help manage the number of concurrent connections and reduce the overhead associated with establishing and closing connections. Connection pools maintain a pool of open connections that can be reused by multiple requests, improving response times and reducing connection-related resource consumption.

Amazon RDS also supports database proxies, such as Amazon RDS Proxy, which acts as an intermediary between your application and the database. RDS Proxy helps improve database scalability and availability by managing and pooling connections, thereby reducing the load on the database and improving the overall performance. It also provides features such as automatic failover and connection multiplexing, which enhance reliability and efficiency.

Optimizing Data Access Patterns

Optimizing data access patterns involves designing your database schema and queries to ensure efficient data retrieval and manipulation. For relational databases, this includes indexing frequently queried columns, optimizing join operations, and structuring your tables to minimize data redundancy and enhance normalization. Proper indexing can significantly speed up query performance, but it is important to balance the number of indexes with the impact on write performance.

For NoSQL databases such as Amazon DynamoDB, designing an effective data model involves selecting appropriate partition keys and sort keys to distribute data evenly and optimize query performance. DynamoDB's use of primary keys, secondary indexes, and query filters allows you to efficiently access and manage data based on your application's access patterns.

It is unlikely that you will be asked to determine the appropriate index or partition key; however, it can appear in the exam, so familiarize yourself with the importance of partitioning.

Configuration Considerations

Configuring your database instances involves tuning various parameters to match your workload's requirements. For Amazon RDS, this includes setting database parameters related to memory allocation, cache sizes, and connection limits. Tuning these parameters can enhance performance and resource utilization, particularly for high-traffic applications.

Amazon Aurora offers additional configuration options such as Aurora Global Database for global applications and Aurora Serverless for variable workloads. Aurora Global Database provides low-latency access to data across multiple Regions, while Aurora Serverless automatically adjusts capacity based on demand, helping to manage costs and ensure scalability.

Selecting the right database engine and configuration involves evaluating your application's needs, choosing between relational and non-relational databases, managing connections and proxies, optimizing data access patterns, and fine-tuning database configurations. By carefully considering these factors, you can design a database architecture that delivers high performance, scalability, and efficiency, aligning with the requirements of your AWS-based solutions.

High-Performing and/or Scalable Network Architectures

Networks form the backbone of cloud architectures, facilitating communication between services, applications, and users. Properly designed network architectures ensure that your applications are resilient, responsive, and capable of handling varying loads while maintaining high availability and performance.

Overview of Network Services

In *Chapter 2*, *Virtual Private Cloud*, you learned about the fundamentals of networking in AWS. Let's recap what you learned. Networking in AWS encompasses a comprehensive set of services and features designed to manage connectivity and communication within your cloud infrastructure. AWS provides robust networking capabilities to ensure applications are secure, scalable, and high-performing.

Amazon **Virtual Private Cloud** (**VPC**) is a foundational service that enables you to create a private, isolated network within the AWS cloud. Through VPC, you define your network's IP address range, establish subnets, set up route tables, and configure network gateways. This control over network topology, security, and connectivity allows you to manage resources such as EC2 instances and databases effectively.

Within a VPC, you can create subnets to segment your network and isolate resources. Subnets can be designated as public, which allows internet access, or private, which restricts direct internet access. IP addressing within VPCs is managed using CIDR blocks, and routing is controlled via route tables that direct traffic both within the VPC and to external destinations.

For internet and VPN connectivity, AWS offers several solutions. Internet gateways provide direct internet access, while NAT gateways or NAT instances allow private subnets to access the internet for outbound traffic. To establish secure connections to on-premises networks, AWS provides virtual private gateways and VPN connections.

ELB plays a crucial role in distributing incoming application traffic across multiple targets such as EC2 instances and containers. ELB includes different types of load balancers: ALBs for HTTP/HTTPS traffic, NLBs for TCP/UDP traffic, and **Classic Load Balancers** (**CLBs**) for both HTTP/HTTPS and TCP traffic.

AWS Global Accelerator enhances the performance and availability of global applications by routing user traffic through AWS's extensive global network. This service provides static IP addresses and directs traffic to the nearest AWS edge location, thus reducing latency and improving application performance.

Security groups and network **access control lists** (**ACLs**) are key components for managing traffic security. Security groups act as virtual firewalls for EC2 instances, controlling inbound and outbound traffic with stateful rules. Network ACLs, on the other hand, provide additional security at the subnet level with stateless rules that must be defined for both inbound and outbound traffic.

AWS Direct Connect offers a dedicated network connection between your on-premises data center and AWS. This private connection can provide more consistent network performance and lower latency compared to internet-based connections.

Lastly, Amazon Route 53 is a scalable DNS service that handles domain name resolution for applications. It offers routing features based on latency, health checks, and geographic location to ensure high availability and optimal performance.

Now that your memory is refreshed, learn how to build scalable network architectures.

Designing Scalable Network Architectures

A well-designed network architecture can adapt to changing demands, support growth, and provide seamless user experiences. This section explores key considerations and strategies for creating scalable network architectures in AWS.

Creating Scalable Network Topologies

A scalable network topology starts with a solid design that can grow and adapt to changing requirements. In AWS, this often involves designing a network with multiple **Availability Zones** (**AZs**) to ensure high availability and fault tolerance. By distributing your resources across multiple AZs, you can minimize the impact of a single AZ failure on your application's overall availability.

Within your VPC, you should create a hierarchical network structure that includes public and private subnets. Public subnets can host resources that need direct internet access, such as web servers and load balancers. Private subnets are used for resources that do not require direct internet access, such as application servers and databases. This separation enhances security and allows for better management of network traffic.

Selecting the Appropriate Load Balancer

ELB is crucial for managing incoming traffic and ensuring that it is distributed efficiently across your resources. To design a scalable architecture, choose the right type of load balancer based on your application's needs:

ALB: Ideal for applications that require advanced routing features at the application layer, such as URL-based routing or host-based routing, an ALB can handle HTTP and HTTPS traffic and supports WebSocket connections, making it suitable for web applications and microservices.

NLB: Best for applications that need to handle high-throughput and low-latency TCP or UDP traffic, an NLB operates at the transport layer and provides static IP addresses, which is useful for applications with high-performance requirements or those that require a fixed IP address for incoming traffic.

CLB: Provides basic load balancing at both the application and transport layers. While a CLB is suitable for legacy applications, it lacks some of the advanced features offered by the ALB and NLB.

For the exam, the right load balancer is more than likely not going to be the CLB. AWS recommends not using this load balancer type, and for that reason, it's unlikely to be the correct answer. This means that, when determining the most appropriate load balancer, you'll be selecting between the ALB and NLB. Two of the key differentiators between these load balancers are the supported protocols and static IP support. If your application is a web application communicating with HTTP/HTTPS, then you will need to use an ALB. Likewise, if your application requires that your load balancer has a static IP address, you will need to use an NLB.

Network Configurations for Global and Hybrid Architectures

For applications with global reach, AWS Global Accelerator can enhance performance by routing user traffic through AWS's global network. This service optimizes the path from users to your application, reducing latency and improving response times. It provides static IP addresses and intelligently directs traffic to the closest and most available endpoints, which is particularly beneficial for applications with a global user base.

In hybrid architectures, where you integrate on-premises infrastructure with cloud resources, AWS Direct Connect can provide a dedicated, high-bandwidth connection between your on-premises data center and AWS. This connection offers more consistent network performance and lower latency compared to internet-based connections, making it ideal for data-intensive applications or those with stringent performance requirements.

Implementing Redundancy and Failover

Designing for scalability also involves planning for redundancy and failover to ensure uninterrupted service in the event of a failure. Utilize multiple load balancers and redundant network components to avoid single points of failure. For instance, deploying ELBs across multiple AZs ensures that if one AZ becomes unavailable, traffic can still be routed to healthy instances in other AZs.

Designing scalable network architectures in AWS involves creating flexible and resilient network topologies, selecting appropriate load-balancing strategies, configuring networks for global and hybrid scenarios, implementing redundancy and failover mechanisms, and optimizing performance with edge services. You will now look at optimizing network performance.

Optimizing Network Performance

Effective network optimization involves minimizing latency, maximizing throughput, and ensuring reliable connectivity. In AWS, several strategies and services can help you achieve these goals and enhance the performance of your network architecture.

Using Edge Services

One of the key strategies for optimizing network performance is leveraging edge services, such as Amazon CloudFront. CloudFront is a **content delivery network** (**CDN**) that caches and delivers content from a network of globally distributed edge locations. By serving content from locations closer to end users, CloudFront reduces latency and improves load times for both static and dynamic content.

CloudFront also integrates with other AWS services such as Amazon S3 for content storage and AWS Lambda for serverless computing, allowing you to implement custom logic and processing at the edge. This reduces the need for data to travel back and forth between your origin servers and end users, further enhancing performance.

Optimizing Network Connection Options

Optimizing network connection options is another important aspect. AWS Direct Connect establishes a dedicated network connection between your on-premises data center and AWS. This private connection bypasses the public internet, offering lower latency, more consistent performance, and higher bandwidth compared to traditional internet connections. Direct Connect is particularly useful for applications requiring large data transfers or with stringent performance requirements.

Amazon VPC Peering facilitates connecting two VPCs within the same Region or across Regions, enabling resources in different VPCs to communicate as if they were within the same network. This setup optimizes traffic routing and reduces latency by keeping communication within the AWS Backbone network rather than routing through the internet. Additionally, AWS Transit Gateway simplifies the management of inter-VPC and on-premises network connectivity by acting as a central hub. It allows connections between multiple VPCs and on-premises networks through a single gateway, reducing complexity and streamlining network architecture.

Placement of Resources

Strategically placing your resources within AWS can significantly impact network performance. When designing your network, consider the following:

Proximity to users: Deploy resources in AWS Regions and Availability Zones that are geographically close to your user base to reduce latency. For global applications, use services such as AWS Global Accelerator to direct user traffic to the nearest AWS edge location.

Load balancer placement: Position load balancers in a way that optimizes traffic distribution and minimizes latency. For instance, placing ALBs in front of your application servers can help handle incoming requests efficiently and route them to the appropriate backend resources.

Subnet configuration: Properly configure subnets to ensure efficient routing and isolation of network traffic. Use public subnets for resources that require internet access and private subnets for internal resources to optimize traffic flow and security.

This is actually an important thing to remember for the exam. You may be asked a question about the best location to deploy infrastructure, given the geographical location provided in the question.

Monitoring and Troubleshooting

Continuous monitoring and troubleshooting are essential for maintaining optimal network performance. Amazon CloudWatch provides monitoring and logging capabilities for AWS resources, including network-related metrics such as latency and throughput. CloudWatch allows setting alarms and automated actions based on predefined thresholds. AWS X-Ray offers tracing and analysis of network requests, helping identify performance bottlenecks and troubleshoot issues within distributed applications. X-Ray provides insights into request flows and latency, enabling precise diagnosis of performance issues. VPC Flow Logs captures and analyzes network traffic within your VPC, offering visibility into traffic patterns, detecting anomalies, and troubleshooting connectivity issues. Flow Logs helps you understand the source and destination of traffic, optimizing network performance and security.

These considerations for optimizing network performance lay the groundwork for handling the complex challenges of data management. As we transition into the next section, you will delve into data ingestion and transformation solutions, exploring how to effectively capture, process, and analyze data to drive informed decision-making and operational efficiency.

High-Performing Data Ingestion and Transformation Solutions

Data ingestion and transformation play pivotal roles in handling and processing the vast amounts of data generated by modern applications. This section delves into the important aspects of designing efficient data ingestion and transformation solutions within AWS environments. As businesses increasingly rely on real-time data for decision-making and operational efficiency, it becomes essential to understand how to effectively capture, process, and analyze data streams.

Overview of Data Ingestion Services

Data ingestion is a fundamental process for managing the flow of data into your AWS environment. It involves collecting and transferring data from various sources into your data storage or processing systems, where it can be analyzed and utilized. You have learned how to ingest data into AWS. Some of these services include Amazon Kinesis, AWS DataSync, and AWS Storage Gateway.

Amazon Kinesis is a powerful service for real-time data streaming. It enables you to collect, process, and analyze large streams of data records in real time. Amazon Kinesis provides three main components: Kinesis Data Streams, Kinesis Data Firehose, and Kinesis Data Analytics. Kinesis Data Streams allows you to build custom, real-time applications by processing data streams from sources such as website clickstreams, database events, or social media feeds. Kinesis Data Firehose simplifies the process of loading streaming data into other AWS services, such as Amazon S3, Amazon Redshift, or Amazon Elasticsearch. Kinesis Data Analytics enables you to query and analyze streaming data in real time using standard SQL queries.

AWS DataSync is a managed service that simplifies the process of transferring large amounts of data between on-premises storage and AWS storage services. It supports data transfer to and from Amazon S3, Amazon EFS, and Amazon FSx for Windows File Server. DataSync automates and accelerates data transfers while ensuring data integrity and minimizing the operational overhead associated with manual data migration tasks. This service is particularly useful for data migration projects, backup and restore operations, and ongoing data synchronization.

AWS Storage Gateway is a hybrid cloud storage service that enables on-premises applications to seamlessly use AWS cloud storage. It offers three gateway services: File Gateway, Volume Gateway, and Tape Gateway. File Gateway provides a file interface for accessing objects in Amazon S3, allowing you to store files in the cloud while maintaining a local cache for frequently accessed data. Volume Gateway offers iSCSI block storage volumes that can be backed up to Amazon S3 or Amazon EBS, and Tape Gateway provides a virtual tape library interface for backup applications, enabling you to archive data to Amazon S3 Glacier or S3 Glacier Deep Archive.

Each of these services plays a crucial role in the data ingestion ecosystem, offering various capabilities to address different use cases. Whether you need real-time streaming, large-scale data transfers, or hybrid cloud storage integration, AWS provides the tools to effectively manage and ingest data, ensuring that it is readily available for analysis and application use.

Designing Data Streaming Architectures

Designing data streaming architectures is essential for efficiently managing and processing real-time data flows. With the growing need for instant insights and timely decision-making, it is critical to implement robust architectures that can handle high-velocity data streams while ensuring scalability and reliability. This section discusses the key considerations and components for designing effective data streaming architectures using AWS services.

Data streaming architectures are ideal for scenarios where timely processing of data is critical. Examples include monitoring and analyzing social media feeds, processing log files for real-time analytics, online gaming, and handling financial transactions. These use cases benefit from architectures that can ingest and process data in near-real time, allowing for rapid insights and responses.

Implementing Data Lakes

A data lake is a centralized repository that allows you to store structured and unstructured data at scale. It enables you to collect data from various sources and process it as needed. To design a data lake architecture, start by selecting a storage solution such as Amazon S3, which provides durable and scalable storage for large volumes of data.

To integrate data streams into a data lake, use services such as Amazon Kinesis Data Firehose to continuously stream data into your storage solution. Kinesis Data Firehose can automatically batch, compress, and encrypt data before loading it into Amazon S3. Once the data is in S3, you can use AWS Glue to catalog and transform the data, making it available for analytics.

Securing data ingestion points is critical to protect your data and ensure compliance with security and privacy regulations. Implement access controls and encryption for data in transit and at rest. AWS services such as AWS **Identity and Access Management (IAM)** and AWS **Key Management Service (KMS)** can help manage access permissions and encrypt data. Additionally, configure network security measures such as **Virtual Private Cloud (VPC)** endpoints and security groups to control data traffic and access to your data ingestion services.

Designing for Scalability

Scalability is a key consideration in data streaming architectures to handle varying data loads. Use managed services such as Amazon Kinesis Data Streams and AWS DataSync that automatically scale to accommodate increased data volumes. Implement partitioning and sharding strategies in Kinesis Data Streams to distribute data across multiple shards, ensuring that your system can handle high throughput.

To further enhance scalability, consider using AWS Lambda functions in combination with data streams. Lambda functions can process data in real time as it flows through Kinesis Data Streams or Amazon S3, enabling you to build event-driven processing pipelines that scale automatically with the data load.

Data Transformation and Processing

Effective transformation and processing enable you to derive meaningful insights from diverse data sources, ensuring that data is accurate, structured, and ready for use.

Transforming Data Formats

Data transformation involves converting data from its raw form into a format that is suitable for analysis or integration with other systems. AWS Glue is an **extract, transform and load (ETL)** service that simplifies this process by allowing you to prepare and transform data. Glue can automatically discover and catalog metadata from various sources, making it easier to clean, enrich, and transform data. It supports a range of transformations, including data cleansing, schema evolution, and format conversions.

AWS Glue provides a serverless environment for running ETL jobs, eliminating the need to manage infrastructure. It integrates with other AWS services such as Amazon S3, Amazon Redshift, and Amazon RDS, enabling seamless data movement and transformation across different storage and database solutions. If a question requires a service with ETL capabilities, then Glue will almost certainly be the correct answer.

Selecting Compute Options for Large-Scale Data Processing

When dealing with large-scale data processing, selecting the right compute resources is crucial. AWS offers several options tailored to handle extensive data tasks. Amazon EMR provides a managed cluster platform for running big data frameworks such as Apache Hadoop, Apache Spark, and Apache HBase. It distributes workloads across multiple instances, allowing for the rapid processing of large datasets. EMR automatically provisions and scales the necessary infrastructure based on workload demands and integrates with other AWS services for data storage and analysis.

AWS Batch is another solution designed for managing and executing batch computing workloads efficiently. It handles job scheduling, provisioning, and scaling of compute resources based on job requirements, making it ideal for processing large volumes of data, running simulations, or executing complex computational tasks. For more specialized needs, Amazon EC2 offers virtual servers that can be tailored to meet specific computational requirements. EC2 instances are versatile, supporting custom scripts or applications for parallel data processing, with a range of instance types and sizes to balance performance and cost.

Implementing Visualization Strategies

Visualization is an important aspect of data analysis, as it transforms processed data into actionable insights. AWS provides several tools for effective data visualization. Amazon QuickSight is a scalable business intelligence service that enables the creation of interactive dashboards and visualizations. It supports data sources such as Amazon S3, Amazon RDS, and Amazon Redshift, offering features such as machine-learning-powered insights, ad hoc analysis, and customizable visualizations to help explore and understand data.

Amazon Athena provides an interactive query service that allows analysis of data stored in Amazon S3 using standard SQL queries. It is particularly useful for ad hoc querying and can be integrated with visualization tools such as QuickSight to present query results visually. AWS Glue DataBrew is a visual data preparation tool that simplifies data cleaning and normalization without requiring code. It offers an interactive interface for transforming data, preparing datasets, and creating visualizations.

Summary

This chapter outlined the key elements for designing high-performing architectures on AWS, essential for the *SAA-C03* exam. It covered the task statements for designing high-performing storage, compute, networking, and data ingestion architectures, recapping relevant services where necessary, and giving tips for answering *SAA-C03* exam questions. The final exam domain, *Design Cost-Optimized Architectures*, will be covered in the next chapter.

Exam Readiness Drill - Chapter Review Questions

Apart from mastering key concepts, strong test-taking skills under time pressure are essential for acing your certification exam. That's why developing these abilities early in your learning journey is critical.

Exam readiness drills, using the free online practice resources provided with this book, help you progressively improve your time management and test-taking skills while reinforcing the key concepts you've learned.

HOW TO GET STARTED

- Open the link or scan the QR code at the bottom of this page

- If you have unlocked the practice resources already, log in to your registered account. If you haven't, follow the instructions in *Chapter 16* and come back to this page.

- Once you log in, click the START button to start a quiz

- We recommend attempting a quiz multiple times till you're able to answer most of the questions correctly and well within the time limit.

- You can use the following practice template to help you plan your attempts:

Working On Accuracy		
Attempt	Target	Time Limit
Attempt 1	40% or more	Till the timer runs out
Attempt 2	60% or more	Till the timer runs out
Attempt 3	75% or more	Till the timer runs out
Working On Timing		
Attempt 4	75% or more	1 minute before time limit
Attempt 5	75% or more	2 minutes before time limit
Attempt 6	75% or more	3 minutes before time limit

The above drill is just an example. Design your drills based on your own goals and make the most out of the online quizzes accompanying this book.

First time accessing the online resources? 🔒

You'll need to unlock them through a one-time process. **Head to** *Chapter 16* **for instructions**.

Open Quiz

https://packt.link/SAAC03Ch14

OR scan this QR code →

15
Design Cost-Optimized Architectures

The *Design Cost-Optimized Architectures* exam domain forms the smallest component of the *SAA-C03* exam at just 20% of the questions. However, it is a really important area to be familiar with. A good grasp of cost optimization will help you not only in the exam but in your jobs as well. A good architect will balance cost against value, so it is crucial to understand the various areas for improvement. This domain has four task statements:

- Design cost-optimized storage solutions
- Design cost-optimized compute solutions
- Design cost-optimized database solutions
- Design cost-optimized network architectures

You will begin with the first task statement, *Design Cost-Optimized Storage Solutions*.

Design Cost-Optimized Storage Solutions

Storage is a critical component of any cloud architecture, and its costs can quickly escalate if not properly optimized. In this section, you will explore techniques for designing cost-effective storage solutions on AWS. You will begin by understanding the pricing models and cost characteristics of the various AWS storage services, such as Amazon S3, Amazon EFS, and Amazon EBS. You will then delve into strategies for leveraging storage access patterns to minimize costs, including optimizing for batch uploads, implementing storage tiering, and managing data life cycles. Next, you will learn how to select the most cost-effective storage service for your workloads based on factors such as access patterns, throughput requirements, and retention needs. Finally, you will cover best practices for managing data transfer costs and designing cost-optimized backup and archival solutions. By the end of this section, you will have a solid understanding of how to design storage architectures that balance performance, durability, and cost to meet your business requirements.

Understanding AWS Storage Services and Cost Characteristics

In *Chapter 5*, *Storage*, you learned all about the various storage services that AWS offers, and you have recapped these in the previous exam domain chapters. It is important to now focus on those same services through a cost-optimized lens.

Amazon S3

S3 operates a tiered pricing model based on storage, requests, and data transfer. This means that the more you store in S3, the more you are charged. You are charged for data transfer out of S3 to the internet or out of the Region that your S3 bucket is stored in. You are not charged for the transfer of data into AWS.

The more you store in S3, the cheaper the per-GB price becomes. For example, in us-east-1, for the first 50 TB you store in S3, the price is \$0.023 per GB. After 50 TB, the price decreases to \$0.022 per GB, and then after 500 TB, the price reduces again to \$0.021. This is built into S3 pricing and automatically applied to your billing. This particular fact is unlikely to appear in the exam but it is a useful fact to note.

Amazon S3 Glacier

The key pricing difference from S3 is that there are retrieval fees for retrieving data from Glacier. How large these fees are depends on the storage class; classes in which data is retrieved quickly will have a higher retrieval fee.

Amazon EFS

EFS also has tiered pricing based on storage, but unlike S3, EFS pricing is also based on the throughput provisioned, that is, whether you have provisioned burst or provisioned throughput. There are also charges for data transfer.

Amazon EBS

Finally, EBS is charged based on the volume type, amount of storage, throughput, and IOPS provisioned. EBS has several volume types:

- General Purpose SSD (gp3)
- General Purpose SSD (gp2)
- Provisioned IOPS SSD (io2)
- Throughput Optimized HDD (st1)
- Cold HDD (sc1)

The gp2 volumes are charged on provisioned storage only, with performance in IOPS and throughput increasing in line with the amount of storage provisioned. On the other hand, with gp3 volumes, IOPS and throughput can be configured separately to the storage provisioned. Not only does this give you greater flexibility but it often works out cheaper than gp2 volumes because you are not having to provision more storage than required to get the performance that you need. For the exam, remembering that gp3 is more performant than gp2 should be sufficient to help you select the right answer if you need to select between them.

You will also be charged for the storage of snapshots that are taken of your EBS volumes. EBS snapshots are incremental, however, so after the initial full snapshot, you will only be charged for the blocks that have changed.

Leveraging Storage Access Patterns for Cost Optimization

Beyond understanding the pricing models of AWS storage services, it's crucial to design your storage solutions with access patterns in mind. The way you interact with your storage can have a significant impact on your overall costs. In this section, you will look at strategies for leveraging storage access patterns to optimize your storage expenses.

Batch Uploads versus Individual Uploads

Remember that for S3, AWS charges per PUT, COPY, POST, and LIST request. It may, therefore, be cheaper to place data into larger batches to reduce the number of requests being made to S3. S3 Batch Operations is a service that can help you with this, but the base pricing is $0.25 per job as well as $1.00 per million object operations, so this should only be used when working with millions and millions of objects. Otherwise, for small, ad hoc uploads, it will be cheaper to upload as normal.

Storage Tiering and Lifecycle Management

In *Chapter 5, Storage,* you learned that S3 storage has several storage classes that affect how you are charged for your data storage as well as how readily accessible your data is. These are as follows:

- Standard
- Standard-Infrequent Access
- One Zone-Infrequent Access
- Express One Zone
- Glacier Instant Retrieval
- Glacier Flexible Retrieval
- Glacier Deep Archive

Standard is the most expensive storage tier and Glacier is the cheapest in terms of data storage. But Glacier has retrieval costs and may take time to retrieve data depending on the class of Glacier selected. This means that each storage class has use cases that it is appropriate for. In exam questions about S3 storage classes, make sure you identify the data use case and whether there are any availability or cost requirements. The question will often state that the data is needed regularly for X months, after which it is still needed but rarely accessed. In this case, you would keep the data in the Standard class for the X months, then move the data to Glacier. This means that the data is accessible for the time it is regularly accessed, and then you can take advantage of the super cheap storage of Glacier.

There is one additional tier, **Intelligent-Tiering**. This will move your data between Standard and Infrequent Access, depending on the access patterns of the data. This enables you to automatically benefit from cost savings for data with sporadic or changing data access patterns.

Both EBS and EFS also have archiving cold storage options that are cheaper but have lower performance. EFS also has an Infrequent Access tier.

Managing the movement of data between storage classes manually is a tedious job and can definitely be a full-time job for businesses with lots of data. It is important to leverage lifecycle policies to move data between storage classes automatically. This can be done in S3 and EFS. This way, you can move data to cheaper archive classes when the data is not needed regularly. This is useful for regulatory workloads that need to keep data for a certain number of years but do not need to access it except in rare circumstances.

For EBS snapshots, you can leverage Amazon Data Lifecycle Manager to help you configure retention schedules for EBS snapshots.

Now that you have reviewed cost optimization for storage, you can move on to compute solutions.

Design Cost-Optimized Compute Solutions

Compute is an area in AWS that can lead to spiraling costs if not optimized correctly. Several strategies can be employed to help you optimize your compute spend, such as selecting the best pricing model for your workload, selecting the right compute platform for your workload, and leveraging regional savings.

AWS Compute Service Pricing Models

In *Chapter 4, Compute*, you learned about the different instance purchase models:

- **On-Demand**: Standard instance purchase option where you pay for the instance family type, length of operation, and OS type on a per-hour or per-second basis, depending on the OS selected.

- **Reserved Instances**: Reserve instance capacity for 1 or 3 years, paying either all upfront, partial upfront, or none upfront.

- **Spot**: Bid for spare compute capacity.

- **Savings Plans**: Reserve compute capacity for 1 or 3 years. Includes EC2 instances, Lambda, Fargate, and SageMaker.

- **Dedicated Hosts/Instances**: Reserve hardware just for your use.

Savings Plans and Reserved Instances can potentially provide savings of up to 72%, while Spot Instances can offer up to 90% savings. Remember that Savings Plans and Reserved Instances are best for consistent, known workloads, whereas Spot Instances are better for spiky, unpredictable workloads. So, read the question carefully to pick the correct answer. If the choice is between Savings Plans and Reserved Instances, look for whether the question states the need for Fargate or Lambda compute. Only Savings Plans can address compute other than instances.

Dedicated Hosts/Instances should be the correct answer if the question states that dedicated hardware is required. If the question states that the customer has licenses already that they would like to use, then the correct answer will be Dedicated Hosts.

Selecting the Appropriate Compute Service and Instance Type

The easiest way to save money with EC2 is to ensure that you select the right instance type. If you have general workloads such as web applications, then use a general-purpose instance family such as the t3 family and make sure it is sized appropriately. You can increase the size of your instance where necessary so there is no need to select a large instance "just in case."

Further to this, use the latest generation instance types where possible. They have improvements in performance that should result in lower costs.

EC2 is only the answer for certain workloads, however. It is a great option for steady, known workloads. But if you have unknown compute requirements, then Lambda may be a much cheaper alternative. You only pay for the compute when the Lambda function is actually running, which is perfect for spiky workloads.

Fargate is also good for workloads with variable or unpredictable resource requirements and is perfect for longer-running operations that Lambda can't handle because of its timeout limit. Because it's billed by the second, it's perfect for intermittent workloads.

For the exam, the key thing to look for in the question is whether the workload is consistent and steady or whether it is intermittent.

By carefully selecting the appropriate compute service for your workloads and applying the relevant cost-optimization strategies, you can significantly reduce your compute-related expenses. The key is to align your choice of compute service with the specific requirements and characteristics of your applications.

Optimizing Compute Utilization

For EC2 and Fargate/ECS, it is crucial to take advantage of autoscaling to help you balance the need for more compute against saving money. Autoscaling will allow you to scale up your compute when you need it and scale it down when you don't so that you don't pay for more than you need.

Also, remember that EC2 only charges for instances when they are running, so consider stopping instances if they are not in use. You could even consider scheduling instances to shut down when they are not needed using a Lambda function.

Leveraging the AWS Global Infrastructure for Cost Optimization

Different Regions are priced differently according to resource availability or the size of the Region. While cost may not be the primary factor when deciding where to deploy compute, it is a factor to consider. Also, consider whether you will need to transfer data to other regions and what service availability is like for the region you want to deploy to.

Try to minimize inter-region data transfer to keep costs low, and if you do have globally distributed applications, use AWS Global Accelerator to reduce the data transfer costs. You can also leverage a **content delivery network** (**CDN**) such as CloudFront to reduce data transfer costs, making sure to store unchanging static content at the edge.

Design Cost-Optimized Database Solutions

After exploring strategies for cost-optimizing storage and compute, you can now turn your attention to the database layer of your cloud architecture. Databases are a critical component of most applications, and their costs can quickly escalate if not properly managed. In this section, you will dive into techniques for designing cost-optimized database solutions on AWS. You will start by evaluating the various database services offered by AWS, such as Amazon RDS, Amazon Aurora, and Amazon DynamoDB, and learn the key factors to consider when selecting the most appropriate service for your workloads. From there, you will explore specific cost-optimization strategies for each database service, covering topics such as right-sizing instances, leveraging pricing models, and optimizing data models and access patterns. By the end of this section, you will have a comprehensive understanding of how to design database architectures that balance performance, scalability, and cost-effectiveness.

Choosing the Right Database Service

In *Chapter 7, Data and Analytics*, you learned about the three main database services: Amazon RDS, Amazon Aurora, and Amazon DynamoDB. Choosing the right service for your database can greatly impact your costs, and there are some considerations for each service.

RDS is a managed relational database service that supports a number of SQL-based database engines. When you provision an RDS database, you select which instance type you would like your database to run on. Make sure you select an appropriate instance type for your database. Do not select one that is too large; remember that you can increase the size of your instance as needed. You can also leverage Reserved Instances and Savings Plans for RDS instances.

Aurora is also a managed relational database service, but Aurora only supports MySQL or PostgreSQL. One of the key cost-optimization strategies for Aurora is to leverage its autoscaling capabilities. It can automatically provision additional read replicas and remove them when no longer required.

Finally, DynamoDB is a managed NoSQL database, perfect for unstructured data with unpredictable workloads. With DynamoDB, you provision capacity for read and write, so ensure you do not provision more capacity than you need. This can be changed later if required.

Database Capacity Planning and Optimization

Selecting the right instance type for RDS-based databases is a crucial skill for the *SAA-C03* exam. You will not need to necessarily know the exact CPU and memory requirements for each instance type, but you should understand which instance types are memory-optimized, which are compute-optimized, and which is best for each workload. Memory-optimized instances are typically better for in-memory data processing workloads such as real-time analytics and caching, while compute-optimized instance types are usually better for data transformation or write-heavy tasks.

For platforms such as Aurora and DynamoDB that use capacity units to measure performance, understanding how these capacity units work and how to plan for them can help you select the right database configurations to meet performance needs and control costs.

Leveraging Database Features for Cost Savings

Database services in AWS have a number of features that can help with cost optimization, including read replicas, serverless options, and caching strategies.

Read replicas can help offload read-heavy workloads from the primary database, leading to cost savings. By distributing read operations across multiple read replicas, you can scale your read capacity without needing to scale the primary database, which is typically more expensive. This means that you might be able to use a less expensive database instance for the primary database.

Serverless databases can be good for cost optimization when you have spiky workloads because serverless databases charge based on the actual usage of resources (e.g., compute and storage), rather than requiring you to provision and pay for a fixed capacity. They can also scale automatically based on the workload's demands, ensuring that you don't have to pay for increased costs all the time. Finally, because the database is fully managed by AWS, it can reduce the operational overhead and administrative tasks, which can translate to a reduction in cost to the business.

Finally, by caching frequently accessed data in memory, you can offload read-heavy workloads from the primary database, reducing the load and potentially allowing you to use a smaller, less expensive database instance. This also has downstream performance impacts, by improving the response times of the application.

Managing Database Backup and Retention Costs

To ensure that a database is resilient and highly available, it is best practice to perform regular backups, but you have to pay for the storage of these backups and this can accrue costs.

When optimizing backup storage strategies, remember that backups stored in S3 can take advantage of the S3 storage classes, so ensure that lifecycle policies are configured to move backups to cold storage as required. Make sure to pay attention to any **recovery time objective** (**RTO**) and **recovery point objective** (**RPO**) requirements in the exam question to ensure you select the correct storage class. If data is required immediately, then it is unlikely that Glacier is the correct answer.

RPO is also a good thing to consider for exam questions about backup frequency. To ensure good cost optimization, you do not want to take more backups than you need to meet your RPO.

With compute and databases considered, you will now learn more about designing cost-optimized network architectures.

Design Cost-Optimized Network Architectures

When designing cost-effective network solutions, it is essential to consider the various AWS services and features that can help you optimize your network-related expenses. The exam covers a wide range of networking concepts and services, and your ability to leverage them to achieve cost savings will be a key differentiator in your performance.

Network Connectivity Options and Their Costs

In *Chapter 2, Virtual Private Cloud*, you learned about the various network connectivity options as well as their costs. At the most expensive end of the scale, there is Direct Connect, which provides a dedicated network connection between an on-premises data center and the cloud. This option is not only expensive but also time-consuming, taking months to configure. You can usually rule out Direct Connect fairly easily by looking through the question for mentions of low-cost or quick implementation requirements.

There are then VPNs, and AWS Site-to-Site VPN is a cost-effective option for securely connecting on-premises networks to the cloud using an internet-based connection. Make sure you are familiar with VPN redundancy and how it might impact cost, as this may appear on the exam.

You can always use AWS Transit Gateway to simplify network management and reduce data transfer costs by centralizing network routing and connectivity. By using Transit Gateway, you can connect multiple VPCs and on-premises networks through a single gateway, avoiding the need for costly VPC peering arrangements. This can lead to significant cost savings, especially for architectures with a large number of interconnected networks.

Optimizing Network Routing and Traffic Patterns

When designing cost-optimized network architectures, it is important to carefully consider the routing and traffic patterns within your AWS environment. Inefficient routing can lead to unnecessary data transfer costs, which can significantly impact your overall cloud spending. Make sure you understand when you are charged for data transfer. The general rule of thumb is you don't pay for data transfer into AWS but you do pay for data transfer out of AWS. This is not always the case, but it's a good guideline to follow.

Remember that for accessing internal AWS services, you can use PrivateLink without incurring data transfer charges for internet egress or NAT gateway usage, using VPC endpoints.

Try to minimize cross-region traffic. You pay for data transfer out of a region, so if the question is specifically asking to keep costs low, don't choose an answer with a multi-region approach, unless the question specifically asks for it.

Make sure routing rules route traffic efficiently. Although this is less important for the exam, it's an important area of knowledge to have.

AWS Global Accelerator can help optimize network traffic and reduce data transfer costs, particularly for globally distributed applications. By using Global Accelerator's static IP addresses and optimized routing, you can minimize the need for costly network egress charges.

Finally, implement throttling strategies to control unintended spikes in data transfer costs. Depending on the service being used, you may be able to throttle traffic. This is particularly useful for workloads with variable or unpredictable data transfer patterns, and can also help to mitigate the effects of **distributed denial of service (DDoS)** attacks.

The key area to remember with this part of the domain is controlling data transfer costs. Those are typically the largest costs incurred and the ones to be avoided. So, remember to understand when you are and are not charged for data transfer, and you should be good.

Utilizing AWS Cost Management Tools and Services

Controlling costs in AWS is an important topic, and you learned about this in detail in *Chapter 11, Management and Governance*. But to recap, there are several tools to help you to understand your costs in AWS.

AWS Cost Explorer is a comprehensive tool that provides detailed cost and usage analysis for your AWS resources, including network-related services. Use Cost Explorer to analyze your network traffic patterns and data transfer costs, and identify areas where you may be able to optimize your network architecture. Create custom cost reports and alerts to monitor your network-related spending and identify any unexpected increases or anomalies.

AWS Budgets allows you to set custom budgets for your AWS resources, including network-related services. You can configure budgets for specific network services, such as data transfer costs, AWS Direct Connect usage, or NAT gateway charges, and then receive alerts when your actual or forecasted costs are approaching your budget thresholds.

AWS **Cost and Usage Reports** (**CUR**) provides detailed, line-item data about your AWS usage and associated costs. You can use the CUR data to identify optimization opportunities, such as opportunities to leverage VPC endpoints or adjust network connectivity options.

Consider implementing a comprehensive tagging strategy to categorize and track your network-related resources and their associated costs. Leverage the tagged data in your cost analysis and reporting to make informed decisions about network architecture optimization.

Through these tools, you can stay well informed about the cost of your infrastructure and also make well-informed decisions about your spending forecast. Make sure you understand the limitations of each tool because you may be asked a question about which way costs should be monitored and remediated.

Summary

In this chapter, you have learned about designing cost-optimized architectures, which forms a critical 20% of the *SAA-C03* exam. You began by exploring techniques for designing cost-effective storage solutions on AWS. You gained an understanding of the pricing models and cost characteristics of various AWS storage services, such as Amazon S3, Amazon Glacier, Amazon EFS, and Amazon EBS. You then dove into strategies for leveraging storage access patterns to minimize costs, including optimizing for batch uploads, implementing storage tiering, and managing data lifecycles.

Next, you shifted your focus to cost-optimized compute solutions. You reviewed the different compute service pricing models offered by AWS, including On-Demand, Reserved Instances, and Spot Instances. You learned how to select the appropriate compute service and instance type based on the specific requirements of your workloads, as well as techniques for optimizing compute utilization through autoscaling and instance scheduling.

Moving on to database solutions, you explored methods for designing cost-optimized database architectures. You evaluated the key factors to consider when choosing between Amazon RDS, Amazon Aurora, and Amazon DynamoDB, and discussed strategies for capacity planning, leveraging database features for cost savings, and managing backup and retention expenses.

Finally, you explored network architectures, examining the various connectivity options and their associated costs. You learned how to optimize network routing and traffic patterns to minimize data transfer expenses, as well as how to utilize AWS cost management tools such as Cost Explorer, Budgets, and CUR to monitor and analyze your network-related spending.

With all of this information, you should be equipped to answer any question in the *SAA-C03* exam. Coming up next, we have a practice exam so you can try answering some questions in the style of those asked in the *SAA-C03* exam.

Exam Readiness Drill - Chapter Review Questions

Apart from mastering key concepts, strong test-taking skills under time pressure are essential for acing your certification exam. That's why developing these abilities early in your learning journey is critical.

Exam readiness drills, using the free online practice resources provided with this book, help you progressively improve your time management and test-taking skills while reinforcing the key concepts you've learned.

HOW TO GET STARTED

- Open the link or scan the QR code at the bottom of this page

- If you have unlocked the practice resources already, log in to your registered account. If you haven't, follow the instructions in *Chapter 16* and come back to this page.

- Once you log in, click the START button to start a quiz

- We recommend attempting a quiz multiple times till you're able to answer most of the questions correctly and well within the time limit.

- You can use the following practice template to help you plan your attempts:

Working On Accuracy		
Attempt	Target	Time Limit
Attempt 1	40% or more	Till the timer runs out
Attempt 2	60% or more	Till the timer runs out
Attempt 3	75% or more	Till the timer runs out
Working On Timing		
Attempt 4	75% or more	1 minute before time limit
Attempt 5	75% or more	2 minutes before time limit
Attempt 6	75% or more	3 minutes before time limit

The above drill is just an example. Design your drills based on your own goals and make the most out of the online quizzes accompanying this book.

First time accessing the online resources? 🔒
You'll need to unlock them through a one-time process. **Head to** *Chapter 16* **for instructions**.

Open Quiz	
https://packt.link/SAAC03Ch15	
OR scan this QR code →	

16
Accessing the Online Practice Resources

Your copy of *AWS Certified Solutions Architect - Associate (SAA-C03) Exam Guide* comes with free online practice resources. Use these to hone your exam readiness even further by attempting practice questions on the companion website. The website is user-friendly and can be accessed from mobile, desktop, and tablet devices. It also includes interactive timers for an exam-like experience.

How to Access These Materials

Here's how you can start accessing these resources depending on your source of purchase.

Purchased from Packt Store (packtpub.com)

If you've bought the book from the Packt store (`packtpub.com`) eBook or Print, head to `https://packt.link/SAAC03unlock`. There, log in using the same Packt account you created or used to purchase the book.

Packt+ Subscription

If you're a *Packt+ subscriber*, you can head over to the same link (`https://packt.link/SAAC03practiceres`), log in with your `Packt ID`, and start using the resources. You will have access to them as long as your subscription is active.

If you face any issues accessing your free resources, contact us at `customercare@packt.com`.

Purchased from Amazon and Other Sources

If you've purchased from sources other than the ones mentioned above (like *Amazon*), you'll need to unlock the resources first by entering your unique sign-up code provided in this section. **Unlocking takes less than 10 minutes, can be done from any device, and needs to be done only once**. Follow these five easy steps to complete the process:

STEP 1

Open the link `https://packt.link/SAAC03unlock` OR scan the following **QR code** (*Figure 16.1*):

Figure 16.1: QR code for the page that lets you unlock this book's free online content

Either of those links will lead to the following page as shown in *Figure 16.2*:

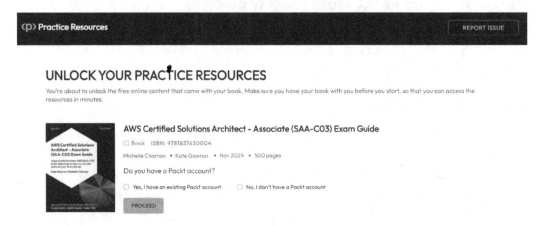

Figure 16.2: Unlock page for the online practice resources

STEP 2

If you already have a Packt account, select the option `Yes, I have an existing Packt account`. If not, select the option `No, I don't have a Packt account`.

If you don't have a Packt account, you'll be prompted to create a new account on the next page. It's free and only takes a minute to create.

Click `Proceed` after selecting one of those options.

STEP 3

After you've created your account or logged in to an existing one, you'll be directed to the following page as shown in *Figure 16.3*.

Make a note of your unique unlock code:

`NZZ3045`

Type in or copy this code into the text box labeled 'Enter Unique Code':

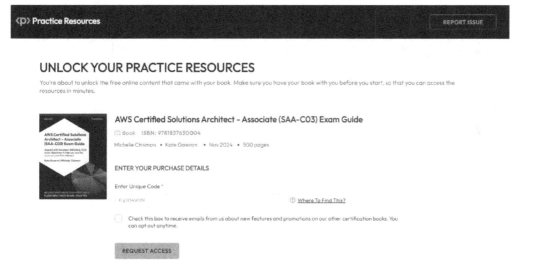

Figure 16.3: Enter your unique sign-up code to unlock the resources

---

Troubleshooting tip

After creating an account, if your connection drops off or you accidentally close the page, you can reopen the page shown in *Figure 16.2* and select `Yes, I have an existing account`. Then, sign in with the account you had created before you closed the page. You'll be redirected to the screen shown in *Figure 16.3*.

STEP 4

> **Note**
> You may choose to opt into emails regarding feature updates and offers on our other certification books. We don't spam, and it's easy to opt out at any time.

Click Request Access.

STEP 5

If the code you entered is correct, you'll see a button that says, OPEN PRACTICE RESOURCES, as shown in *Figure 16.4*:

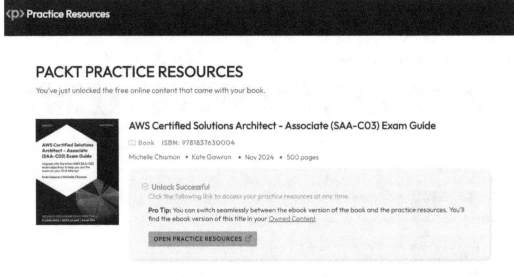

Figure 16.4: Page that shows up after a successful unlock

Click the OPEN PRACTICE RESOURCES link to start using your free online content. You'll be redirected to the Dashboard shown in *Figure 16.5*:

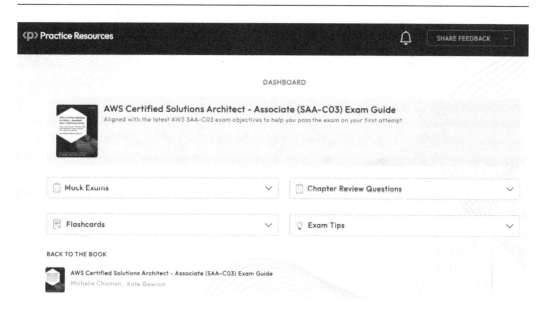

Figure 16.5: Dashboard page for AWS SAA-C03 practice resources

Bookmark this link

Now that you've unlocked the resources, you can come back to them anytime by visiting `https://packt.link/SAAC03practiceres` or scanning the following QR code provided in *Figure 16.6*:

Figure 16.6: QR code to bookmark practice resources website

Troubleshooting Tips

If you're facing issues unlocking, here are three things you can do:

- Double-check your unique code. All unique codes in our books are case-sensitive and your code needs to match exactly as it is shown in *STEP 3*.

- If that doesn't work, use the `Report Issue` button located at the top-right corner of the page.

- If you're not able to open the unlock page at all, write to `customercare@packt.com` and mention the name of the book.

Share Feedback

If you find any issues with the platform, the book, or any of the practice materials, you can click the `Share Feedback` button from any page and reach out to us. If you have any suggestions for improvement, you can share those as well.

Back to the Book

To make switching between the book and practice resources easy, we've added a link that takes you back to the book (*Figure 16.7*). Click it to open your book in Packt's online reader. Your reading position is synced so you can jump right back to where you left off when you last opened the book.

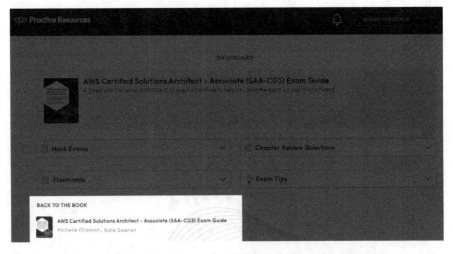

Figure 16.7: Dashboard page for AWS SAA-C03 practice resources

> **Note**
> Certain elements of the website might change over time and thus may end up looking different from how they are represented in the screenshots of this book.

Index

Security groups: 28, 29, 33, 36, 37, 39, 92,
      94, 98, 156, 187, 247, 278, 283

Software as a service: 9, 163

Spot instances: 77, 78, 79, 90, 91,
      161, 168, 291, 297

Storage class: 105, 106, 107, 109, 111, 112,
      180, 266, 267, 288, 289, 290, 294

Subnets: 11, 27, 28, 29, 30, 31, 32, 33, 35, 36,
      38, 39, 40, 41, 42, 44, 46, 47, 48, 49, 50,
      51, 55, 93, 96, 228, 247, 254, 277, 278, 281

T

Tape gateway: 181, 184, 282

Task definition: 85, 86, 96, 97, 98

Transmission control protocol: 5, 130

W

Web application firewall: 215, 246

www.packtpub.com

Subscribe to our online digital library for full access to over 7,000 books and videos, as well as industry leading tools to help you plan your personal development and advance your career. For more information, please visit our website.

Why subscribe?

- Spend less time learning and more time coding with practical eBooks and Videos from over 4,000 industry professionals

- Improve your learning with Skill Plans built especially for you

- Get a free eBook or video every month

- Fully searchable for easy access to vital information

- Copy and paste, print, and bookmark content

At www.packtpub.com, you can also read a collection of free technical articles, sign up for a range of free newsletters, and receive exclusive discounts and offers on Packt books and eBooks.

Other Books You May Enjoy

If you enjoyed this book, you may be interested in these other books by Packt:

AWS Certified Solutions Architect – Professional Exam Guide (SAP-C02)

Patrick Sard and Yohan Wadia

ISBN: 978-1-80181-313-6

- Design and deploy fully secure, dynamically scalable, highly available, fault-tolerant, and reliable apps on AWS

- Integrate on-premises environments seamlessly with AWS resources

- Select appropriate architecture patterns and AWS services for designing and deploying complex applications

- Continuously improve solution architectures for security, reliability, performance, operational excellence, and cost-efficiency

- Plan and execute migrations of complex applications to AWS

- Implement cost-control strategies to deliver cost-effective solutions on AWS

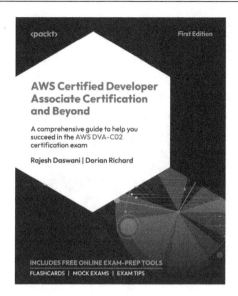

Microsoft Azure Fundamentals Certification and Beyond

Rajesh Daswani and Dorian Richard

ISBN: 978-1-80181-929-9

- Host static website content using Amazon S3

- Explore accessibility, segmentation, and security with Amazon VPC

- Implement disaster recovery with EC2 and S3

- Provision and manage relational and non-relational databases on AWS

- Deploy your applications automatically with AWS Elastic Beanstalk

- Use AWS CodeBuild, AWS CodeDeploy, and AWS CodePipeline for DevOps

- Manage containers using Amazon EKS and ECS

- Build serverless applications with AWS Lambda and AWS Cloud9

Share Your Thoughts

Now you've finished *AWS Certified Solutions Architect - Associate (SAA-C03) Exam Guide*, we'd love to hear your thoughts! Scan the QR code below to go straight to the Amazon review page for this book and share your feedback or leave a review on the site that you purchased it from.

https://packt.link/r/1837630003

Your review is important to us and the tech community and will help us make sure we're delivering excellent quality content.

Download a Free PDF Copy of This Book

Thanks for purchasing this book!

Do you like to read on the go but are unable to carry your print books everywhere?

Is your eBook purchase not compatible with the device of your choice?

Don't worry, now with every Packt book you get a DRM-free PDF version of that book at no cost.

Read anywhere, any place, on any device. Search, copy, and paste code from your favorite technical books directly into your application.

The perks don't stop there, you can get exclusive access to discounts, newsletters, and great free content in your inbox daily.

Follow these simple steps to get the benefits:

1.   Scan the QR code or visit the link below:

https://packt.link/free-ebook/9781837630004

2.   Submit your proof of purchase.
3.   That's it! We'll send your free PDF and other benefits to your email directly.

www.ingramcontent.com/pod-product-compliance
Lightning Source LLC
LaVergne TN
LVHW080112070326
832902LV00015B/2542